P9-DCY-137

Storycatcher

Storycatcher

Making Sense of Our Lives through the Power and Practice of Story

CHRISTINA BALDWIN

New World Library
Novato, California

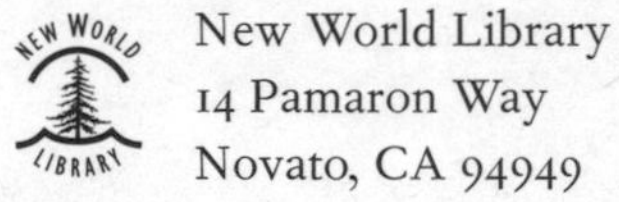
New World Library
14 Pamaron Way
Novato, CA 94949

Text design and typography by Tona Pearce Myers

Library of Congress Cataloging-in-Publication Data
Baldwin, Christina.
Storycatcher : making sense of our lives through the power and practice of story / Christina Baldwin.
p. cm.
Includes index.
ISBN-13: 978-1-57731-491-2 (pbk. : alk. paper)
1. Autobiography—Authorship. 2. Autobiography—Psychological aspects.
3. Storytelling—Psychological aspects. I. Title.
CT25.B25 2005
808'.06692—dc22 2005013340

First printing, October 2005
ISBN-13: 978-1-57731-491-2
ISBN-10: 1-57731-491-3

New World Library is dedicated to preserving the earth and its resources. We are now printing 50% of our new titles on 100% chlorine-free postconsumer waste recycled paper. As members of the Green Press Initiative (www.greenpressinitiative.org), our goal is to use 100% recycled paper for all of our titles by 2007.

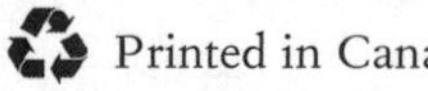
Printed in Canada on 100% postconsumer waste recycled paper

A proud member of the Green Press Initiative

Distributed to the trade by Publishers Group West

10 9 8 7 6 5 4 3 2 1

To my mother, Connie McGregor,

and to my father, Leo E. Baldwin Jr.

Thank you with my whole heart.

Contents

Preface

Every person is born into life as a blank page — and every person leaves life as a full book. Our lives are our story, and our story is our life. Story is the narrative thread of our experience — not what literally happens, but what we make out of what happens, what we tell each other and what we remember. This narrative determines much of what we do with the time given us between the opening of the blank page the day we are born and the closing of the book the day we die.

We make our lives bigger or smaller, more expansive or more limited, according to the interpretation of life that is our story. Whether we speak or write these stories, we constantly weave life events into narrative and interpret everything that happens through the veil of story. From our smallest, most personal challenges to global issues that affect nations and generations, we make the world fit into the story we are already carrying. This unceasing interplay between experience and narrative is a uniquely human attribute. We are the storytellers, the ones who put life into words.

Events become real when we organize experience into narrative: we literally cannot think without words. People become real when we put interaction into words: story is the foundation of relationship. With words alone we can create connection, establish community. With words alone we can recognize ourselves in each other's lives. We share the earth with over seven billion people; each one of us a book of bones and flesh, filling our daily pages with stories that make sense out of our lives. From the corner chair in an American living room, to the cook-fire in an African village, story conveys what it is to be human and gives humanity its voice.

This book explores three premises about story:

• *How we make our experience into story determines how we live our personal lives:* At the end of the school year, on a day called "Flowers and Stars," the children and their parents gathered at the local elementary school for celebrations and awards. All the fifth graders received summer journals for writing during vacation, and the teachers nominated one first grader who was in the advanced reading and writing group in her class for a special award. She told her mother, "I'm getting a surprise; let's sit up front."

But her mother was sure the girl was mistaken and insisted they sit in the back row of the auditorium in the middle of a row of chairs. "That way you can stand up and see better," she said. And so the ceremony began. Child after child was recognized for something special about each of them, and the little girl stood faithfully on the folding chair watching and waiting.

Finally, the principal called her name: "And for advanced reading and writing, Anna Grace receives her own blank book and a box of pens." The little girl was so excited. She squeezed out of the row and walked the long center aisle to the front of the room and up on the school stage where the principal handed her the award. She shook his hand, clutched the book and pens to her chest and looked into the mass of grownup faces until she saw her mother, "See!" She announced across the space. This is a moment of interpretation that will shape her life story: *See, I know what I'm talking about.... See, I was brave enough to come get my gift.*

• *What we emphasize and retell in our collective story determines whether we quarrel or collaborate in our community:* After 9/11, the most profound stories that emerged from those hours in the World Trade Center were hundreds of affirming statements, "We got out of the towers because we helped each other get out.... Once we got in the stairwells we realized that our lives totally depended on the person in front of us making it... and so we helped each other and forgot about ourselves, and the person behind us took care of us and we made our way down those endless flights and lived. Thousands of us who should have died... lived."

These people had been strangers, competitors in different companies, bosses who never knew their clerical staff, cubicle workers who never talked directly to upper administration, people of different colors, religions, nationalities. Their stories of cooperation teach us as powerfully as anything else that happened that day. The uprising of love, compassion, altruism is the response the terrorists could not predict: fear, yes, but the unleashing of renewed community life, that is what still works in us as these stories become part of the legend of who we are and how we imagine ourselves behaving in similar circumstances.

• *What we preserve in larger human story determines what we believe is possible in the world:* On Christmas Eve in 1914, two lines of homesick soldiers, one British, one German, were dug into trenches on the Western Front in the midst of World War I. Between them was a fire zone called no-man's land. On this moonlit, snowy night, the Germans lifted army issued Christmas trees twinkling with tiny candles over the edge of their trenches and set them in plain sight. The British shouted and cheered in delight. The Germans began to sing "Stille Nacht..." and the British began to sing along with "Silent Night." This encouraged the Germans and they set down their guns in the moonlight and heaved themselves from their trenches carrying candles, cake, and cigars toward their enemies. The British responded in kind carrying steamed pudding and cigarettes. The men met in the middle of the forbidden zone, exchanged gifts, sang carols, and played soccer. This seemingly spontaneous truce extended for hundreds of kilometers among thousands of soldiers. They couldn't shoot each other. The war essentially stopped. Horrified commanders on both sides had to transfer thousands of men to new positions until the enemy became faceless and storyless again, something killable, not a brother. Almost a hundred years later, scholars are still studying this event, reading soldiers' journals and letters that refer to it, seeking to understand "the breakdown in military mindset," or seeking to understand how a spontaneous peace movement could spread within the heart of war.

SOMETHING IS HAPPENING in the power and practice of story: In the midst of overwhelming noise and distraction, the voice of story is calling us to remember our true selves. In chapter one, I tell of two families: one that shares its stories, one that withholds its stories. And in chapter four, I recall thirteen days when nuclear war threatened to destroy the whole story. And in chapter five, we listen while a sister who was a peacenik and a brother who was a soldier talk at last about Viet Nam. In chapter six, we watch a young African woman return to her devastated country to help train community leaders. In chapter seven, a grandmother works to heal the effects of alcoholism in five generations. In chapter eight, we see how story preserves or destroys organizations. And in chapter nine, two priests and two ministers wrestle with grace and judgment. And page by page, we will join in the art and craft of storycatching.

Something is happening in these stories and in this book and in our lives. It is the time of the Storycatcher. It is the time when those who understand the value of story and practice the art of connection have an essential role to play. Storycatchers come whenever we are in crisis to remind us who we are. Storycatchers entice our best tales out of us: they turn with a leading question, a waiting ear, and their full attention. In return, we speak…we write…and we are heard. Storycatchers invite the stories we most need to come forward into the community. Storycatchers know that the mix of wisdom and wit and wonder that spills into the room in story space will reconnect us. Come into these stories and listen for what will connect your life, and mine, and ours.

Storycatcher

CHAPTER ONE

Following the Beeline

HOW STORY CONNECTS US

Life hangs on a narrative thread. This thread is a braid of stories that inform us about who we are, and where we come from, and where we might go. The thread is slender but strong: we trust it to hold us and allow us to swing over the edge of the known into the future we dream in words.

Story — the abundance of it, and the lack of it — shapes us. Story — the abundance of it, and the lack of it — gives us place, lineage, history, a sense of self. Story — the abundance of it, and the lack of it — breaks us into pieces, shatters our understanding, and gives it back over and over again, the story different every time. Story — the abundance of it, and the lack of it — connects us with the world and outlines our relationship with everything. When the power of story comes into the room, an alchemical reaction occurs that is unique to our kind: love or hate, identification or isolation, war or peace, good or evil can be stirred in us by words alone. The power of story is understood by the powerful, yet the power of story belongs to all of us, especially the least powerful. History is what scholars and conquerors say happened; story is what it was like to live on the ground.

THE GROUND WHERE I WAS BORN is the butte country of western Montana, a land of reds and oranges, sweeping wheat fields and brown tufts of cattle grass. Here the days begin with a pinkening line along the flattened east horizon like a great eye opening, and the days end with marauding sunsets that disappear like ghost riders into the western crags. I was set down in this landscape, placed into the arms of family, community, nation, and nature.

I have traveled far, but come back from time to time in search of some elusive sense of origin. Driving west out of Great Falls on Interstate 15, the one freeway that dissects these plains, running north like an artery to Shelby and Sweetgrass and the turnoff to Glacier Park, I join a bloodstream of tourists, ranchers, Indians, all going to the sun. Just north of the junkyard, truck stops, and cattle yard I swing onto Trunk Highway 21 — Vaughn Junction — where the roadbed follows a path as ancient as buffalo, as tribal migrations, as the sure-footed Sacagawea, who led her band of white men into the same vista that lies before me unchanged. Unchanged, as soon as my back is turned to the slash of interstate. Unchanged, as soon as the sun hits the pavement on a slant that transforms the road into a shimmering ribbon that might be grass, might be water. I drive half-blind into glint and shadow until the road catches me up and I follow it as mesmerized as a deer.

Beyond Vaughn Junction, there is nothing in the way. Nothing to break the sight line. The first ridge of the Rockies rises beyond the buttes, the Continental Divide drawn invisibly along the upper crest of peaks, deciding what flows back toward me, what flows west toward the sea.

My immediate sight is filled with the shape of Square Butte, an overturned, brown-wrapped box of land sticking straight up out of gullied pastures and wheat fields. The terrain around me is tucked away this October day in tidy strips of harvested grain and baled hay. I am heading toward sixty years of age and this is the first time I have seen my birth lands in any season other than high summer. The land waits for winter, though this afternoon is cool breeze, bright sun, a cheery day to find myself sitting on a pink marble headstone with my name on it: BALDWIN. Here lie Leo Elmer and Mary Hart Baldwin, my grandparents; Grace Baldwin Ho, Dorothy Baldwin Humphreys, two middle-aged aunts brought back to the bosom of the family to lie. My feet sink ankle deep into the thatch of grave grass.

Fatherland

My father's father, Leo Sr., was a Methodist circuit rider in the butte country of Montana in the early decades of the twentieth century. First by horse and buggy, and later by Model-T, followed by an assortment of farm trucks, he drove the valleys of the Sun and Judith rivers east and west of Great Falls, tending to the spiritual needs of pioneering homesteaders, farmers, and ranchers — marrying, baptizing, burying. He was a smallish man, wiry and strong, with deep-set blue eyes, a strong nose that is still coming down the family line, and composure based on faith and practice. He preached a straightforward gospel of deep reverence for God's creation, not too rigid, not too brimstone. My grand-father loved the Lord, and believed the Lord loved him and his flock in return.

> *Language is the road map of a culture. It tells you where its people come from and where they are going.*
>
> — Rita Mae Brown

I didn't know him during these early years. By the time I came along, fifteenth out of twenty grandchildren, a caboose born after World War II with cousins nearly old enough to be aunts and uncles, Grandpa was a settled presence in the tiny town of Fort Shaw. The town was barely a bump on Highway 21, the back road to Helena, or a sneak through the mountains to Missoula. Over the years, to support a large family, Leo had become a beekeeper six days a week and a preacher on Sundays at Simms Methodist Church.

I was born here in 1946, in Great Falls Deaconess Hospital, in the same ward where my father had been born in 1920, the seventh of Mary's eight children, his birth the first time anyone thought to drive his mother into town.

There was no question that they'd drive my mother to town. She was young and skittery, enough like her mother-in-law, Mary, that I wonder if tensions blossomed that spring after the war as wildly as flowers. In a time when all civilized births happened in hospitals, women drugged into half slumber, my mother studied a book on natural childbirth and panted her way proudly through contractions, producing her first child — which happened to be me — after only four hours of labor.

Though my parents soon moved and I grew up in cities a thousand miles east, we made frequent summer pilgrimages to the Sun River valley homestead. Heading out of the driveway on the west suburban edge of Minneapolis, we'd drive straight into the eye of the sun, nearly twenty-four hours on road that was two-lane blacktop most of those years: the summers I was 5, 7, 9, 11, 13, 14, 16, and 22. We didn't stop except for breakfast until Square Butte filled our vision and we rolled over the foothills. Home.

For decades, a passel of kinfolk, changing crews every year, would show up for several weeks in August to bring in the honey crop. Grandpa and the uncles would drive out to raid the hives, five hundred colonies of bees strategically placed in those irrigated valleys to bring in the pure gold of alfalfa and sweet clover. I got used to seeing men in long-sleeved canvas shirts and leather gloves, pants cuffs tucked into boots, bee bonnets draped over their heads and buttoned into collars. Every afternoon the flatbed truck would rumble into the driveway, groaning from the heavy load of hive boxes, or "supers," taken from the hives. Buzzing with drowsy bees still riding on the honeycomb, it would back up to the honey house loading dock. Sweating a combination of man smell and honey, the men hefted the heavy wooden hive boxes into the extracting shed. There they would slice the wax caps off the combs, run the supers through the centrifuge extractor, and warm the honey just enough to make it trickle down troughs, through filter screens, and into big metal vats.

One evening my grandpa called me into his study with a small glass bottle of honey in hand. Under the glow of his desk lamp he spread open the huge old Bible that had been his father's before him. The scent of honey rose from his skin and his clothing and maybe the Bible itself. "Lookee here, Chrissie," he said, holding the capped jar like a magnifying glass over the words. "Our bees make such pure honey you can read right though it." The letters were slightly wiggled, but I could see them. "Isaiah," he said in his hoarse whispery voice, "that's a good book. Here, read me this." His hands were square with a fleshy palm, the fingers all sinew and big knuckled. Outdoor hands, callused palms. His fingernail, cleaned with a pocketknife at the horse trough where the men sluiced off the dirt of the day before coming in to dinner, pointed to the middle of the page.

I stood on tiptoe, balancing myself with my hands on the edge of the roll top desk. "Isaiah, 55:12," I said, just like they began in church, "*For you shall go out in joy, and be led forth in peace; the mountains and the hills before you shall break forth into singing, and all the trees of the field shall clap their hands.*"

"Good," he said, and where he touched my hair I thought it smelled of honey. And where he touched my heart, there is honey still.

> *What's truer than truth? The Story.*
>
> — Hasidic wisdom

Story opens up a space between people that is unbound from the reality we are standing in. Our imaginative ability to tell story, and our empathetic ability to receive story, can take us anywhere and make it real. In the act of telling story, we create a world we invite others into. And in the act of listening to story, we accept an invitation into experiences that are not our own, although they seem to be. Story weaves a sense of familiarity. We are simultaneously listening to another's voice and traveling our own memories. We are looking for connectors, making synaptic leaps linking one variation of human experience to another. You come with me to the glowing light in the tiny farmhouse study, but you also stream through memories of your own childhood. Who put honey in your heart?

The distances all seem reasonable now. The thirty-one miles west of Great Falls to the homestead is simply thirty-one miles. Years ago, fueled by impatience and the belief in destination, it seemed to take as long to drive these last thirty-one miles to Grandma and Grandpa's as it had taken to drive all the way from Minneapolis. We hung over the backseat, myself, eventually two brothers, a sister, breathing hotly on the neck of whichever parent was driving — Mother usually, as we would be gone for a month or more at a time, cruising in that year's carefully outfitted station wagon through the homes and hospitality of relatives. My father would join us only for the first or last two-week stretch when the caravan of his family ventured into ancestral territory.

Many years later I discovered there were families who went to the lake cabin, children who spent weeks at fancy camps, tours made to Europe or the cities of the East. We went to visit relatives. Most of my father's brothers and sisters stayed in a constellation to the family home, scattered throughout the West like pony express stations until I thought we Baldwins, like Wyatt Earp or Annie Oakley or Buffalo Bill, had some claim on the place. *Our* butte, *our* benchland, *our* mountains. With two brothers in California and a sister in Oregon, my mother's country was a string of lighthouses that introduced me to the sea: the landscape between Minnesota and saltwater was fatherland.

When we opened our suitcases, our clothes would steam with released Minnesota humidity. They dried out fast — my shorts and flounce-edged halter-tops, one Sunday dress, jeans, and sneakers. I shed my city self and dashed straight into the landscape, filled my nostrils with dust and earthy scents of cows and horses. I hung over fence railings at my uncle's ranches and strode, veiled and brave, in and out of my grandfather's honey house.

There was a railroad spur at the edge of town, out near the grain silos. Each year, little vials of honey, like the one through which I had read the blessing of Isaiah, were sent to food marketing cooperatives such as Sue Bee in Iowa and the Finger Lakes Honey Co-op in New York. The companies sent back their orders and "Baldwin and Sons Beeline Honey" left in boxcars sending our sweet cache to blend with the darker nectars of eastern fruit trees, buckwheat, and sorghum. Harvest over, school looming in the shortening days, my parents, my brothers and sister, and I would turn reluctantly east and head into the darker strains of our life in Minneapolis the other eleven months of the year. We always took a sixty-pound tin home with us. We prayed before we ate, and we ate a lot of honey.

The stories of the West, the homestead, the history of this family, were fed to me with dinner, the table buzzing with jokes and repeated tales. One of the uncles would start, breaking into the raucous stream of words with the beginning of a story, "Did I ever tell you children about the time your father got caught climbing the water tower?" He pointed a long table knife down the row of family faces. The knife was veneered with honey, and lined along the flat edge of the blade was a row of peas that he slathered into his mouth with one smooth curl of his tongue. Even if we had heard this story a dozen times, we'd shake our heads, "Nooo...," and off he'd go. I don't know if Uncle Willard always ate his peas with honey, or just did it for effect. My little brother, Carl, who avoided green food as much as possible, shivered and rolled his eyes in my direction. The renditions of our father's exploits around the town were always slightly changing, embellished here and there, sometimes causing him to jump in and defend himself, or come up with a story of one of his brother's misadventures. No matter the variation and how it differed from the night before, Willard always concluded with a chuckle and the phrase, "Now, that's the gospel truth. Yes it is, yes it is."

I eat my peas
with honey,
I've done it all my life.
It makes them taste
so funny,
But it keeps them
on my knife.

— Children's rhyme

The Essential Element of Narrative

We understand that story is not the gospel truth, or journalism, or courtroom testimony. Story is life seen through the honey jar, slightly distorted by personal experience, perception, inclination, and fancy. This is the nature of story. The fish gets a little bigger, the storm gets a little wilder, the love gets a little stronger, our bravery or disappointment gets a little exaggerated in the telling over time. There is creative tension in story. When we hear it, when we read it, when we speak it, when we write it, we filter words through our own experiences and our need for meaning. We shape the tale to reinforce our understanding of how life is.

The Baldwins are storytellers: Celts, of Scots-English-Irish background, some of them traceable back to the seventeen hundreds in Massachusetts, then traceable back to England — tinkers, tailors, farmers, loggers. The current generations inherit a legacy of stories and the embellishment that goes with them. Right before our eyes we children watched our uncle change our father's story. And then we watched our father change another story and another, and who knows where the gospel truth resided? And does it matter?

Storytelling is not testifying before some arbitrator of "truth" who will judge us; and yet we say earnestly, "Believe me, this is a true story." The stories in this book are true: your responses to them and retelling them, and even how you change them, make them truer. This is the nature of the tale and part of our delight in the power of story. I adored the repartee between my aunts and uncles and father, hung on their words, fed off their liveliness for months, doling out the taste of these tales as sweetly as we doled out the summer's honey, dollop by dollop, making it last. A day without honey is like a day without story: a day without story is like a day without honey.

Not every word that comes out of our mouths is a story. Story is narrative. Words are how we think; narrative is how we link. Story narrative has a sense of beginning, middle, and end. Story features characters, place, things happening; tension between what is known and unknown, between what is expected and what is surprise. Story takes life events and combines what's happening with all our thoughts, feelings, and reactions. And all these elements combine inside story into sense making. Story is the sweet nectar of language. Story is the crystallizing of thought, turning it into something digestible, sweet on the heart, even when the details are hard to bear. Story is the way we dribble sweetness over the often harsh realities of life's everyday grind, dollop by dollop, rolling what happens on the tongue until we discover the nugget of meaning, humor, heartbreak, insight.

Story adapts to fit the media and the times. In the rush of a day, if we only have a minute for story, then story is told to us in a minute. Even when stories are abbreviated, trivialized, or commercialized they are offered within a narrative framework that we recognize: a beginning, middle, and end that make a point, that teach or entertain, or that tug the heart and mind in an intended direction.

Without Story, information is nothing but a lot of bricks lying about waiting for someone to make constructive use of them.

— Aidan Chambers

A television commercial is a story:

A beautiful woman is preparing to meet a handsome man. We watch her flip her hair. We listen to her humming a wordless tune. She reaches for a product — deodorant, hair spray, perfume, whatever — and strides confidently out the door. The man of her dreams is overjoyed to see her. They kiss. We know they will live happily ever after (because this is a story!), and the mysterious Voice of Authority says something glowing about the product. We go buy the product because we liked the story.

Email chains are stories:

I got this from a friend. Read it for inspiration, and send it to five people to bring them good luck. Once there was a field of daisies . . . or Once there was a man who found a dog . . . or Once there was a little girl who was lost . . . or A schoolteacher someplace is trying to prove the power of the Internet to her students. *If you get this, send Miss Thompson's second grade class an email. . . .* (And later we hear the server crashed so many responses were coming through.)

Coworkers gathering on Monday morning present each other with stories:

I promised my wife I'd go straight to the grocery store and bring back stuff she needed for dinner. But you know me and bargains . . . there was a flea market in the strip mall parking lot, so I swerved in, parked, and found a weed whacker for half price . . . now I'm considering how to explain this to Beth, and when I get in the car the battery is dead. I mean d-e-a-d and I'm nowhere near the grocery store! But as luck would have it, I am parked in front of an auto parts store, so I get a new battery, saving myself money and time I would have spent waiting for AAA. On one hand I'm thinking this was an act of fate, and on the other hand I'm thinking I'm going to be in trouble . . . and then, boy this really was a godsend, I notice this flower shop . . . well, you know the rest of the story — I'm a sweet, thoughtful guy . . . with a new weed whacker and a new battery.

The news is presented through story:

Today police roped off the 1300 block of Oak Street after reports of gunfire. . . . Later a neighbor reported, "I was in the backyard when I heard this big bang and hit the dirt. I thought it was me who was shot, but when nothing hurt, I crawled into the house and called 9-1-1. . . . And then . . ."

Every one of these examples features characters, place, things happening, and an abbreviated narrative structure the brain recognizes as story.

Embedded in every human language, narrative is the organizational thought process that carries story. Through chronology and symbology, narrative makes the association between events, thoughts, and feelings that creates meaning — that makes sense. Even when story is shortened, even when the story rambles, we count on our minds and our listeners' minds to fill in the pieces we've skipped and follow the thread.

Story is narrative. I think of narrative not as a path, but as three-dimensional space, or landscape; through which (by our choice of words) we can take a path.

— Bob Hughes

There are seven billion story-filled people in the world: all of us talkers, all of us listeners. We live in a breadth of conditions almost unimaginable to each other. Yet if we can find a common language in which to communicate, we can find the commonality in who we are. Embedded in the narrative of our lives are common human values, impulses, and longings.

The ways that children hang on summer days in a mix of playful fantasies and practical chores serving the family or the village are universal. The ways men grunt in the rhythm of hard work, and the stories that pass from hand to hand along with honey supers, or construction tools, or mud bricks are the same in a thousand tongues. The gestures and stories among women making food, tending children, washing clothes, and cleaning house bequeath knowledge from generation to generation. We understand our commonality when we remember ourselves at this level of the human story.

Among Hasidic Jews, when a child first approaches the Torah to study the history and wisdom of "the law," the rabbi puts a drop of honey on a tiny plate and sets it on the page. The child licks the honey from the holy word so she or he will always associate sweetness with learning. In Islam, references to honey, and the sweetness of paradise, sing throughout the Qur'an. And among the Tzutujil Indians of Guatemala, their parting blessing to each other is expressed as a wish for "long life, honey in the heart, no evil, thirteen thank-yous."

During honey harvest, the dry fields around the homestead clicked with grasshoppers and I stepped tentatively with my citified feet, jumpy with warnings about rattlesnakes and gopher holes. Pointing to the butte that filled the western horizon, Uncle Willard once informed me, "There's a cliff over there, you can't quite see it from here, but Indians used to run buffalo off that ledge. The ground would shake for miles from the thump of their hooves."

In 1904, ten local Native girls from the Indian school at Fort Shaw traveled all the way to the St. Louis World's Fair. Despite the terrible abuses and hardships Indian children faced during this time when so many of them were being removed from their families and cultural roots, these girls became world basketball champions and role models in a hostile world. In 2004, a marble obelisk was installed at the edge of the old fort, with a laser photograph of the team in their uniforms and a brass basketball glinting in the Montana sun. Their names were honored by their own descendants, and descendants of white settlers: Minnie Burton, Lemhi Shoshone; Genie Butch, Assiniboine; Genevieve Healy, Gros Ventre; Belle Johnson, Piegan; Rose LaRose, Shoshone-Bannock; Flora Lucero, Chippewa; Sarah Mitchell, Assiniboine; Emma Sansaver, Chippewa-Cree; Catherine Snell,

Assiniboine; and Nettie Wirth, Assiniboine. It doesn't make this history right, but it adds a story of cross-cultural respect for those who still live on the land.

"Were you there? Did you ever see the hunters . . . or the buffalo?" I asked my uncle.

"No," he shook his head. "I just heard tell. Your grandpa knew them though. You ask him. He taught at the Indian school when I was your age. He respected them. They taught him things, showed him places."

My eyes filled with tears. "I wish I was there. I wish I was there, then."

"So do I," he said. "It must have been a real marvel."

Every day I had jobs to do, mostly in the garden gathering fruits and vegetables and lugging the bounty into the kitchen. My grandmother and the aunts canned beans and tomatoes and peaches, made jam and pickles, salted cabbage, filled bins with potatoes and onions. It was a different kind of heat in the kitchen than in the honey house, women's heat. My grandmother ruled the room. Her daughters had been raised in the routine and moved through the work in rhythm with their mother's sense of control. The daughters-in-law, however, often serious women who had been attracted to the jocularity of the men, could never quite get it right. Their helpfulness was like grit in the salad; it grated the teeth, it spoiled the sense of perfection. Yet by 5:00 PM, when almost in unison they raised their apron skirts to pat the perspiration that flushed their cheeks and foreheads and turned their attention toward preparing dinner, they had produced a row of jeweled jars: fruits and vegetables glowed red and green and pink and yellow inside the glass. Labeled and dated, everything went into the root cellar and pantry for the coming months of winter feasting. I would be gone by then, back in the Midwest, surrounded by the taciturn Scandinavians of my mother's family.

Mother Country

The Hansons lived long and said little. My great-grandmother was a tiny blackbird of a woman, with pinched lips and gnarled hands. She was 102 when I met her. I was nine years old at the time and we had just moved to Minnesota. Before the boxes were even unpacked, we drove west into the farmlands to Benson, to stare at this living relic of my other bloodline. Britta Hanson had come over from the old country, a girl on a schooner, nine weeks at sea. Then she had ridden an oxcart from the end of the railroad into the unplowed prairie of the Great Plains. My mother told us these bits of information, shushing us in the car, during the five hours it took us to drive across our new state.

Mother knocked on the door of the small frame house, and we hung at her skirts like we were going to the circus, ready to pay a nickel to see The Hundred-Year-Old Lady. I don't remember if we even went inside, don't remember if the door opened to our impossibly young energy — age nine, age seven, age four, and my mother pregnant again. We have a photograph taken in sunlight, after Britta tottered out of her house on the arm of my Great-Aunt Ellen, another old woman who looked more like her sister than her daughter. We are standing in a spread of life from my mother's grandmother to my mother's children all squinting in the sun.

After paying our respects we went out to see the farm Britta (long called Betsy) and my great-grandfather had built along the river. The property is still in the family, belonging to a second cousin who never moved away: Oak Grove Farm, H. R. Hanson, proprietor. Great-Grandpa Hanson had two claims to fame: he had returned to Norway in 1907, bringing greetings from the Norwegian immigrant communities of western Minnesota, and somehow managed to meet the king. When he returned from that triumph, he built the biggest barn in Swift County. Dead before I was born, and buried in Six Mile Grove cemetery along with half a dozen of his children, and since joined by all of them, I know him only from a few photographs. He always wore what they called a "walrus mustache," a huge brush of hair on his upper lip that completely covered his mouth. I used to wonder how he could eat... or talk. And since he was always skinny, and few stories have come down about him, perhaps this really was a problem, and not just a fantasy of my child-mind.

It took me years to get even this much information out of my grandmother. Emma Hanson Anderson lived to be 106, and though she retained her mind, she didn't speak in details about the long journey of this life. From the time I was in my early twenties I would visit her with a notebook in my pocket or a tape recorder ready to receive any story she might share. I wanted to be prepared to catch the gems I believed were in her. If one side of my family had story, the other side must as well.

Maybe I didn't know the right way to elicit her stories, but I always came away slightly disappointed. I was her oldest grandchild. I loved her and I know she loved me, but the details of my heritage were never fleshed out. Emma and my grandfather had divorced in 1937, when the family was living in North Dakota. My grandmother had only one sentence to say about this, "One man in my life was enough."

There once was a Norwegian farmer who loved his wife so much he almost told her.

— Minnesota folk saying

Left to fend for herself at the height of the Great Depression, she eventually relocated to Oregon and her sons went in the military just in time for World War II. My mother had already driven west, seen the mountains and the ocean for the first time, and imprinted on the region that would always call to her. She ended up working in the college library and taking as many courses as she could afford at Willamette University in Salem, where she met Leo Baldwin. Grandma worked in the Portland shipyards during the war as one of thousands of Rosie the Riveters. From the time I began to know her, in the 1950s and on, she always worked as a live-in — a maid, a cook, and then a nurse for people rich enough to hire help or to die at home. My grandmother had only one thing to say about this: "It's hard to get good references when all your patients die."

All her life she remembered pleading with her father to take her along to Norway, and how summarily he had dismissed her, leaving her with two older brothers to work the farm. Finally, after decades of hinting, her youngest son took her to Norway when she was eighty years old. I showed up at her apartment a few months later eager to hear the tales. "How was the trip?" I asked excitedly.

"Fine," she said. "It was real nice of Dean to take me with."

"Yes, yes it was.... What does Norway look like?"

"The fjords are beautiful. We saw Hafslo, where we come from."

"Does anyone remember our family?"

"The place is full of Hansons, but that wasn't our name there. Hanson is what they handed out when my father got to America. He was Hans Rasmus Rasmussen when he got on the boat."

Story is both the great revealer and concealer. There is the story of what gets said, and the story of what remains unsaid. There is the story that covers up story. There is the blanket of silence thrown over secrets, like people putting sheets on the furniture when leaving home. It's all still there, the shape of the lamp, the length of the sofa, the arrangement of things on the coffee table, just cloaked, and in many ways revealed more definitively by the attempt to hide, the desire to protect.

When I was thirteen years old, my Grandfather Anderson and his second wife took me along in the backseat on their drive to the coast to visit my aunt and uncles. I packed my bag of summer clothes and a copy of *Gone with the Wind*. Head bowed in the hot breeze, the white noise of unair-conditioned travel, I filled the void in conversations with the great story of the South and the Civil War. I had read all 1,065 pages by the time we got to Oregon.

When I was getting into the car, excited to be off on my own for the first time, gloating a little that as the oldest I was deemed ready for such adventure, my mother fussed with last instructions. She seemed nervous that I would not remember my manners without her drill. Then, just as we were ready to pull away, my beautiful, mannerly mother poked her head through the rolled-down window and whispered her parting words, "Thumb your nose at North Dakota for me when you go by...." Then she pulled her head back into the morning air and stood waving, my grandfather gunned the engine, the dog jumped out of the way, the little kids bounced at the edge of the lawn, and we were off.

"Thumbing your nose" was not good manners. I wasn't even sure what it meant, but I knew it was bad, like that other gesture with the raised middle finger. My mother's message was a secret code. What had happened to her in North Dakota that made her hate the place? What did she not want me to know about her, about her childhood, her family? And why wouldn't she tell me?

THE TENSION BETWEEN what is said and what is not said is not just a peculiarity of my family: this is the dilemma of the human family. It takes courage to tell our stories. It takes belief that our stories will be received and held in respect. It requires that some mechanism is alive and structured in the community around us to hold who we are individually in the context of who we are collectively.

These structures have traditionally existed throughout human evolution and history. There was always a place for story in daily life. There was always time. There were always people ready to talk and others ready to listen. And beyond that, there was an understanding that story was essential to the quality of personal and communal life. The practice of story creates a social net that makes us capable of seeing each other's unique contribution and incapable of simply dismissing someone as "not like me."

Sometimes it is a great joy just to listen to someone we love talking.
— Vincent McNabb

As long as we share our stories, as long as our stories reveal our strengths and vulnerabilities to each other, we reinvigorate our understanding and tolerance for the little quirks of personality that in other circumstances would drive us apart. When we live in a family, a community, a country where we know each other's true stories, we remember our capacity to lean in and love each other into wholeness.

I have read the story of a tribe in southern Africa called the Babemba in which a person doing something wrong, something that destroys this delicate social net, brings all work in the village to a halt. The people gather around the "offender," and one by one they begin to recite everything he has done right in his life: every good deed, thoughtful behavior, act of social responsibility. These things have to be true about the person, and spoken honestly, but the time-honored consequence of misbehavior is to appreciate that person back into the better part of himself. The person is given the chance to remember who he is and why he is important to the life of the village.

I want to live under such a practice of compassion. When I forget my place, when I lash out with some private wounding in a public way, I want to be *remembered* back into alignment with my self and my purpose. I want to live with the opportunity for reconciliation. When someone around me is thoughtless or cruel, I want to be given the chance to respond with a ritual that creates the possibility of reconnection. I want to live in a neighborhood where people don't shoot first, don't sue first, where people are Storycatchers willing to discover in strangers the mirror of themselves. I want to be surrounded by a story-based culture that itself remembers story is essential to human survival.

Until he extends his circle of compassion to include all living things, man will not himself find peace.

— Albert Schweitzer

Martin Buber, a great archivist of Jewish wisdom, tells this story: "My grandfather was lame. Once they asked him to tell a story about his teacher. And he related how the holy Baal Shem used to hop and dance while he prayed. My grandfather rose as he spoke, and he was so swept away by his story that he himself began to hop and dance to show how the master had done. From that hour on he was cured of his lameness. That's the way to tell a story!" In the strength of a storytelling heritage, Buber understood that telling story was help enough.

In the tens of thousands of years before writing, before popular literacy, before we recorded what we know in books and on computers, story was the way we transmitted everything. Story was the carrier, the link, the way we taught each other how to be human and to see each other's humanity as we crossed paths on the long walk out of Africa to populate the world.

As soon as our ancestors began to talk, we began making the social container that would hold what we had to say. We gathered around the campfire and practiced speaking and listening. We literally grew our mental capacity by putting our thoughts into stories. We delighted and entertained and informed and inspired and socialized and governed and worshipped through story. Today, the deterioration of that understanding in dominant culture, and the obliteration of that understanding in indigenous culture, are two of the greatest threats humanity faces.

We require story in order to link our lives with each other. Story couples our experiences, mind to mind and heart to heart. Story is the electromagnetic conductor that brings us close enough together to make the leap of association and identification, to see that another person is a variation of ourselves. We are in grave danger if we lose our link to our own stories.

And so I have become dedicated to re-creating a sacred common ground for story. What underlies this book is a deep belief that only by telling each other our authentic stories will we come upon our wisdom and make the new road map we need for survival. Underlying this book is my experience that story is a skill we can remember and practice and encourage in each other.

More, more, more story. That's what I wanted. I was the child in the corner of the kitchen, snapping beans or washing dishes under the voices of the women. I was the child curled up with a book at the end of the sofa pretending to read while the men watched sports or talked of the news. I was the one who woke in the night when voices were raised and the hidden tremors of my parents' marriage stormed between them. I was the one who stayed after school to sharpen pencils and clean chalkboards and listen to teachers talk when the students were gone. I was the one who sat in the front seat with my father when we drove east through the night covering a thousand miles of highway between my aunt's ranch and our suburban home, urging stories out of him to keep him awake. I was the one who listened.

Two or three things I know for sure, and one of them is that to go on living I have to tell stories, that stories are the one sure way I know to touch the heart and change the world.

— Dorothy Allison

I was also the child who chattered in class, and at the supper table, and when being tucked in at night. I was the one who kept jumping into the stream of consciousness, getting my feet wet, figuring out how to join the tale. Hopscotching from rock to rock, making my way into words, practicing how to get in the story. My mother says I announced when I was three, "I wish God gived me two mouths, one to eat with and one to talk." And I remember the first joke my father taught me when I was five years old, carefully memorizing the story of two little skunks so I could say something funny to my uncles when we got to Montana. I was the one who talked.

Story as Our Self

My story is myself: and I am my story. This is all you will know of me; it is all I will know of you. This is all that will survive of us: the stories of who we are, the ways that people speak our names and remember something we did, an event we lived through, a clever story we were known for, or hopefully, some wisdom. They are mostly gone now — grandparents, aunts and uncles — and you and I will soon be gone, too. What is left of their lives, and what will be left of ours, is story.

> *I am the only one who can tell the story of my life and say what it means.*
>
> — Dorothy Allison

Once the closets are cleaned, and the house is sold, a few artifacts may remain that someone wants: photographs, journals or letters, a voice caught on tape, a birthday party recorded on video. We may pass along a recipe in fading ink and spidery handwriting that reveals the secret spice in Great-Grandma's Swedish meatballs. We may hand over the DVD that archives the old 16 mm family movies, a CD of our family's genealogy.

The rolltop desk from my grandfather's study lives at my house, and my cousin across town has Pa's big Bible. After dinner recently, we laid it out on the dining table, paged through the records of births, marriages, deaths, and found a letter written in the hand of our great-grandfather, Andrew Walker Baldwin. I've seen only one photo of him, taken at age twenty-one, though he lived to seventy-four: dark hair and the first notice of those deep-set eyes; that nose, familiar to the whole family. I've seen the photograph, but what brings Pa alive is the letter, the story he is telling. The Bible is more precious as an heirloom when I think of the letters tucked throughout the pages of the New Testament: Paul's Letter to the Ephesians, Andrew's letter to Ora.

Whatever detritus we leave after ourselves, story is what makes it valuable. Without story, the artifacts of ordinary lives quickly lose significance and preciousness. An old chipped teacup is no treasure unless you know this is Aunt Grace's artwork; unless you know she had polio as a young girl, that her siblings pulled her around in a small wagon until the family could afford a wheelchair. She only went to school three years, had to stop when her younger brothers could no longer lift her up and down the schoolhouse stairs. But she had a sweet voice and the family scrimped to give her piano lessons so she would always have some beauty for herself. Grace lived with her brother, Arthur, their whole lives, contributing modestly to their living by hand painting china. This cup comes down in our family with stories of Aunt Grace's music, her acceptance of her crippling, and a photo of her sitting corsaged and crookedly proud in her wicker wheelchair the day she won some recognition for her art.

We need language to tell us who we are, how we feel, what we're capable of — to explain the pains and glory of our existence.

— Maya Angelou

And somewhere, in another family, a woman is holding a teacup up to the lamp, showing a child how the light comes through, the china is so thin. She turns it over in her brown hands. She wonders whose initials these are, *GH*. This was *her* grandmother's cup, a token gift from the matron she worked for in the 1930s. This cup comes down in this other family with stories of high society among the wives of timber barons and shipping magnates nearly a hundred years ago, women who valued the delicacy of a rose on porcelain in the rough society growing up along the shores of Puget Sound.

Now, the young woman speaks softly to her daughter about what it has been like in their lineage. "Your Big Mama traveled to Tacoma all alone on the train from Arkansas, worked in other people's houses, raised other people's children, and sent money home to her family so they could live through the Depression. Finally, at age thirty-five, the man who had loved her since she was little hitchhiked up and found her, proposed, and took her home. They moved to Chicago, and she had my daddy when she was nearly forty years old." She smiles and then pours tea. "Be proud of who you come from," she says.

Once there was a quiet, crippled woman, singing softly to herself, dipping porcelain in an alabaster glaze, painting flowers in delicate brushstrokes. She worked in the back room, catching the rays of sunlight, or wrapped in shawls against the damp of rain and fog. When the doorbell rang, the ladies and their maids would come to buy. Maybe they sat down for a little talk, started the story moving off in all directions, giving meaning to a little piece of ceramic. We are connected through a hundred teacups. We may never discover the source of our connection, but that doesn't remove it.

I want to know who you are. I want you to know who I am. I want us to make our own story in the world. I want our grandchildren to say about us that there was a time when many things looked dark, when people felt separated from each other and wars and pestilence and fear were rampant in both rich nations and poor nations. And people were distracted and busy, driven along in the deterioration of many things they held dearly. But then, in the nick of time, something that no one could see, and no one could stop, began to restore hope and instill them with wisdom and action: people began to remember the sweetness of story. People turned away from the behaviors that had ravaged neighbors and nature; people turned away from the machinery of war they had perfected; people turned back to each other, and sat down and talked and listened.

The invariable mark of wisdom is to see the miraculous in the ordinary.

— Ralph Waldo Emerson

I want to know who you are. I want you to know who I am. We may not even know why, until I hear your stories, until you hear mine. We may not even know why until something sparks between us that makes us smile or cry with recognition — not out of sentimentality, but out of commonality, waking our remembrance that we are each other.

Who put honey in your heart?

Let's start there.

Tell me that story.

Becoming a Storycatcher

Each of us has someone who put the honey in our heart. That person is often an ordinary person who becomes extraordinary through the power to touch another life. Teaching ourselves to recognize these persons and remember these moments is essential to becoming a Storycatcher.

Tell Me This Story...

These story beginnings can be used in writing or in conversation to enhance storycatching in your life.

- Describe one of your earliest memories. Who is with you? Bring in all five senses. Do you know if this is an actual memory or a story you have heard others tell about you?
- Describe your relationships with grandparents or elders. How involved in your life were they? Do you know much about how they grew up? What effect did having elders around (or not having elders around) have on your life?
  Imagine a conversation with a grandparent or elder who is no longer around: What questions would you ask? What do you wish you knew?
- Describe the place you come from. What is the landscape? Who lives there? Use all of your senses to describe the way you remember this place. Do you still visit?
- Choose a family heirloom or artifact and write down as much of its history as you know. Where did it come from? How old is it? How did it come to be valued in your family? Who has it now? What will happen to it in the future?

CHAPTER TWO

The Ear in the Heart

THE ART OF STORYCATCHING

Story is the song line of a person's life.
We need to sing it and we need someone to hear the singing.
Story told, story heard, story written, story read
create the web of life in words.

Dusk, and the room glows only in candlelight for no one has wanted to move toward the lamps. Though twilight sits at our shoulders, we do not want to disturb the delicate attentiveness that hangs suspended between us. There is a palpable sense of compassion and respect in the room. Eyes glisten with tears and laughter. This is story space. This is what happens when people set aside everything else and listen to each other with such quality of attention that speaking and listening become like meditation. Our whole way of being with one another subtly shifts: we become the ear in the heart.

I can tell you a hundred stories:

How a parent and child had trouble understanding each other until they went camping and sat around the fire…

How a couple set aside one hour a month to sit in a quiet place and read to each other from their journals…

How a team of people assigned to a difficult task decided to write their strategic plan as a mythic story and then to fulfill their roles as heroes and helpers to each other…

How soldiers sat down and admitted the pain of fighting a particular war….

I can tell you these stories, and I will. Come listen. Come read. Lean into this space ready to receive and to give the gift of story. What is accentuated here in my living room is the reciprocal nature of story space. One by one we take turns speaking or reading while everyone else listens: one offers, eleven receive, the next one offers, eleven receive again. The rhythm of this, the tempo and cadence of our words, and the quality of attention to our listening connect us to tens of thousands of years learning just this — how to catch stories.

Learn to be quiet enough to hear the sound of the genuine within yourself so that you can hear it in others.

— Marian Wright Edelman

There is a television in this room, but it is unplugged and the convex distortion of its blank screen turned discreetly aside. There is an audio system in the corner with rows of CDs and an iPod and it is silent. The telephone ringer and email alert are muted. The digital melodies and buzzers and vibrators are turned off on the cell phones and pagers in our pockets. Beyond this room, families and friends carry on the business of our lives and allow us to attend for a while just to each other. Beyond this room, the pace of modern life goes racing by, but we are not caught up in it. We are storycatching.

Storycatching is an experience of time out of time; there is a rich complexity to what happens that is deeper than what we expect in minute-by-minute time. Inside the weave of attentiveness, we make intuitive and imaginative leaps. We who are listening follow the thread of narrative; the one who is speaking takes us into another time and place, an event and setting, and introduces us to a cast of characters who become real to us solely through the magic of language. We anticipate where the story is heading and it creates a kind of synergy, a way we hold the speaker to the track of the tale. We bring our words to each other in the flickering light.

The stories we share tonight build a connectedness that will sustain itself long after we have parted and returned to our separate lives. Months from now, one member of this circle, a woman named Stormy, will fly in to a remote cabin in Alaska intending to spend the winter working on her memoirs of life as a Wyoming police officer. By radiophone and email, she will reach out for the support of this group and we will understand what to offer because we know her story. Two months from now, Karen, another woman in this weave of twilight, will be diagnosed with advanced cancer and her friend Patsy will let us know. Her death must already be in her, spreading undetected while we sit laughing at her exuberance and wit. She will move into the home of her daughter to leave her final story in the hearts of two young granddaughters.

Storycatchers are

- *intrigued by human experience;*
- *inquisitive about meaning, insight, and learning;*
- *more curious than judgmental;*
- *more in love with questions than answers;*
- *empathetic without overidentification;*
- *able to hold personal boundaries in interpersonal space;*
- *able to be present while others experience emotions;*
- *able to be present while others have insight;*
- *able to safeguard the space for listening;*
- *able to invite forgiveness, release, and grace;*
- *aware of story's power and use it consciously;*
- *practitioners of the heart of language.*

One day in early autumn, I will see another member of this group at the local ice cream stand. He will say, "Sometimes that circle seems so far away...but when I got the word about Stormy...about Karen, it all came right back. I could even see where each of them was sitting."

We are sitting this evening in low chairs in a circle around a coffee table illuminated with candles and decorated with objects that each of us has brought because of their relationship to the stories we share. *Here is a stone from the beach in France ... here is a photo of our wedding day ... here is a button off my grandfather's favorite sweater ... here are the immigration papers ... the adoption papers ... the old wooden spoon ... an heirloom brooch ... a lock of baby hair ... a photo of my granddaughters dressed as faeries....* Each object has served as the source of the story.

This time we are a dozen people, women and men ages thirty-seven to seventy, from across the United States and Canada. We have spent five days together in a creative process that focuses on writing a defining moment in our lives. We have met in this circle to talk about the craft of story, to respond to questions that open the mind's internal gateways, and to write in our journals and notepads and laptop computers. Housed on the grounds of a small local retreat center, we have gathered on an island just north of Seattle, Washington, and settled into story-time. We have gone hiking and beachcombing, taken restorative naps, eaten delicious meals, and curled up in cubbyholes of solitude supported by the quiet presence of the group. We have talked and talked and listened and listened. All this while, we have engaged in a profound and simple act: we are remembering who we are and seeing others for who they really are.

Storycatchers are people who value story and who find ways in the midst of their everyday lives to honor this activity. They signal to the rest of us that something important is happening in the moment and invite us to notice and pay attention. Perhaps we're at a party and someone starts to speak about what at first seems an ordinary anecdote but soon grows into something more important. A Storycatcher notices and says, "Come, let's sit down on the sofa. I want to really hear you."

Own only what you can carry with you; know language, know countries, know people. Let your memory be your travel bag.

— Aleksandr Solzhenitsyn

The Storycatcher's job is to help us shift into narrative: to make people conscious of the story just beneath the surface of our talk and invite us to speak it. Storycatchers can be little children or frail elders — and anyone in between. In the community hall after church, people are having cookies and coffee and talking casually about their week's activities. A three-year-old seated next to an elderly parishioner announces cheerfully, "You have the best wrinkles."

Though surprised, the old woman recognizes the innocence of the comment and says, "Yes, they are very special wrinkles, and each one has a story."

"Well then," says the child, pointing to a spot on the woman's arm, "tell me the story about that one."

Storycatchers invoke the invisible basket of time and attention that holds story, even when shared in settings less intentional than a candlelit circle. Storycatchers are the ones who ask a leading question, make an inviting comment, or just stop and turn to face the speaker with heightened attention. At the end of a family visit to his parents' house, the oldest son asks everyone at the table, "So, what has been your favorite thing about our all being together?"

Storycatchers believe that the ordinary stories of our ordinary lives have extraordinary gifts coded within them — for the one speaking and for the ones listening; for the one writing and for the one reading. Storycatchers are intrigued with making — perhaps driven to make — sense of experience and to make stories out of our sense. Sometimes Storycatchers are provocative, disturbing the status quo with a probing question or statement. Often Storycatchers are a gift, the people others count on to make a story that will get us through the chaos.

The Ear in the Heart and the Pen in the Hand

There are two modalities of storycatching explored in this book: oral tradition and personal writing. In the modern world, both speaking and writing are vital components in reclaiming and preserving story. Novelist Edmund White once wrote, "When a person dies, a library is burned." White is referring to the library of our stories, our insights into life experience, the map of our learning. I am such a library, and so are you. In the preservation of story there need to be tellers who pass along what they carry about life, and listeners who receive; there need to be writers and readers.

The art of storycatching is our ability to speak and write in narrative.

The art of storycatching helps us treasure our own and each other's stories.

The art of storycatching challenges us to believe that listening to and reading stories is time well spent, and to spend time speaking and listening, writing and reading.

The art of storycatching focuses our abilities to heal ourselves and change the world around us through the stories we share.

Traditional stories, told orally, contained within them the history, social laws, spiritual truths, and cultural values of families and their communities. We continue to pass stories along, year after year, generation after generation, because their timeless elements possess an intrigue, a power, and an ability to transform our lives.

— Robert Atkinson

Both oral and written story traditions are experiencing a renaissance in the modern world. Though we are under incredible pressure to fill our time with chores and distractions, to just keep moving in the race of our days, and to fall exhausted into bed, story remains our companion. People keep claiming the value of personal stories.

In the midst of information overload it is even more essential that we sit down with children and read and talk, that we interview and are interviewed by members of our families, that we share the history of our contributions when we leave a job or retire, that we hang over the neighbor's fence or stop at a coworker's cubicle and get to know each other. We keep finding time to write journals, stories, life histories, and letters to future generations, to leave legacies and narrative wills. Scrapbooking, a form of visual storytelling, has become such a phenomenon that entire stores are devoted to the craft. An estimated fifteen million blank-book journals sell every year in the United States. Somebody is writing. We make videos and DVDs, constantly catching our life stories up to current technology. We take digital photographs and record stories and pictures with every new gadget of the computer age. Cell phones morph into communication hubs. Babies have their own websites.

Story is loose in the world, and the people of the world are communicating as never before. Out on the web, in blogs and other ever unfolding technology, we humans connect and show each other our faces and tell each other our stories, and translation software puts our messages into whatever language we can understand.

The stakes are high. Those who would control the ear in the heart understand that if people truly discover each other, we will make a million circles and sit down and laugh and cry at our commonalities. And then we will not be so easily led to fight wars. We will not so unconsciously exploit other people's lives in order to make our own lives more comfortable. We will not be confused by the manipulation of half-truths and lies. Story is a huge component in what we will make of the world. Direct story: face-to-face and book to book and computer screen to screen — all contribute to a world of storycatching.

Remember your roots, your history, and the forebears' shoulders on which you stand. And pass these roots on to your children and to other children.

— Marian Wright Edelman

Storycatching as a Modern Movement

We have never completely lost storytelling. We can't; our brains are biologically wired for it. But we have lost space for story; and we may also have lost the understanding of how essential storytelling is to who we are. In the world of hyperconnectivity, we tell stories all the time. But are we sharing stories that inform, inspire, or activate us toward the betterment of our communities? In an environment of stimulation overload we tend to tune out rather than tune in, and consequently, we have lost respect for storytelling as an art. But fortunately, whenever we — the human family — lose something, there are those among us who work to preserve it, and those who come in search of it. When the folk art of story is being lost in the noise and pace of modern life, it needs someone to become the catcher, someone who sees value and reverses the trend.

There are many popular examples of movements to preserve and promote storytelling. One modern effort to preserve the oral tradition of story was the publication in the mid-1970s of a series of interviews conducted by Appalachian high school students with the elders in their community: *The Foxfire Books*.

Under the guidance of an innovative high school English teacher, Eliot Wigginton, the students of Rabun-Gap Nacoochee School in rural Georgia set out to document the vanishing culture of the southern Appalachian mountain people. The effort first started as a magazine in 1966, then a collection of intergenerational interviews was published in book form starting in 1972. Teenagers with tape recorders were sent out to interview the old and common hill folk within driving distance of their school. The books happened to coincide with the back-to-the-land movement when tens of thousands of mostly city-raised young adults headed into the hills, where they soon discovered how much they needed advice and practical skills. The Foxfire series gave it to them.

These grandparents were primarily an oral civilization, information being passed through the generations by word of mouth and demonstration, little of it is written down.... If this information is to be saved at all... it must be saved now....

— Eliot Wigginton

The books are a marvelous illustration of story-catching, for while they give instructions on a huge range of subjects — basket weaving, hog butchering, fiddle making, old-time burial customs, wild food gathering, and on and on — all this wisdom is collected through the medium of story. Through the act of sending young people out to talk with old people, people who had not considered their lives as stories worth catching, found a new generation of listeners. The books, numbering twelve volumes published between 1972 and 2004, have sold nearly nine million copies and bridged spoken and written story.

It may be hard to consider our verbal skills an art form when the sound of one another's voices is so often background noise, as though life were a never-ending cell phone call. Mirroring a junk-food diet for the body, we have developed a junk-talk diet for the mind. The cure for junk food is not to stop eating but to eat consciously, carefully balancing our nutrition; the cure for junk talk is not to stop talking but to speak and listen and write and read consciously, carefully determining our communication.

Perhaps we wouldn't eat so much, or smoke, or drink so much if we were paying attention to ourselves. Perhaps we wouldn't talk so much if we were paying attention to each other. All these oral activities are trying to meet a need, and perhaps the greatest need is to be seen and heard. We are often physically and mentally overwhelmed with the wordiness of the human world, yet the cure for wordiness is not less story but *deliberate* story. The cure is catching the essence, stopping in our tracks and turning to listen to one another.

As creatures of story, we long for story: not just wordiness but the quality of interaction story engages in us. Ironically, so many of us experience great loneliness as we jostle around each other on crowded streets, overhear each other on cell phones, or cruise the Internet late at night. As we practice the art of storycatching, we can look for opportunities to insert story space into our daily lives. Story shifts us into connection when only moments earlier we felt isolated.

Attending a conference in California not long ago, I found myself standing in a line waiting to buy fancy coffee. One by one people reached the counter and placed their orders: "skinny latte double-shot tall." I could see I would be in this line a while, so I took a little risk. Turning to the person next to me I asked, "So what's your first memory of coffee?"

The man's face lit up. "Waking to the smell of coffee on school mornings. It meant my mother was already up. It meant we'd get hot breakfast."

"Oh," the next stranger joined in. "Ever heard of Swedish coffee? My mom used to boil the grounds in a pan and drop a raw egg into it to congeal the grounds together." Within minutes, we were storytelling and laughing and the kids behind the counter were saying, "Wait 'til I tell you this one...."

As I left I suggested to the young espresso makers, "Next time you have a long line, just get them talking. It'll keep everybody cheerful." This is the choice to create deliberate story.

When we are paying attention, and when we are paid attention to, we learn to take our place in the story going on around us. I remember a moment when I first took my place on the rim of story.

It was an August afternoon when I was five years old and hanging around the edges of my father's clan during the Baldwin & Sons honey harvest. My mother and one of the aunts had been designated to set the table for all the men and older boy cousins who would come in from the honey house and all the women and older girls who would emerge from the kitchen and the day's garden harvesting. It was going to be a crowded table. They went round and round the dining room squeezing in more place settings. Perhaps thinking I would just sit on her lap, my mother said, "We need fourteen places, if Chrissie doesn't count."

With every experience, you alone are painting your own canvas, thought by thought, choice by choice.
— Oprah Winfrey

Just then I walked into the room with my hands full of silverware. "But I do count! One-two-three-four..." Everybody laughed, but it was a prophetic moment, for I decided from then on I would count... I would be counted... I would represent myself, and remember myself, even if I had to squeeze in between the bigger people.

When I was five I claimed my place verbally; when I was twelve I claimed my place in writing. At Christmas, the year I was in sixth grade, someone gave me a little pastel five-year diary, predated, with five tiny lines an entry. I started off on January first and had just enough room to write down the weather and list what we had for supper: not enough space for story, or feelings, or questioning. Writing in that tiny space quickly became a task I would ignore for days; then I would try to remember something to say about a whole string of days at a time. Pretty soon I gave it up, shoved the little diary to the bottom of my underwear drawer, and just took some three-holed paper, an old black binder, and went freestyle. This was my first journal.

I wasn't a particularly good writer, but I liked the sense of importance I could grant my own experience. I liked how daring it felt to put things on the page I couldn't say to anyone else. Even though those revelations seem trivial now, they were significant then. Keeping a journal is like doing scales on piano, only in words; writing allows us to practice the foundations of our own story. We become more and more articulate the more we practice.

I didn't ask myself why I was writing; I just did it. But one day a little thought tiptoed to the edge of my mind: maybe I was actually supposed to pay this kind of attention to my own life. Maybe paying attention to myself was my job, telling my story was my thing to claim, and my life would be different if I did.

And a lot of people must have come to a similar understanding, for in the last fifty years, particularly since the mid-1960s, we have been living through a literal renaissance in personal writing. I know — the back of my closet is full of my participation. Uncrated, my journals from 1960 on consume nearly twenty feet of shelf space, and I am only one among millions.

Words set things in motion. I've seen them doing it. Words set up atmospheres, electrical fields, charges.
— Toni Cade Bambara

The Power of Personal Writing

People have always had the impulse to record their existence, to mark their territory, and leave hints of their accomplishments. For years I had a shirt silk-screened with designs modeled after the Paleolithic cave paintings of prehistoric Europe: animals and stick-figure hunters. "I'm wearing the first journal entries," I would announce to a new class of writers.

For millennia, people have left their handprints on cave walls and carved pictographs onto boulders. Later, as hunting and gathering gave way to agriculture and communities that flourished in place, societies developed elaborate hieroglyphs that transferred oral tradition to pictorial symbolism.

The origins of writing have mythological roots. In her research, anthropologist Marija Gimbutas traces the credit for early Sumerian tablets to the goddess Nidaba, who is described as the scribe of heaven. And Indian mythology credits the goddess Sarasvati with the invention of the alphabet. Riane Eisler, exploring the origins of culture in her book *The Chalice and the Blade*, says, "The first use of this most powerful tool of human communication seems to have been spiritual: a sacred script associated with the worship of the Goddess."

Then, starting around 3200 BCE (before the Common Era), two civilizations that developed a written language flourished in the area of the Middle East known as the Fertile Crescent, Mesopotamia and Egypt. In his book *The Alphabet Versus the Goddess*, Leonard Shlain makes the case that the switch from dependence on oral tradition to writing changed many things within the brain, requiring that human beings become left-brain dominant for the first time in our evolution. Left-brain dominance also began to change everything about human society, including a shift from the Divine as procreative Great Mother to the Divine as law-giving Great Father. These shifts have both a light and dark side to them.

> *Neolithic art is a kind of language.... And if we let that language speak for itself, without projecting onto it prevailing models of reality, it tells a fascinating — and in comparison to the stereotype, a far more hopeful — story of our cultural origins.*
>
> — Riane Eisler

Writing is the deepest foundation that underlies the rise of modern humanity. The codification of law and the recording of religion, philosophy, and history created huge leaps in human civilization. And the cost of these leaps has been the diminishment of holistic, right-brain values such as oral tradition, respect for the earth and nature, and the preservation of women's social, spiritual, and economic power and partnership.

In the twenty-first century, we live in a world where cultural literacy is a ticket to joining the human community. Any culture discovered in a preliterate condition is quickly provided an alphabet, and the richness of its preliterate worldview and spirit, whatever that has been, becomes subjected to the limitations of writing and translation.

The struggle to cope with this level of change, which can be observed in such refugee cultures as the Hmong, whose people were airlifted from Laos to the United States after the Viet Nam war, is a struggle experienced by every group of people since the invention of writing.

Among some tribes struggling to retain cultural heritage, it is common for elders to say, "The story in English is not the story; and the story written is not the same as the dance."

For most of the history of writing, only selected people within a social or religious hierarchy were educated to become literate. In medieval Europe, for example, it was not uncommon for lords and kings to remain illiterate and to count on scribes to write and read for them. In these same centuries, during the establishment of the Roman Catholic Church, clerics and clergy learned to read and write, but parishioners did not. And until 1450, the entire library of human documents was transcribed by hand. When Johannes Gutenberg invented the printing press, things started to change: Books could be typeset rather than handwritten, and printing made books more widely available. Once people could borrow or own books, the ability to read and write could be taught at the hearth and literacy found its way into the broader population.

If writing is thinking and discovery and selection and order and meaning, it is also awe and reverence and mystery and magic.

— Toni Morrison

With the sweeping arrival of populist literacy, millions of ordinary people had access to the larger story in which they were living. People began to see themselves within a broader context because they could read about the world beyond their personal experience. In the next few centuries, during the immigration of Europeans around the globe, literacy held increasing value as a way to communicate with sponsoring governments or lonesome families back home or as a way to enculturate and convert indigenous populations. Letter writing became a profoundly important global lifeline, a way of transmitting information about the world in which people found themselves. Correspondence led to descriptive writing, which led to literature, which led to leisure reading. And here we are in a world where the Internet and satellite technology keep us instantly in touch — 24/7 in real time.

Born into this evolutionary process, little children understand the power of the written word from an early age. Children practice making letters of the alphabet and writing their names; they scribble pretend correspondence and ask their parents to mail it; they pretend to read, even if they're holding the picture book upside down; and they are very aware that the adults around them, through reading and writing, have access to a mystery they do not. Adults have access to knowledge and story and children want it for themselves. The earlier and more readily a child unlocks the keys to literacy, the more intelligent he or she is assumed to be. The taproot of our way of seeing the world is the written word.

I believe the kinds of writing millions of us are doing in our diaries and journals are attempts to heal the split in the human mind and in the human experience. We are using the linear skill of putting words on paper as a holistic practice. We are bringing the metaphors of story into the raw experience of our lives and making new sense and meaning out of this amalgam. What we create through this kind of writing is neither art nor reality, it is something new: the story of our lives.

"What does Christopher Robin do in the mornings? He learns. He becomes Educated. He instigorates — I think that is the word he mentioned, but I may be referring to something else — he instigorates Knowledge . . ." (said Eeyore).

— A. A. Milne

Journal writing is the ongoing creation of the story of a life, in the littlest and largest sense. It is a story told to the self, by the self, for the benefit of the self. People are highly adaptable and endlessly creative in their journals, and their writing ranges from the notation of the most mundane details to the most profound thoughts the writer is capable of — and everything in between.

The Renaissance in Personal Writing

In 1974, recently returned from living abroad and trying to find my way into the next phase of postcollege work, I went to the University of Minnesota community education program to see if anybody there taught journal writing. I quietly admitted my writing habit and since I did not seem able or interested in giving it up, I wondered if they had anybody on staff who could teach me how to do it better. The registrar looked me over and asked me a few questions. "Journalism?"

"No. Journal *writing*. Like a diary, only I'm not disciplined enough to do it every day. . . ."

"Well, how long have you been doing it?"

"About twelve years."

"Twelve years! Why don't you teach the course?" And so my career began.

I made up a course title, outlined a curriculum, and waited to see who would show up. Twelve people came: ten young women poets, one young man poet, and an antiquarian book dealer who collected first edition diaries and journals and had kept a diary himself every day since he was thirteen. We sat in a circle with our blank books and loose-leaf pages on our laps. I made up things as we went, and they all contributed to my thinking and understanding of how this might go. We felt as though we were breaking ground: admitting the importance of this private writing, writing in quiet communion, then sharing thoughts we'd never spoken aloud. The whole idea of studying journal writing, seeing it as an art form and a life skill was portentous; we knew this intuitively, but we couldn't see the shape and scope of what was coming. It was winter, a time of long darkness in Minnesota. I remember us bundling up, leaving the attic of the little bookstore where we met, journals tucked in gloved hands, following our breath to the tomblike cold of waiting cars. We scuttled off into the night like conspirators: same time next week. Same group.

In 1977, my first book, *One to One: Self-Understanding through Journal Writing*, came out of these classes. By then several of my students had started to teach similar courses in community colleges, and they had called me saying, "You started this, why don't you write the book about it?" I was living in a fourplex, bottom right apartment, trying to financially survive as a freelance writer doing magazine pieces in the regional press. I had given myself until I was thirty to figure out how to "be a writer"; time was running out so I started the book. By the spring of 1976 I was twenty pages into something, I wouldn't exactly call it a book yet, when I saw a miniscule ad in the back of *Ms. Magazine* announcing a women's writing conference on Long Island, New York. I phoned and asked if I could speak about journal writing.

"Journalism?"

"No, journal *writing*...like a diary. I grew up thinking only Anne Frank and Lewis and Clark had ever kept journals...but I'm finding out things, a lost lineage of writing, and I'm teaching classes here in Minneapolis. I think other writers will be interested."

"All the speaker slots are filled," said Hannelore Hahn, director of the conference and founder of a group called the International Women's Writing Guild. "I can give you ten minutes at the end of a plenary."

"That's great! Thanks." By August I had forty pages, a working title, a lot of naiveté, and a round-trip ticket to LaGuardia. At the conference out on Long Island I was surrounded by a faculty of real writers and a community of women who were writing, writing, writing but did not yet call themselves anything. I don't remember what I said in my allotted time, only that there seemed to be interest; women raising hands, wanting to know more. I gave them all my room number and said, "I'll be there during free time, if anyone wants to come by...bring paper!" By 4:15 my room was wall-to-wall women. I was sitting on the back of a chair so I could see everybody. We were writing. And we've never stopped.

These were pioneering times for journal writers. Along with theologian Morton Kelsey, who suggested writing about life's spiritual journey; psychiatrist Ira Progoff, who codified the *Intensive Journal®*; and Tristine Rainer, who combined therapeutic techniques in *The New Diary*, I rode the first wave of interest in reflective writing. When *One to One* was published, the Library of Congress had to create a new category for it: "1. Diaries and journals, therapeutic uses of..."

First mostly women, and then more and more men, started reclaiming our life stories through the act of writing them down. Therapy latched on to the tool, and James Pennebaker at the University of Texas in Austin did research that proved what many of us already knew: story heals. Pennebaker proved that the act of writing, beyond its mental and spiritual benefits and organizational promises, raises the T cell level in the bloodstream, stabilizing the immune system. In the United States alone, tens of millions of people do some kind of private writing that records their personal stories.

From these first few books, a body of literature has grown that now consists of hundreds of titles. This book will join dozens of others in the personal writing section of the bookstore — a section that did not exist a few decades back. And extending beyond the books that show us how to write our stories are the books that tell them: memoir, autobiography, personal fiction, anthologies, even the *Chicken Soup for the Soul* series.

I cannot imagine my life without writing. Writing has changed everything about how I live, though it's hard to say exactly how because I have no comparison self who doesn't write. The reason I spend thousands of lifetime hours creating something 99 percent of which no one else is likely to ever read is that writing itself is the gift. Writing organizes the mind and the actions that lead from the mind. Over time, the decisions and choices we make in the rush of the moment are informed by the self-knowledge our story gives us. We learn that if we have practiced articulating our story, if we have honored the path to this moment by writing it down, the choices we make are congruent with who we say we are. This is one of the primary promises of story: it was true in oral form and remains even more true in written form. For in writing we live life twice: once in the experience, and again in recording and reflecting upon our experience.

We understand that what we write has a great chance of outliving us. Over the years I have worked with tens of thousands of journal writers, and constantly the question is asked, "What do I do with this when I die?" Writing creates an artifact; writing makes our story into an object, something left behind us, something that necessitates custodial care. Our journals place us in the lineage of the unnamed, unknown cave painters, who decorated underground caverns in the Paleolithic era over thirty thousand years ago. We join those who will leave hints and traces of our personal stories for the future to find.

> *A breed apart from the diarists who write simply to collect the days . . . are those who set out in their books to discover who they really are . . . They want to use their diaries to test, and add to, their strength.*
>
> — Thomas Mallon

I don't know what will happen to all this writing. I don't know what will happen to my own writing. I just know I've never quite been able to throw it away, that I've been cheerfully willing to carry heavy boxes of filled notebooks with me move after move in the decades of my life. I just know that every year more people decide to write, and though we may feel very vulnerable to these words while living our story, or when imagining our next of kin reading our writing after we're gone, over time our writing takes on a patina of universality. We know this because we read the diaries and journals of others and experience the universality of human story, presented in a million situations and conditions, yet somehow the same.

There is no historical precedent for what we are doing with our determination to write. This is the first time in human history that widespread and populous literacy can support such a phenomenon. We are laying a new foundation for the future, laying out a grid of millions of stories. Not just those of the famous people or the powerful people, but the stories of ordinary people. With the personal computer a fixture in homes, classrooms, libraries, and senior centers, anyone who can type (and with the growing use of voice recognition technology, anyone who can talk) has a powerful tool for recording his or her story. With digital technology, we can typeset and illustrate and publish our own personal histories. What we need is someone to listen, someone to read.

The story — from Rumplestiltskin *to* War and Peace *— is one of the basic tools invented by the human mind, for the purpose of gaining understanding. There have been great societies that did not use the wheel, but there have been no societies that did not tell stories.*

— Ursula K. LeGuin

In her book *Writing for Your Life*, Deena Metzger closes with the story of a university writing class in which one of the students' assignments was to interview someone very different from themselves, someone with whom they would not normally converse. One particular student was from a privileged background and so terrified of the assignment he almost dropped the class. On the day the interview was due, he arrived with great excitement. "I was at my wit's end," he said, "when it occurred to me to interview our Guatemalan housekeeper. Naturally I was very nervous because I had never really spoken to her, and it was rather late at night. But as I had to do the paper, I went to her room and knocked on the door. When I entered, I explained my need, asking if it would be a terrible nuisance for her to tell me something about her life. She looked at me strangely and my heart sank. After what seemed a very, very long time, she said quietly, 'Every night before I go to sleep, I rehearse the story of my life, just in case someone should ever ask me. Gracias a Dios.' "

The Gift of Story Space

The art of storycatching includes a dedication to holding the space for speaking and listening.

And so, having considered the power of both oral and written tradition, we return to the circle of chairs and notice the delicate web of witness woven between us when we listen to each other through the ear in the heart. We notice the gift of speaking into a container of listening. We take turns speaking or reading while everyone else listens: one offers, the others receive, the next one offers, the others receive again. We notice the rhythm, the tempo and cadence of our words, and how the quality of attention connects us.

Story space is

- *calm, with as little background noise (television, radio, other conversation) as possible;*
- *circular, so that the speaker and listeners can see each other, with space in the center where the words may come to rest;*
- *comfortable, appropriate to the group and setting;*
- *defined by simple agreements for speaking and listening, and an understanding of how the stories shall be treated (defining confidentiality and respect before sharing, for example);*
- *fair and equitable, allowing time for all those wishing to speak or read;*
- *respectfully acknowledging that the story has been heard (thanks or other verbal signals, a bell, applause, hushed silence are all forms of acknowledgment);*
- *agreeing to bear witness, to listen without attempting to fix a person or resolve issues presented in the stories;*
- *rotating leadership roles, such as host, timekeeper, or guardian, and shared responsibility among all present for sustaining the quality of the experience.*

But what if we disagree with what someone is saying? What if we belong to different religions or races or countries or political parties?

What if the storyteller is angry, or frightening, or starts to cry? What do we do then? We bring the conversation back to experience, to speaking the story of what we have lived through. The conversation that deteriorates is the conversation that is dogmatic, opinionated, conceptual, argumentative, and devoid of experience. Story is not opinion; story is experience.

"Dialogue"... is a conversation with a center, not sides. It is a way of taking the energy of our differences and channeling it toward something that has never been created before. It lifts us out of polarization and into a greater common sense, and is thereby a means for accessing the intelligence and coordinated power of groups of people.

— William Isaacs

Several years ago the Public Conversation Project, greatly distressed over violence and the growing polarity of opinion, invited ten people who were adamantly opposed to abortion together with ten people who were adamantly for the right of women to choose. They established basic ground rules for an ongoing conversation: no opinions, just story; no attempts to change minds, just listening. The group met for three years. No one changed her mind about the issue, but everyone changed his mind about the people involved in the other side of the issue. Tensions decreased and tolerance grew for each person's stance because that stance was embedded in story. This tolerance was carried into the larger community.

Storycatchers know story has the power to open the heart, even if the mind does not change. Story is empathy in action between people. And to provide an environment where stories can safely go deep into our vulnerabilities, we need to intentionally create a social structure, up front, before we begin. All social interactions have structure, most of which is culturally encoded and assumed — just as we assume people know which side of the street to drive on and how fast to go; if they don't, they learn quickly! Story space looks casual when everything is going along compatibly, but when painful stories come forward to be held by a community, we need structure in the space, just as we need structure in the story. We cannot follow the story if it loses its narrative thread; we cannot hold the space if it has not been laid down with intention.

Structure is a gift. Once these social structures and roles are in place, members of a group can share leadership and responsibility for the quality of their experience. Articulating a structure that will support authenticity is one of the Storycatcher's skills: we lay out the hearth for hearing each other. The writing group in the living room described at the beginning of this chapter had already put a structure in place.

Stories move in circles. They don't go in straight lines. So it helps if you listen in circles.

— Naomi Newman

Setting the Space

- *We are seated so we can see and hear each other.*
- *We have deliberately placed light (candles) and significant objects in the middle to remind us we are setting our words down in neutral space. Nobody has to pick them up; we can listen without having to agree.*
- *We have adopted a few simple agreements: the story belongs to the speaker and will not be shared without permission; we will practice listening to each other with curiosity rather than judgment; we will take responsibility to ask for what we need and offer what we can; we will pause from time to time to take a breath, recenter ourselves, call ourselves back to our intention.*
- *Our intention is to bear witness to the stories of defining events in our lives that have been at the core of our journeys — in all our diversity.*
- *Our time together has a defined beginning, middle, and end. We know when we are in the heightened attentiveness of listening and when we are relaxing at the dining table.*

We have chosen to slow down our process of speaking and listening by speaking only one person at a time. We resist the urge to jump in and elaborate or comment or take over the narrative. We like the free form of usual conversation, and we also like the gentle discipline of waiting, turn by turn, to speak the tale. Sometimes we pass a smooth stone hand to hand; sometimes we place a pen in the center and one person at a time reaches for it. Sometimes we simply stay in open conversational flow.

We have made a covenant to serve as each other's community of listening. Sometimes we don't know the importance of a story until we tell it in an environment of deep listening and see how our experience and words impact other people. This understanding is part of our genetic encoding: we know how to respond to stories and spontaneously offer each other grunts of recognition, sighs of empathy, shouts of encouragement, laughter and tears, and applause. We smile and frown and gesture and gaze intently and turn our gaze away. We rile each other up and calm each other down.

In the underlying structure of story space, it may help if people volunteer to serve informally in several roles: a host who oversees the physical arrangement and comfort of the group and who convenes and releases the group from its attentiveness; a guardian who watches the time and calls for helpful pauses in action. (I carry a little chime as the signal for stopping and restarting conversations: *ring* — pause — *ring* — continue.)

Once invoked, story space can serve many purposes. Story space is a structure, like the bones in our bodies, that allows us to move in certain ways, and restrains movement in other ways. With the skeletal structure in place, story space fleshes out with as much beauty and diversity as our own bodies do.

STORY SPACE CAN LOOK LIKE THIS:

Sally and Joe came home in the seventh month of her pregnancy to visit her mother and have a baby shower in the community where she grew up. Seventeen people gathered in a circle of chairs and pillows in the living room. We could all see each other. On the coffee table was a candle and an arrangement of cute childhood photographs of the parents-to-be and sonograms of the baby. The mother served cake and coffee and invited everyone to sit down. After Sally and Joe opened presents the mother called everyone into attentive listening. "While we are gathered here as the family and friends of this young couple," she said, "I invite us to spend a few moments providing a bit of story or a blessing for these two people who are taking on the awesome responsibility of raising a child. So that we can hear each other, I'm going to pass around this stuffed toy and ask that we speak one at a time." And so the stories began…

Story space can look like this:

A man whose wife had died of cancer and left him to raise several children, married again. And his children, though longing for good mothering, had a difficult time accepting this woman into their lives. One night the ten-year-old boy wrote an angry letter in a spiral notebook and left it on the table for the woman to find. "I will never call you mother!" his diatribe began. The woman read it late at night. She turned to the next blank page and wrote back. "Dear Jeremy, I do not want to replace your mother, but if you listen carefully to your own heart beating, you'll notice that it makes two sounds, *lub-dub, lub-dub, lub-dub*. That first sound is your mother, who will live in you as long as you live. That second sound is your choice about whom else you will love. One day when I was your age, my father left home and never came back. It took me years to learn the story, and more years to deal with my broken heart. Shall we write each other letters here and see if we can talk about the things that make and break our hearts?" And so a journal writing process began that went on for a year. They did not talk about their writing, but the writing changed how they talked.

Peace is not merely the absence of war. It is also a state of mind. Lasting peace can come only to peaceful people.

— Jawaharlal Nehru

And story space can look like this:

In the brutal disintegration of tribal wars, the guerrilla armies of the hill people stole the young boy children of the valley people and forced them to fight against their own tribe. UNICEF heard of this atrocity and decided to buy back the children and reintroduce them to their villages. The UNICEF workers would drive into these remote villages with several boys who had been gone for two, three, four years; boys whose childhoods had been stolen, whose souls were wracked with the guilt of what they had done. They went to the tribal elders and asked them, "We have brought them home to you, but they are not the same. What will you do?"

"We will light a fire in the center of the village every night for a year," the elders replied. "The boys will be required to come and tell their stories and listen to the reactions of the villagers. We will weep together for what this war has done. We will talk until the war is talked out of them, until the sorrow is healed, until the fire is burned up."

What they will say about us a thousand years from now is waiting for us by the fire. Come speak, I'll listen. Come listen, I'll speak. When the space is set so the ear in the heart can remain open, our stories will serve as a call for us to recognize each other. Tell me any story that has heart for you, and I will listen through the h(ear)t in me.

When did you claim the right to speak or write your own life?

Let's start there.

Tell me that story.

Becoming a Storycatcher

Learning to listen with the ear in the heart enhances our ability to become a Storycatcher. By making agreements about sharing conversation and the responsibility for listening, we help to hold the story space. Recognizing the need for deliberate conversation in place of speaking merely to hear the sound of one's voice increases the power of story for all participants. And writing takes the power of story onto the page, where we can practice the narrative of our lives, looking for what has heart and meaning.

Tell Me This Story...

These story beginnings can be used in writing or conversation to enhance storycatching in your life.

- Think of an important story someone has told you: How did you feel when listening to this story? If you had permission to share this story with others, did you? If so, how?
- Can you keep a confidence? Describe a story about confidentiality. What is important to you about confidentiality?
- What does it mean to be listened to? How can you tell when someone is hearing you?
- If you keep or have kept a journal, tell the story of that writing process: what is easy, what is difficult, what keeps you from writing, and what supports your writing?
- How could you design a space and place and time that would support a writing practice? What are the rules you need to break so writing is pleasurable and intriguing?

CHAPTER THREE

Tending Our Fire

WHY WE MAKE STORY

They say a picture is worth a thousand words,
but we can't get the whole picture unless we have the whole story.
And the magic in words is that the story can make the picture.

The day pulls the rain back into its mouth, giving us a wee bit of time to ramble this ancient valley. I'm visiting Kilmartin, Scotland, the land of my bloodlines, and I feel the cells of my body singing with return. For eight thousand years people have lived here on these rolling knobby hills and in the deep silted rifts that extend back from the sea toward the highlands in great fans of green pasture. The past fifteen hundred years have been a bloody mess, feudal clan fighting feudal clan for the hilltops and the space between.

In the shops of Oban, an hour's bus ride north, you can buy the tartans, the crests, the kilts and sweaters, the tea cozies and little silver spoons, the thimbles and knives — everything blazoned with insignia to wear about town. Look at me, I'm the descendant of a MacDougall, a MacLean, a Brown, and a Campbell: American mongrels doing the tour — and I among them.

I look at the past and I see myself.
— Miriam Makeba

Beyond the edge of modern commerce, the stones have survived: standing stones, cairns of stones, pathways of stones like teeth protruding from the moss and heather of the moors, sometimes for miles leading toward the center of something important. The stones are waiting in the sheep meadows below the small, exquisitely designed Kilmartin House Museum. We start first with a little education, going through the story of this place so that we can better decode the walk we will be taking into the misty silence of the fields viewable through the plate glass walls of the museum café. Here in this western edge valley, the oldest standing stones are dated at 3000 BCE, and the later cairns at 1500 BCE.

Kilmartin seems to have been a sacred gathering site where it is imagined the tribes convened for ceremony and initiation. Like most of the standing circles of prehistoric Britain, these stones are calibrated to the path of the sun with slits along rock face to mark the alignment for solstice and equinox. Along one wall of the museum a diorama shows the positioning of stones spreading out for miles. The pattern suggests a long walk to the ceremonial fire and elaborate rituals of worship and exchange. I can imagine this, yes, but everything is speculation. Whoever erected these monoliths were a people whose stories have fallen with them into dust and silence.

One thing we know: in Kilmartin, in Avebury, in Silbury, in Stonehenge, and in hundreds of sites scattered across the terrain of Wales, England, Scotland, and Ireland, these people were amazing engineers and astronomers. They were scientists and craftsmen. One thing we don't know: *what is the story that inspired them to this work?* What inspired generations of them enough to set aside their fishing, hunting, shelter building and take on the mental calculations and backbreaking work?

And why am I so sure they were driven and inspired by story? Because I am. Because you are. Perhaps our greatest freedom is to nurture the passions on which our life decisions and actions rest. Stories are the source of our decisions and actions. Stories excite our dedication in ways that conceptual thought alone cannot. We need both to motivate such hard work: the thought and the inspiration, the idea and the context, the what and the how come.

I believe that most people desire to be good, desire to live lives of integrity and purpose, desire to have honorable work that sustains them and their families, desire to make a contribution to their communities, desire to leave even a small legacy for their successors. *This statement is a thought, a chosen conceptual basis for how I live.* To sustain this thought, I need evidence, and evidence comes through story. I collect evidence of human goodness by listening to, reading about, passing along in writing and speaking hundreds of stories that support this belief. I am a conduit for stories that give me hope about the nature of humanity and our potential for wisdom. Fortunately, we are storytelling creatures and evidence is not hard to collect.

> *We are the species that has evolved with language; or perhaps we should say, language evolved us.*
> — Mary K. Sandford

We are *Homo sapiens*, "bipedal primates . . . characterized by a brain capacity of 1,400 cc (85 cubic inches) *and a dependence upon language* and the creation and utilization of complex tools." *Homo*, a Latin word meaning "man," derives from the Old Latin word *hemo*, meaning "earthly one." *Sapiens* comes from the Latin word *sapient*, to be wise, to have and to show great wisdom and sound judgment. We have traded everything — fur and claw, size and endurance — to carry around the brain of humanity on this naked, vulnerable stem.

I stand in the valley of my ancestors with my hands on the lichen-covered stones and stare into the swirling mist. My mind takes me back and back and back to another story.

The DNA of Story

Dusk, twenty thousand years ago. The man is wet to the skin and shivers. The lifeless body of a rabbit bounces against his shoulder as he hurries through twilight. The woman trotting at his side pauses in the fading light to gather a few leaves, scratch a surface root free with her toe, and deposit it in the skin pouch at her waist. They move in this fashion along a trail they hope will lead to welcome, warmth, and company for the night. They smell smoke before they can see it, then hear voices. Finally they round a bend and there it is — fire glow on a cave wall. Other travelers have already gathered. Not wanting to be mistaken for prey or foe, the man grunts loudly, making the sound for "man-friend." The people at the fire are alerted now and shush each other, listen cautiously. "Man-friend, man-friend." His word travels through the dark to the fire. There is chatter, then one among them grunts back, "Man-friend, man-friend." The woman opens her throat and ululates the haunting cry of female greeting. The women at the fire call back to her. They have two things to offer: food and story. They will be welcomed. And so it has always been.

Even now, though we live in a world that glows with a manufactured brilliance to dim the stars, when we light a candle on our dining tables, roast marshmallows over the backyard grill, or place a night-light near a child's crib, our twenty-first century bodies remember how important it has always been to find the fire and tend the flame. With offerings that feed the body and stories that sustain the soul, we return to the fire for a primal sense of belonging. Something about firelight welcomes us. Something about story informs, inspires, and connects us. And so it has always been.

For tens of thousands of years getting to the fire or not has been a matter of survival or not. *Before fire*, community could extend only as far as body warmth: a bonded pair, their offspring, maybe a single juvenile. The early hominid's sense of community was immediate and tangible: how many could be fed, how many could keep warm — instinctual, mammalian behavior. *After fire*, hominids could expand their living patterns to include kinship groups: more could be fed, more could keep warm. *Homo sapiens* began to cluster as they realized that more hunters equaled more meat, more females equaled more food gathering and, of course, more babies.

The couple that walked toward the fire twenty thousand years ago had already undergone two hundred thousand years of genetic selection for language and social organization. Scientists now largely agree that several million years ago the great apes and hominids shared a common ancestor with communication abilities, probably similar to those we observe in living apes. After apes and hominids separated, the *Homo* genus began a series of experiments that, while all extinct, may have contributed to the development of our gene pool: *Homo habilis, Homo ergaster, Homo erectus, Homo antecessor, Homo heidelbergensis, Homo neanderthalensis*. We know them only through their skulls, teeth, and skeletal fragments. By the time *Homo sapiens* became the evolutionary link that survived all the earlier models, physical evidence suggests that mutation for language capacity had taken a great leap forward. This evidence shows up in the changed skulls and brain cavities of our earliest direct ancestors, which scientists have studied through endocranial casting.

OH, THAT'S SUCH A BIG WORD: endocranial. There was a time I thought I'd know a scientific term like this better than the words of poetry. I spent fifth grade poring through a cache of *National Geographic* magazines I'd found stacked in my Grandpa Anderson's basement, their muskiness adding an aura of antiquity and authority: these were not comic books. That spring when, for my birthday party, my mother came up with the theme, "Come as what you want to be when you grow up," I was ready. In a room full of nurses, secretaries, and teachers (this was, after all, 1957), I descended the stairs wearing khaki shorts, a big white shirt, and a pith helmet. I had just learned a new word: anthropologist.

Biologists note that brain tissue is "expensive" for the body: it requires more protection, and increased blood and oxygen supply. Animals develop only as much brain tissue as they need to fulfill their function. The mental capacities of a mouse, a horse, and an elephant are all determined in part by the size and configuration of their brains. The mental capacities of a human are determined by brain size, configuration, *and* the ability to retain complex systems of information and bodies of knowledge that are based on symbolic transfer: language.

Lest we get too enamored with our specialness, in his book *The Language Instinct*, Steven Pinker writes, "Though language is a magnificent ability unique to *Homo sapiens*... in nature's talent show we are simply a species of primate with our own act, a knack for communicating information about who did what to whom by modulating the sounds we make when we exhale."

Pinker makes the case that language is biologically innate. He says, "Language is not a cultural artifact that we learn the way we learn to tell time or how the federal government works. Instead, it is a distinct piece of the biological makeup of our brains. Language is a complex, specialized skill, which develops in the child spontaneously, without conscious effort or formal instruction, is deployed without awareness of its underlying logic, is qualitatively the same in every individual, and is distinct from more general abilities to process information or behave intelligently...."

What is most important to me must be spoken, made verbal and shared, even at the risk of having it bruised or misunderstood.

— Audre Lorde

According to scientific theory, language development does not remove us from the animal realm; it distinguishes our place within it. I believe that nature is a manifestation of the Divine, and that anthropological studies of evolution based on fossil skeletons and DNA, and a growing scientific exploration of brain development and language, are not in conflict with religious belief. Both are true. Religion and science are complementary views of how we got here: religion is the story of what we can imagine; science is the verification of what we can observe.

Science and story have always been partners. The impulse to understand our lives and the world through science is almost as ancient as the impulse to understand our lives and the world through story. Science-mind led to capturing the secret of fire tending, studying the properties of plants, learning from animals, figuring out the seasons and the stars, and building the standing stones of Great Britain and Easter Island, the pyramids of the Mayans and Egyptians, and every marvel under heaven. Story-mind fills in the significance and embeds information inside narrative so that we remember it.

Later in his book, Pinker *tells the story* of the discovery of the Papua New Guinea peoples between 1930 and 1960. "By the 1920s," Pinker says, "it was thought that no corner of earth fit for human habitation had remained unexplored. New Guinea, the world's second largest island, was no exception. The European missionaries, planters, and administrators clung to its coastal lowlands, convinced that no one could live in the treacherous mountain range that seemed to run in a solid line down the middle of the island. But the mountains visible from each coast in fact belonged to two ranges, not one, and between them was a temperate plateau crisscrossed by many fertile valleys. A million Stone Age people lived in those highlands, isolated from the rest of the world for forty thousand years."

In 1930, Michael Leahy, a gold prospector following a river upstream and cresting the first ridge, found himself staring into previously undiscovered terrain. As night fell, he noticed a number of firelights flickering below and realized that he was not alone. The next day, he and his companions met the peoples of the Neolithic era, and these people met pale-skinned modern man. In the isolated plateau, various tribal groups had developed eight hundred languages, each capable of expressing "abstract concepts, invisible entities, and complex trains of reasoning."

Pinker *uses the story* of this discovery to make several scientific points:

- All groups of people develop language; no mute cultural group has ever been discovered.
- Though certain regions and societies have been labeled "cradles of civilization," no region or group has served as a "cradle of language" conferring speech to previously languageless groups.
- While the technologies of a culture vary widely in their sophistication, the sophistication of language is consistently complex.
- Children will learn language and when necessary will develop grammatical complexity that surpasses that of their parents or teachers (deaf people, who cannot learn auditorily, create sophisticated grammatical languages of sign).

The biological and neurological wiring that makes us human has been in the developmental stages for several million years. The skulls of

Homo habilis, which lived 2.5 to 2 million years ago, show the faint imprints of their brains clearly enough to determine that the language areas of the left hemisphere were already present. And *Homo sapiens*, which appeared in Africa about two hundred thousand years ago, and began migrating out of Africa about one hundred thousand years ago, had skulls like ours. As Pinker notes, "It is hard to believe that they lacked language, given that biologically they *were* us, and all biologically modern humans have language."

The Necessity of Language to Know the Story

In about 250 CE, an Irish tribe called the Scotti began to sail across the Irish Sea and settle on the Inner and Outer Hebrides and coastal lands of western Scotland, moving in amongst those who were already residents.

We don't know much about these people, not even what they called themselves. The Picts is what the Romans named this tribe, from the Latin word *pictis*, meaning "painted," supposedly in honor of their heavily tattooed bodies. The Picts left art and stones but no records of their stories other than several quotations attributed to their chiefs and written down in Latin during the era when they held the line at the end of the Roman Empire. (One wonders how this translation occurred, since the Picts were certainly not speaking Latin.)

> *We the most distant dwellers upon the earth, the last of the free, have been shielded . . . by our remoteness and by the obscurity which has shrouded our name. . . . Beyond us lies no nation, nothing but waves and rocks.*
>
> — Attributed translation of the Pictish chief Calgacus, 300 CE

At first, it seems, the Scots and the Picts joined together to keep the Roman Empire at bay, but once successful at fighting back a common foe, they turned on each other and the English in an age of bloodletting that went on for centuries and still erupts in the modern era. The Scottish and the English remain; the Picts are gone. Standing on a small rise, looking northeast, I see the landscape as a plaid of blood and bones.

Through it all, the stones have stood in their mysterious placements.

For five thousand years, they have withstood everything humans and nature have done in and to this valley. The original stone circles from the earlier Largie period were piled over with fifty-foot cairns of local stones. As climate has changed, they have been covered over by seawater, embedded in peat bog, eroded and stripped back into view. The cairns have been deconstructed to build walls between pastures and carried off to pave village streets. The people come and go and change and adapt. The people forget and remember and change the story. The stones stand.

As a great-great-granddaughter of the Baldwins, Knights, Harts, and Purdys, standing in Scotland, England, Kilmartin, and Avebury, placing my hand on these rough-carved obelisks of mystery, is as close as I can come to decoding the stories of my patrilineal origins. And this is true of any modern human: what we know about ourselves quickly disappears into the mist. Story itself goes back, but we have not, as a species, always taken good care of our stories. And until the very recent invention of writing, the only form of preservation was mouth to mind.

> *Science can explain us, but it can't save us. . . . Story can.*
> — Mary K. Sandford

This day on the moors, in the timelessness of stones, I stand within a technology of communication that can save story as never before. Yet the question remains, what stories will we save? And the question arises, what stories might save us? And the question walks with me down the path, what decisions will ensure that the stories told about us in the future — the seven-billion-member "us" of the extended human family — speak of the uprising of human goodness?

We have been evolving for this moment for millions of years. And considering the state of the world, it seems a good time to step fully into the capacities bequeathed us in our name: *Homo sapiens, the earthly ones with the capacity for wisdom and sound judgment*. Scientific inquiry informs us we are biologically wired to talk and listen; we are psychologically wired to empathize. An invisible lightning strike flashes in the brain and opens our minds to story. This is our brightest hope. Story is the heart of our language capacity. In the right context, given the respect it deserves, story heals, reminds, and guides us. Story is the most powerful tool ever granted ordinary people. Story is power.

Behind all the distraction and gadgetry and technological hyperbole, dusk is gathering in the real world. We need to find our way to the fire. We need to bring what we hold dear and sit down and stare a while into the flickering and unembellished light that holds the darkness at bay. We need to call out to each other, "man-friend... woman-friend...," and have that call returned. We need to sing our coming into the circle around the flames, and to hear the chorus of welcome that gives us courage to step into the light. We need to proceed boldly, arms open with the fruits we have to share and mouths already singing the tales of our journey.

We need to recover both our voice and our heart, even when the process is hard, and even in the face of people who will do their best to deny the very core of our being.

— Paul Rogat Loeb

Story as the Heart of Language

So, here I am, not an anthropologist but an English major with twenty books on brain theory and linguistics piled under my desk, trying to distill a vast body of scientific inquiry and relate it to my interest in story. The point that fascinates me from my foraging is that human beings are biologically wired for verbal activity: we have to tell stories! And it seems obvious that any skill embedded this thoroughly into the biological structure of our brains deserves attention; more than attention, it deserves preservation, study, and tending.

In terms of preservation, language teaches us without our having to directly experience. Every other living thing must learn through direct experience, which is much riskier. Baby bunnies and baby humans should not play in the road. The bunnies who survive are the ones who figure out how to hop out of the way at the sound or vibration of wheels. The children who survive are the ones whose mothers effectively communicate danger and watch over them until reasoning capacity sets in (which can vary from age four to thirty). When my niece was still in preschool, I remember squatting with her over the pancaked carcass of a dead rabbit, driving home my point about why she should never run into the street.

In terms of study, language emotionally moves us to love and hate, and can motivate us to change the whole course of our lives based on secondhand information, hearsay, and example. This aspect of language has been a blessing and a curse throughout history, and probably the source of a lot of history itself! Language soothes or riles the heart, even if we are not directly affected by the events or experiences recounted. Simply hearing stories about other people can cause us to either embrace or expel those people from our hearts and consideration. I was born an American because the stories of the New World that filtered back to Britain and Norway inspired my people to leave everything they knew, their families, their countries, their languages, and their ancestral homes to seek new lives in a new land.

The stories people tell have a way of taking care of them. If stories come to you, care for them and learn to give them away where they are needed. Sometimes a person needs a story more than food to stay alive. That is why we put these stories in each other's memories.

— Barry Lopez

And in terms of tending, language can lift us beyond the borders of our individual lives to imagine realities of other people, other times and places; to empathize with other beings; to extend our supposing far into the universe; to even imagine God. Through the power of words, language expands the borders of our self-concept and places us in a context and continuum of human experience. In just five to seven million years our use of language has evolved from a survival technique to remind us to get out of the road, to encompass and communicate our capacities for contemplation, imagination, and the ecstasy of insight!

The split that occurred in the course of our evolution from ape to human is mirrored in the brain: we have two lobes, two ways of thinking, two ways of processing language. And while the language center is located in the left hemisphere, the capacity to generate poetry, art, and story seems to be located in the right. We are cognitive/left-brained and metaphoric/right-brained. Scientists, being cognitive, have focused most of their study about language on brain theory and I, being creative, have focused most of my study about story on experiential observation and participation in its power to heal and motivate.

To my way of thinking, the ultimate aim is to be whole-brained: to take in information and anchor it in narrative so that language fulfills its amazing functions. Whole-brained responses create language patterns that are associative. We take information and embed it in story and we take story and embed it with information so that skills and information can be passed from generation to generation, or from group to group. This is automatic. It's how we teach children. It's how we socialize the individual to the group. It's how we create culture.

Ninety percent of everything we know has been passed along through story.
— Laurens van der Post

And for most of human history, whole-brained learning has been how we preserved and taught all the wisdom we accrued. Story and information were chanted and drummed and danced around the fire. Decisions were made within a spiritual context, and elaborate prayers and rituals accompanied the counsel offered by elders and leaders. Only recently, in the rise of the Euro-American culture, has this holistic modality split severely in two, with intellect and science given more credence than story and wisdom. We need both: the cognitive and the creative, the statement and the story.

The Four Gifts

In serving as the heart of language, story imparts four distinct gifts. Each of the descriptions of these gifts below is followed by a corresponding chapter in the story of my Scottish sojourn.

1. *Story creates context.* Context is the comprehension of what the story means. Context is the *lived* experience of understanding that resides underneath the *spoken* experience. Context sets events in time and place. "Once upon a time..." or "It was a dark and stormy night..." or "Last Tuesday after the ballgame..." are all examples of context setting. Context verbally places us in the world of the story. It opens the portal of imagination and identification.

Rain finally caught us in the Scottish valley. We hustled into the museum café for tea, shaking off wet jackets. The sounds of passing cars on the highway outside changed to that slick whine of tires on wet pavement. Cupping cold hands around hot milky tea, we sipped, ate scones, and read our educational brochures. We settled into the shelter of the Kilmartin House to write in our journals while dusk gathered around us. We would look up from time to time and stare out into the valley, drawing the reality of the place into our words. This is what we would take with us: the story we made of this moment; the emotional sense of connection to the land, to the people who walked here thousands of years ago depositing stones, and to the people who left here hundreds of years ago depositing themselves in America.

2. *Context highlights relationship*. When context is set, the story starts happening to real people, and the events in the story activate relationships. With or without names, people in a story are identified by relationship: "I had this friend...," "I knew this woman at work...," "My great aunt Ellen...," "This little boy in Costa Rica..." are all examples of identification by relationship to the speaker. Even if the characters in the story are far removed, we begin to see them and to imagine a relationship to them as well.

Only when we got back to the B&B did we hear about the accident. An American schoolteacher had been killed when a lorry going around a curve had tipped over and crushed the man inside his rental car. My traveling companion and I were busing around these backroads because we had not trusted ourselves to drive in a country where every instinct for left and right would have to be reversed. We were shaken at this news. How far to come to die in another country, body and metal twisted together. People came up to us in the pub and said how sorry they were. We wondered aloud, "Where did he come from? Was he traveling alone? Are there students who miss him tonight? How will they inform his family? Is the lorry driver all right?" We could not answer these questions and went to bed tenderly aware of life's precariousness.

3. *Context and relationship change behavior and lead to holistic and connected action.* When story starts happening in a real scene with real people involved we start putting ourselves into the story. This is vicariousness, the human ability to imagine ourselves into relationship with experiences that are not our own but are — through story — able to inform, inspire, and activate us as though they were direct experience. While we listen to such stories, we evaluate the actions and reactions of the characters in the tale. We identify with the person who behaves most like we would behave, or would want to behave. We are critical of people who behave differently, and learn from their experience: to anticipate and prepare ourselves to behave well in a similar situation.

This part of Scotland is a series of small towns with a lot of rolling pastureland in between. The next day we headed back toward Oban on the local bus and listened as the local people got on and off and talked amongst themselves. One woman knew the lorry driver's cousin. Another woman was the neighbor of the ambulance driver. Something had happened that stirred them more than usual. When the accident occurred it had blocked both lanes of the highway and required crews from several communities to clear the scene. A story began to emerge: There was a woman who had been driving just behind the schoolteacher's car. She skidded to a halt and ran toward the vehicles. Without seeming to worry for her own safety, she checked on the lorry driver, who was conscious and hanging securely in his seat belt, then she eased her way into the squashed car and stayed with the man until authorities arrived.

"The man's dead," she told the constable, "but the lorry driver doesn't seem too badly hurt." She gave the police the details of her witnessing and asked that her name be kept private, except she wanted to know how to contact the man's family. She wanted them to know he had not died alone.

We were the last off the bus when the driver turned and stopped us for a moment. "You're Americans, aren't you?" he said. "I know you didn't know the man, but I know the woman. Her father died in a car wreck when he was vacationing in France ten years ago. She made a vow that if God ever gave her the chance to help a stranger, she would do what she wished had been done for him — she'd be the arms of an angel."

4. *Connected action becomes a force for restoring/restorying the world.* When we come upon a story like this one, or participate in a moment that has such rich potential to teach us how to be better human beings, we want to pass it along. We want the story to live, to outlive the participants. We are drawn to our heroic nature, particularly to the private unsung moments that are often our finest interactions. When these elements combine into real scenes, real people, real inspiration, the personal becomes universal — the characters lose their specificity and become everyman/everywoman. Whether this story takes place in Scotland, or France, or India doesn't really matter, because of course it has taken place everywhere and forever. Like the story of the Good Samaritan, it is an archetypal story that reminds us that the choice to be our best self is always with us, waiting for that skid in the road.

So the bus driver respected her privacy, but told us in parting, "I dunna think she'd mind you tell the tale. It's what I'd wish myself, wouldn't you?" We stood in silence a minute, each of us imagining ourselves being the one who was held, being the one with the courage and heart to hold. And as we exited the bus we made a vow — if ever God gives us the chance to help a stranger, we will do what that moment calls for, attempting to be the arms of an angel, in honor of a lady in Scotland, in honor of her father, in honor of an unnamed schoolteacher, in honor of putting goodness back into the world.

Tending Our Fire

Some of the people who left the hills and valleys of Great Britain ended up in the hills and valleys of Kentucky and Tennessee in the southeastern United States. They burrowed into the landscape to preserve a way of life that honored their origins. The Appalachian hill folk kept their Celtic dances and music and their southern drawl remained spiked with brogue and burr. They made a variety of homemade whiskey and proudly — sometimes violently — kept their clans.

At the onset of World War II, under an agency called the Tennessee Valley Authority, the U.S. government decided to provide electricity to southeastern rural America by constructing a huge hydroelectric dam on the Tennessee River. Riding on heightened patriotism and the need for defense, the agency pushed the project forward with apparent populist support. The folks most deeply affected, those whose valley would be logged and flooded and who would be required to relocate from lands where they had subsisted for generations, were enlisted to work on the project as a way of buying their cooperation. In her book *The Wild East: A Biography of the Great Smoky Mountains*, Margaret Lynn Brown writes, "TVA relocation experts emphasized the importance of employment connections to speedy, cooperative removal. State and county government officials actually provided TVA with lists of families receiving public welfare...."

Brown later writes, "TVA targeted [the towns of] Bushnell, Judson, and Almond first, because soon after the gates of the dam closed, all three would be underwater. To achieve these removals, TVA exercised extraordinary power of eminent domain.... By statute, TVA could decide which lands were needed, employ its own appraisers, and make a nonnegotiable offer to landowners. If an owner refused to accept this onetime offer, his property was condemned."

In its own way, the Fontana Dam is a version of a standing stone. In an inflammatory atmosphere of threat, pressure, and red tape, the poor, disrespected hill folk were worked hard and scattered. "As families left and removed their homes, communities were reduced to unsightly heaps of unwanted lumber and buildings and then burned by TVA clearance crews." Like the hills and valleys of Scotland, change was coming to the Tennessee River valley, and no one could stop it.

In one of these valleys where residents were required to move, everyone had taken the government's offer and relocated except one old woman. Whenever TVA officials or social welfare officers approached her cabin, she chased them off with a burning brand lifted out of the fire she kept in a pit in the dirt yard of her dilapidated cabin. To the officials, the property didn't look like much, certainly not worth saving, but they could not convince her to leave.

In a news report published in the *Sylva Herald and Ruralite* newspaper in October 1943, such a situation was described to reporters: "There is an old woman who lives back in the Proctor area, two miles up in the cove, where it is impossible to take a car. She's rather feeble. [Her son] said his mother had not been to Proctor in forty years and had never been to Bryson City, twenty-five miles away. She had never been in an automobile."

When officials expressed their dilemma to one of the woman's former neighbors, he promised to help. "I know what to do. I'll go get her." The man drove his tractor with a front loader onto the old woman's property, scooped up the fire, and carried it down the valley to a relocation site where he deposited the fire. Soon behind him came the woman pushing a wheelbarrow with her worldly goods.

"What did you do?" asked the officials.

"Well, this woman is a keeper of the flame. That's been her family duty in these hills for long as we remember. They kept the fire, made sure it never went out, so we always knew where to get a new coal if we needed it. She's the last. She'd never leave the fire."

In the misty hills of Scotland where this woman's family left the old fire for the unknown, I wonder if this is what I came for — not the stones but the spark. I came to get a coal from the hearth because I needed to rekindle my dedication to the story, to the long, long story that is older than anything we know. Once this understanding starts to live in me I am ready to come home, to find my relocated people; to take two stones, rub them together, make fire, and enter the story again.

What we call the beginning is often the end and to make an end is to make a beginning. The end is where we start from.

— T. S. Eliot

What is the story you're tending, the one you'll never let be put out?

Let's start there.

Tell me that story.

Becoming a Storycatcher

Tending the story is a privilege bestowed on Storycatchers by their willingness to receive, report, and protect the world's stories. Storycatchers become the librarians, taking care of the stories that are already there, adding stories to the shelves, and ensuring that the stories remain available for the future.

Tell Me This Story...

These story beginnings can be used in writing or conversation to enhance storycatching in your life.

- What do you know about the origins of your family? Is your family history recorded someplace? Ask the oldest member of your family to tell you about how things were when she or he was growing up.
- The ancient stones are one of life's mysteries. What other life mysteries are you curious about? Can you imagine a story that explains the mystery?
- Describe a time when language inspired you. It might be a speech, a letter, a book, or a conversation. What about these words inspired you? How did you react?
- Who is a keeper of the flame in your life? Why is this important to you? How do you support or hinder this action?
- What stories are you tending for your family? How are you preserving them? Have you written any of the stories down? Who will keep them after you are gone?

CHAPTER FOUR

It Was a Dark and Stormy Night

STORY WAKES UP

Story is the mother of us all. First we wrap our lives in language and then we act on who we say we are. We proceed from the word into the world and make a world based on our stories.

The autumn wind was chilly and dry leaves rattled in the tree branches. I was sixteen years old and it seemed possible that the world was about to end and take me with it. It was October 1962, and humanity was living through thirteen days when the United States and the Soviet Union sparred with the idea of unleashing nuclear war. We all seemed frozen in place, reciting over and over in our minds: *no they wouldn't — but what if they do?*

I was a sophomore in high school in suburban Minneapolis. My girlfriends were driving me crazy talking about who would sit next to whom on the school buses fleeing toward Minnesota farmland and a fantasy of safety. "How can you be boy crazy at a time like this?" I yelled at my friend Jane.

"Everything else is crazy," she countered. "If I'm going to die, I want to do it in the arms of Kenny Corens. He is such a dream." And she flounced off, ponytail bobbing perkily, walking with a posture that told me she was still imagining balancing a book on her head the way we had practiced in home economics.

You've got to wish for something the whole time you're seventeen. You've got to or there's nothing to live for.
— Charlotte Bingham

"Great," I thought, "she'll never grow old, but she'll die with her head up." How could anyone — young, old, American, Russian, world onlooker — possibly cope with the idea of our own extinction? Yet extinction is a shadow that never leaves us — not since August 1945 and the bombing of Hiroshima and Nagasaki that initiated the Atomic Age, and not since we continue to turn our backs on the laws of nature.

At Wayzata High School, we lived through those days in an atmosphere where the consequences of our country's political action and reaction were overwhelming; it seemed to make the consequences of everything else drop away. Couples were necking in the corridors, and kids who barely knew each other's names were holding hands. Teachers roamed the hallways reciting a litany, "Okay, knock it off, get to class, you'll be tardy..." I suppose it gave them something to do. Though too insecure to join in the love fest — this was before the sexual liberation that would begin to surface a few years later — I have to admit I was wondering about the real need for studying algebra in light of world conditions. But under the watchful eyes of my parents I dutifully trudged through equations, in case we didn't die.

These thirteen days have become a blip in the stream of time, a political memoir by Robert Kennedy, followed by a Kevin Costner movie illustrating how very, very close we came to The End. This event now merits only a few paragraphs in high school American history textbooks subheaded "The Cuban Missile Crisis," a test question my teenage nieces and nephews don't remember after the midterm exam. But it was a defining moment that shaped my life and work, and I believe it is one of the stories that continue to shape the lives of those who were alive then and those born since, even if we have lost track of its influence.

I was born in April 1946, eight months after the United States dropped the Bomb, wiping out 105,000 people in the course of a few minutes and ending World War II. Anthropologist Margaret Mead described this event as "a line in the sand drawn through human history." In her book *Culture and Commitment*, Mead wrote: "Even very recently the elders could say: 'You know, I have been young and *you* never have been old.' But today's young people can reply: 'You never have been young in the world I am young in, and you never can be.' The older generation will never see repeated in the lives of young people their own unprecedented experience of sequentially emerging change. This break between generations is wholly new: it is planetary and universal."

My fellow citizens: let no one doubt that this is a difficult and dangerous effort on which we have set out. No one can see precisely what course it will take or what costs or casualties will be incurred.... But the greatest danger of all would be to do nothing.

— John F. Kennedy, televised speech to the American people, October 22, 1962

Mead predicted that as we comprehended the magnitude of this power shift — the capacity to completely erase ourselves and destroy the planetary ecosystem — it would change the human psyche in ways we would study for centuries to come, assuming we had those centuries. And by 1962, we had thousands of nuclear warheads — bigger, better, lethal beyond our imagining — sitting under the trigger fingers of the politicians in power. And so it is still today. We live by precarious grace that no one has twitched at the wrong moment in the great power plays that plague our kind.

By 1964, the official end of a generational cycle, I had been joined by seventy-seven million brothers and sisters in the largest generation ever born: the baby boomers. Every house on Oak View Lane had at least three kids, and the Catholic families had seven, or eight, or more. Classrooms were full, the district was adding new schools, and suburbs were starting to ring every major city. Population was the rock dropped on the water, rippling out in concentric circles into the farmlands, into the wildlands, demanding domestication of the planet to feed us, clothe us, shelter us, give us stuff and stuff and more stuff. We didn't think about this yet, the other bomb — population — and what was coming if we *didn't* die. But in this moment in 1962, we weren't thinking about anything except getting the Soviets to stop installing missiles on the island of Cuba, in our backyard. John Kennedy was forty-five years old; Nikita Khrushchev was sixty-seven. It was their dance, and we were all at the ball.

Our lives are lived in story. Story is how we organize experience. In the constant stream of things happening, what we remember are the interactions we cull from our experience and call into our story. And the stories we remember are the ones in which we made a significant choice or decision about what things mean.

Generations can be divided according to essential impression around age seventeen. Modern psychology has proven that impressions received in those years are deep and persistent. This holds especially true for a generation of adolescents which goes through experiences of weight. This gives them a unity, a common style, a new approach to life.

— Dr. Sigmund Neumann

I remember October 1962 because suddenly I understood that my story and history were inextricably linked. What happened to the world would happen to me. The Cuban Missile Crisis occurred just at a moment in my life when I was ready to start waking up.

Poised at the garage door, I struggled to carry a garden shovel in one hand and a square green metal box in the other. Not wanting to explain to my mother what I was doing, and not wanting to be questioned by that rambunctious passel of boys who ran with my brother from yard to yard along the dead-end gravel road of our neighborhood, I waited until dusk. In the fading light I looked furtively both ways, then made my dash across our back lawn to the edge of the woods and over the rise, disappearing down the slope that extended a quarter of a mile through stands of oak toward a swamp below. I leaned up against a tree and caught my breath.

I had found this file box in our basement, full of my parents' old tax records. Considering that death might come before taxes came again, I stashed their papers and replaced them with my own contents: a recent issue of *Life* magazine, photos of myself and my family, a map, a copy of Anne Frank's *The Diary of a Young Girl* (at that time, required reading in eighth grade English), my own diary, a small Bible, and a brief, dramatic note. "Dear future, if there is one, this is who I was before the Bomb.

This is what life looked like. Here are the faces of those I loved. Here is the girl who inspired me to write. Here is the basis for a religion we did not follow. Remember me."

I chose a large tree, scraped away enough dirt to create a shallow hole, popped the box into its makeshift grave, and marked the site by chipping an X on the bark with the shovel blade. I climbed up the hill, arms emptied of my life treasures, dragging the shovel and myself reluctantly back to the family's evening routines.

My mother looked up as I eased in the side door. "Where have you been?" It was a rhetorical question; she didn't expect an answer. "Set the table, please, your father will be home soon." Opening the silverware drawer, I resigned myself to acting normally while the back of my mind zinged with unthinkable possibilities.

SOMETHING IS HAPPENING IN THIS MOMENT. Something is happening to our story and we don't yet know it. We are just in it. We live in story like a fish lives in water. We swim through words and images siphoning story through our minds the way a fish siphons water through its gills. We cannot think without language, we cannot process experience without story.

We are the story-making creatures. We are the species that has evolved a language that leads to self-consciousness. Self-consciousness is based on the ability of the mind to take one step back from experience, to filter and interpret and reflect. This is our great and sometimes lonely differentiation from the rest of the animal realm: that step back, the mental requirement that we run everything through the brain's word processor before we know what's happening.

Sometimes I get a little jealous of the rest of nature, which seems unburdened by this need to interpret and understand and find pattern. I'm jealous that the rest of nature doesn't have to spend time trying to explain, justify, forgive, accept, and go on. A cat is not confused about the meaning of life, and you never see a dog limping down the street howling, "Why me? Where did that car come from? What is the lesson in this?" These are human questions and concerns. Everything else around us just *is*; we are the ones who struggle to *be*. And this is who we are: we are human *beings*.

And what a world we have created through language and consciousness — songs and stories, art and culture, myths and traditions and religions, astounding bodies of knowledge, theories about the nature of the entire universe, science and philosophy, and promises about what we might become. So we might as well leave the cat purring on the windowsill, pat the dog on the head, and carry our consciousness as cheerfully as we can.

Without words, without writing and without books, there would be no history, there could be no concept of humanity.
— Hermann Hesse

There are many tools we humans have developed for molding and influencing our journey on the earth, many technologies and social experiments: story is the oldest and the most consistent survivor of all these tools. Story is the mother of us all, for we become who we say we are.

Individually, we first put our lives into language, and then we act upon what we have said and how we have defined ourselves. Our stories about ourselves become the basis for our identity and the way we hold each other accountable for our individual actions. A man who proclaims himself "a good father" should not be beating his children.

Collectively, the community, tribe, or nation first creates a mythic self-image and history and then acts to fulfill this declaration of place and promise in the world. A nation that declares peaceful intent should not be running over borders with an army.

When story and behavior are consistent, we relax; when story and behavior are inconsistent, we get tense. We have a deep psychological desire for our stories and behaviors to be consistent. We need to be able to trust the story, because it's the lens through which we see reality. We will go to great lengths in the attempt to make a story that explains an action and supports or restores consistency. If we cannot make story and action fit, we either have to make a new story or change the action. Eventually, the good man either has to change his story of self-proclaimed goodness or stop beating his children; eventually the peace-loving nation either has to admit what it's up to or stop invading other countries. However, language can be cleverly used to befuddle and confuse and spread falsehood. The good man may find a way to include brutality in his story and self-definition, and the peace-loving nation may find a way to explain aggression as a peaceful, even altruistic, intervention.

Our personal lives are to a great extent shaped by decidedly impersonal forces. And we have far more power to influence those forces than we know.

— Paul Rogat Loeb

The drive for consistency and the ability to redefine abhorrent action so it fits the story are very complex issues. We have a huge ability to continue believing stories we are told are true in order to stay comfortable with actions we don't want to change, or don't feel capable of changing. Individually and collectively we maintain areas of prescribed silence, a sort of "don't ask, don't tell" complacency so that we don't have to live with the tension of inconsistency.

In October 1962, we were living in a collective moment where all these forces were in play — silence and breaking silence, consistency and inconsistency, threat to the status quo, and huge psychological disorientation as we struggled to understand the story we found ourselves acting out in the world.

A Rude Awakening

I am setting the table for six, the perfect family size according to my mother, who jokes among friends about how it makes grocery shopping easier: half a dozen eggs, half a dozen doughnuts. Four kids, two parents, a three-bedroom rambler on a half acre of lawn, ten miles from downtown: the American dream. Car lights swing double orbs of moonlight on the dining room wall. Daddy's home from work and the house noises up as the younger children race from bedrooms and homework and the flickering gray faces of black-and-white TV to greet him at the door. He is snatched over the threshold, pulled through the dining room, and pushed onto the sofa or carpet by his sons and daughters, who all want a piece of this ritual — fifteen minutes of roughhouse tolerated because he is in the middle of it, the core of it, the bear in his den covered with cubs.

At sixteen, I am too old for this game. It's my job to catch his coat and hat and accept the handoff of his briefcase so he can surrender and rumple his suit, which I assume my mother keeps ironing. Too self-conscious to be rolling on the floor with my father and siblings, I stand over the family tumble and ask him, "Did you have a nice day?"

When I turn around my mother is leaning in the doorway, wiping her hands on her apron and glaring at me. This look later becomes a sentence whispered into my ear late at night when she is tucking my sister and me into bed. She bends over me and whispers, "Don't you wife him. . . ." She rises, opens and closes the door. My room is illuminated in a flash of hallway bulb, followed by total darkness.

After she's gone I whisper back, "Why don't you do it?" And then we both forget this ever happened.

We forget because it is not anything we can talk about; nobody is yet talking about such things, not then, and maybe not now. There is rivalry that lives in a family; there are stories we tell in order to explain it; there are silences we keep in order to deny it. To remember requires language: to heal requires story. Healing has come into this scene for my mother and myself and for tens of thousands of mother/daughter pairs who grew up trapped in the societal silences of this time.

My fingers itch with desire to write, to reach for the notebook I keep of my life, but it is buried out in the woods waiting for the end of the world. And if I had it, if I opened to a blank page, cribbed under the tent of the sheet, what would I write? *Dear Diary: Today President Kennedy got on television and told us to be brave because he and Mr. Krushchev are thinking about starting nuclear war. Great. And I have a zit on my nose, and I can tell by the way John MacDonald looks at me that he's not going to ask me to homecoming. And I can tell by the way David Dayon looks at me that he might. What shall I do? And my mom . . . we're always mad at each other. She doesn't understand me at all, which I guess is fair enough. I don't understand her either.*

There are not yet words for the story we are swimming through. Things are happening that we cannot say, or even perceive, because no one admits they are happening. This is where the limitations of human consciousness show up: we need words in order to make things real. If we don't talk about something, it's as though it's not happening. And yet it is happening.

At Christmas, Jane's mother disappeared. We gathered in a shocked circle prying information out of her. "I don't know where she is," Jane admitted. "My dad says it's a hospital, that she's not going to die, but he doesn't know when to expect her back. He's hired a housekeeper — a stranger named Mrs. Hinkleman — and told her to teach me how to cook."

"What are you going to do?"

"Learn to cook."

In May, Ginny's mother died. The school nurse came, got her out of class, and drove her home. Four days later I went to my first funeral, watched a family figuring out grief. Could someone just die without warning? Ginny was almost as perplexed as her friends: "Mom said she was sick...she never said she was dying..."

"Sick how?"

"I don't know — she never said." We sat on her front porch overlooking the minty green of Minnesota in May, isolated in our thoughts. This is what I mean: it's not happening, and yet it's happening. I guess I was lucky that the worst thing at our house was that Mom and I didn't understand each other.

We record unspoken experience in the mind and body, but unless we can story it out, experience remains inside us shrouded like fog hanging over water. We may act on these unspoken tensions, but we act blindly. We whistle bravely forward, a small, lost skiff, sounding a horn in the mist. And often we crash upon unseen shoals. Unarticulated experiences that are not allowed into the story can show up years later as trauma, disease, mental illness, or a midlife crisis. But when these same experiences are shifted into language and successfully worked through in the healing power of story, they lay the groundwork for transformative personal development.

I lay in the autumnal night, gazing out the window through shadowy oak leaves, breath by breath waiting for sleep or death, breath by breath waiting for John MacDonald to realize he loved me, just as Peter van Daan had finally realized he loved Anne Frank. I lay in the autumnal night, breath by breath waiting for my story to find me, praying that my story wasn't over.

In July 1997, in the personal essay column of Newsweek *magazine, a woman named Irma Sonnenberg Menkel commemorated her one hundredth birthday by writing a story she had never told before. In a barracks in Bergen-Belsen, a Nazi concentration camp during World War II, she had helped look after the children housed among the women. One of these girls was Anne Frank. ". . . Typhus was a terrible problem, especially for the children," Mrs. Menkel writes. "In the morning, it was part of my job to tell the soldiers how many had died the night before. . . . When Anne went into a coma, I held her in my arms. She didn't know that she was dying. . . . At Bergen-Belsen you did not have feelings anymore. You became paralyzed. In all the years since, I almost never talked about Bergen-Belsen. I couldn't. It was too much."*

Irma Menkel concludes her essay with these words: "There are many stories like mine, locked inside people for decades. Even my family heard only a little of this one until recently. Whatever stories you have in your family, tell them. It helps."

I identified with Anne Frank like a sister. One day she had been a chatty, seemingly vapid seventh grader in an Amsterdam middle school; the next day she and her family and an assortment of friends were hiding in a previously abandoned floor of her father's office building while Nazi occupation soldiers rid the Netherlands of Jews. And finally, betrayed by an informant, on August 4, 1944, the little group was dragged away into the gruesome archipelago of labor and extermination camps. Anne and her sister Margot died in Bergen-Belsen only a few weeks before its liberation. She was not quite sixteen years old.

The Territory of the Said and Unsaid

In the 1950s and early 1960s, in the comfortable isolation of white middle-class America, we weren't yet ready to say our deeper truth. We didn't know it would help, or even that we needed help. We lived in a bubble where — it seemed — nobody drank too much, nobody suffered too much, nobody was angrily discontented. Though I did not know it yet, this resistance to diverse reality and all its inconsistency is the prison of privilege.

All societies develop a circumscribed territory of what is articulated. As socialized citizens, we live within this territory. We agree to talk about certain things and to not talk about other things. Or we agree to talk about certain things only in a certain way. These agreements create a social story. Social story stresses how we belong and who belongs. Because the desire to fit in is a universal human trait, someone who breaks the trance of social story does so at great risk, and sometimes, great reward. We call this leadership.

Social involvement may simply be the rent we pay for living.

— Marian Wright Edelman

In his book *Soul of a Citizen*, Paul Rogat Loeb says it this way: "The illusion of powerlessness can just as easily afflict the fortunate among us. I know many people who are confident and successful in their work and have loving personal relationships, yet can hardly conceive of trying to work toward a more humane society. Materially comfortable and professionally accomplished, they could make important social contributions. Instead they restrict their search for meaning and integrity to their personal lives. Their sense of shared fate extends only to their immediate families and friends. Despite their many advantages, they, too, have been taught an 'explanatory style' that precludes participation in public life, except to promote the most narrow self-interest."

In the 1950s, while little children were taught to hide under their school desks and never look an atomic bomb in the eye, the social story Americans told each other was that life was about progress and prosperity. Inside our idealized social story, where Ozzie and Harriet came over for dinner and father knew best, life experiences that didn't fit the social norm were driven deep into the silence of collective unconsciousness.

Of course people drank too much, then as now. People suffered. People of color were discriminated against. Jews could not get into certain countries or country clubs. Victorious or not, men came home from the war horrified at their capacity for violence, heartbroken by their experiences of man's inhumanity to man.

Every gun that is made, every warship launched, every rocket fired signifies, in the final sense, a theft from those who hunger and are not fed, those who are cold and are not clothed. This world in arms is not spending money alone. It is spending the sweat of its laborers, the genius of its scientists, the hopes of its children. This is not a way of life at all in any true sense. Under the clouds of war, it is humanity hanging on a cross of iron.

— Dwight D. Eisenhower

Women were shooed out of jobs and education they had enjoyed during the war to make way for veterans. They got married and had babies and lived with frustrated expectations for which they had no words. When pioneering feminist Betty Friedan broke this particular silence, she wrote about it as "the problem that has no name."

The solidarity engendered by the war effort crackled into issues of race and class that festered at the edge of collective consciousness. People strove to make it into the middle-class picture of American life depicted through advertising and appearing on that new invention — television.

Senator Joseph McCarthy held sway in the Congress, attacking anybody he pleased while international militarism and ideological splits divided the world into democracies and dictatorships. The industrial revolution was transmogrifying into corporatism, and colonial occupation was morphing into the global market economy.

Unarticulated collective experience that is not allowed into the social story shows up years later as political upheaval, violence, resistance, revolution, fundamentalism, spiritualism, disconnection, apathy, and dissociation from reality. But when these same experiences are shifted into language and successfully worked through, they lay the groundwork for transformative cultural development.

Standing under that bare oak with the threat of nuclear war thumping loudly in my chest and holding my girlish hope that this time *my* story would be *the* story to be saved, I realized that I would live my whole life balancing between the little story of myself and the Big Story of the Times. Just as one drop of water is part of the river, my one life was part of Life, and my one story was part of Story. It is not one particular drop of water that flows: it is the River. And it is not one life that survives: it is Life. It is not my story that leads us: it is Our Story.

Through my identification with another girl who could write what I couldn't even begin to think, I discovered a way to break out of the socialized story into something else, something new — my own voice. I began to see how the story that gets one person through offers a map that gets more of us through. And when we reveal details that we think are excruciatingly personal, we discover that the personal is universal.

In an atmosphere where at home we did not talk about the trouble in our family, and at school we did not talk about the trouble in the world, I practiced telling my own life story through the end of a #2 pencil onto the pages of my secret notebook. I wasn't a very good writer because I wasn't very good at breaking silence. And I didn't think I was under the kind of pressure Anne had been: I had all the time in the world. That October, all the time in the world shrunk down to a few days.

October 1962 was a watershed moment for story, for shifting from silence to saying, not only with my little epiphany in the woods, but for the society holding its breath around me. History provides these moments again and again, and each time, more people and more story wake up. The Kennedy assassinations, Martin Luther King Jr.'s assassination, Three Mile Island, Chernobyl, Rwanda, the collapse of the Berlin Wall, the end of Apartheid, the end of the Soviet Union, Y2K, 9/11, the tsunami, and whatever's happening tomorrow — all these crises call us to notice that our story and history are linked.

Perhaps we were all in shock, reeling from our recent immersion in our dark capacities. Perhaps in the sunny lands of victory all we wanted was the social story — perhaps our parents thought it would heal them and protect us. They had lived through the Depression. They had lived through the War. Didn't they deserve to just get on with it? In America, we thought so. But whenever a society disowns the stories created by its actions, the storyline goes underground like a coal seam sliced deep into bedrock, building pressure, smoldering.

Women were smoldering. My family was poor those first ten years after the war, and never more than just comfortable as long as I lived at home. My mother accepted the role assigned women in the 1950s, but like millions of women was not suited for it. Poverty and need for security held her chafing in place. She had three, then four, children, no job, seemed to parcel out the money my father brought home as carefully as she could. It was a big deal when I got a secondhand bike. Our Christmases had lots of bright paper but simple gifts: new underwear, new socks, one doll, one truck for my brother, one orange in the toe of each stocking. She made a lot of our clothes and sometimes hand-me-downs showed up, which we wore without questioning. I didn't think anything of it, as other kids seemed to live the same way, not like the suburbs today, not like what is now called middle class. There just wasn't as much stuff in the world.

The politicians used to ask us why we wanted the vote. They seemed to think that we want to do something particular with it, something we were not telling about. They did not understand that women wanted to help make the general welfare.

— Carrie Chapman Catt, founder of the League of Women Voters, 1919

Most nights mom urged us to sleep playing Debussy and Schubert on a Baldwin piano, her prized possession. She took us downtown to the art museum and to children's day at the symphony. She taught us manners, to chew with our mouths closed, what fork to use, and instilled in her unruly children a sense of decorum that has provided me social entrée wherever I've needed to go. We ate dinner together every night and were each required to speak intelligently about our day. But despite all this mothering, when I was thirteen it seemed we just woke up angry at each other and I didn't get over it for twenty years.

In her seventh decade, with tears in her voice she told me, "I had my awakening too, you know. You weren't the first. It was still the fifties and I looked all around, for friends, for someone in our family, asking myself: if I say what I'm thinking, is there anybody here who can respond? This was before the Great Books discussion clubs. I couldn't find a chapter of the

League of Women Voters. I had read Carl Jung but didn't know anybody who went for analysis. We didn't have money. I didn't have education."

"What did you do?" I asked her.

"I went back to sleep. I forgot myself." My mother, and probably many in her generation, discovered what it's like to face the collective agreement of silence: when you cannot know what you know, everything else goes blank. There were no words to say what she wanted; there were no words to say what I wanted. It would take a huge cultural shift, spearheaded by individual voices breaking silences the rest of us didn't even know we were keeping, that would lead us to create a healing story from these times.

Only looking back can we see the universality in the personal story. In the past few decades, I have heard a thousand variations of my girlhood; stories told from the mother's point of view, the daughter's point of view, the father and brother's points of view. Every one of these stories represents a triumph of shifting silence into language, molding pain into compassion. If the pervasive, socialized silence of the 1950s is our story driven into that smoldering coal seam, then our current political, environmental, and spiritual crisis is this coal seam ignited. If thousands — millions — of us have tenaciously spiraled through the lies, secrets, and silences of personal life and arrived at healing, then we are a population capable of applying these skills for healing collective story. The references to my family's pain are a donation by my parents, especially my mother, to this understanding: the personal is the universal; the universal is the personal. Explored to its fullest, all our work with the power and practice of story is such a donation. Breaking silence changes the world.

THE FOURTEENTH DAY DAWNED with the nuclear talons in retreat. My history teacher, a tall angular cross between Abe Lincoln and Ichabod Crane, was elated. "More history!" he announced. "Open your books." Life was going to go on. I was going to have to pass algebra. Late that afternoon I set out to retrieve my treasure box and carried it up the hill.

Stealing into the basement, I carefully removed my contents and replaced my parents' tax papers. I wiped the outside clean and put everything away so there was no trace of my foolishness. How mortifying my drama seemed, how unpatriotic to have doubted the president's ability to pull off the embargo. In my room, I put the photos back in their envelopes, put the Bible back on my nightstand, tucked the *Life* magazine under my bed, hid my journal in the back of my closet, and tore my note to the future into tiny tiny pieces. And then I began to shake. "How dare they!" I whispered through clenched teeth. "Who gave them permission to risk the world?"

Story Wakes Up

We had almost lost the whole story, and the shock to me was that I hadn't even known there was another story until I glimpsed the largeness of the world. I have asked a dozen people recently, "Does the date October 1962 mean anything to you?" Mostly I get quizzical looks and people draw a blank or make a wild guess. "Oh yeah, something political happened... was that when Kennedy was shot? Or Martin Luther King...? Jeez, I wasn't even born yet... were you...?"

We have been given a new story. When it is time for a new story to emerge, holding on to the past... only intensifies our dilemma.
— Margaret J. Wheatley

Yes, actually, I was born — born to the story.

And I wonder if this was one of the moments in history when Story was reborn. Was the bigness of the loss being contemplated so drastic that story itself woke up and broke loose of its tethers? For in light of what has happened since, story has shaken off its complacence and is shouting back against its own extinction. Story is bigger and wilder and more faceted than anyone could have imagined. It's disruptive and raucous, heartbreaking and tender. It offends us and outrages us, enlightens and guides us.

Since 1962, both I and the American society that frames my life story have shifted from a culture that spoke in platitudes about almost nothing to a culture that speaks graphically and obsessively about almost everything. We have shifted from a constrained social story to an unconstrained, desocialized story. This was not just an American phenomenon: people in every culture have had to deal with the deconstructing of social mores and values. They have had to re-create ways to put life back in order. This is no easy task, for individuals or societies. We are in transition from an old map to a new map. The movements that have swept through cultures worldwide are movements based on talking: movements based on finding each other through story, and then attempting to influence society based on what has first been learned in story.

People of all religious and political persuasions experience themselves as under siege in one way or another. The core values that used to hold us seem threatened by chaos. Perhaps story is to blame. Perhaps if we just put story back in the box, life will get back in the box. Perhaps we can return to simpler times, simpler thinking, and simpler stories. Personally, nationally, and internationally, forces we barely understand polarize us. And we can hardly find ways to get away from all the noise and think things through.

So what Is asked of us, the tellers of the new story, is our voice and our courage.

— Margaret J. Wheatley

As we enter the twenty-first century, one-third of the U.S. population holds a politically and religiously conservative worldview that can become increasingly dogmatic when pressed by social experimentation. Things people accepted in high school, like the study of evolution or the realities of World War II, are rejected — the Holocaust never happened and the creation story of the Bible is literally true. The collective attempt is to simplify story, to put it back into a frame of reference that seems more manageable.

One-fifth of the U.S. population holds a politically and spiritually progressive worldview that can become increasingly outlandish when pressed to reconform. People invent all kinds of stories — about angelic intervention, walk-in souls, conspiracies, and the New Age of planet

Earth. The collective attempt is to expand story into the broadest possible considerations until they discover a map for conscious evolution.

And the remaining half of the population wants to be left alone in the mainstream with their belief that life has not so radically changed, and that they can progress through the patterns of modernity laid out by their parents and grandparents. Their story is that good education leads to good work, and a stable family life contains all the rewards of the middle path. The collective attempt is to moderate story, to contain the parameters of change, and preserve traditional secular and spiritual values.

None of these positions can manage reality or the story of reality. Story is out. Story is bouncing around in all our technology and insisting that we become aware of the full range of our humanity and inhumanity. It is literally impossible to keep a secret anymore. Anything in the world we want to know about we can "Google" on the Internet and find on a website. We can put diaries and journals into weblogs. We can make mobile phone calls from a crashing plane or while freezing to death on Mount Everest. We have created a web of technology that frees story as never before. And it can nearly drive us mad with distraction.

Because remembering is the mind's first step toward understanding . . .

— Toni Morrison

Sometimes in the deepest layer of sleep I see images of those shaggy *Homo sapiens* stretching their spines into full upright position, scratching their heads that contain the same brains we carry today, and with a compulsion they may not have understood, starting their hike out to populate the world. I see them fanning like butterfly wings across the Middle East, some heading into Asia, some heading into Europe. I see the canoes and rafts slipping into Pacific waters, the ice bridge from Siberia to Alaska, the rise and fall of ancient civilizations. And then, like something careening out of control, the dream increases in speed, machinery and technology layer over our relationship to nature, and I wake in rising panic that something is wrong, something so big we cannot hope to fix it.

In *Dark Age Ahead*, what she calls "a gloomy and hopeful book," the octogenarian social architect Jane Jacobs searches out the root causes of cultural decline and calls our attention to what is happening around us in North America. After noting the cyclicality of the rise and fall and complete obliteration of cultures, she writes: "Writing, printing and the Internet give a false sense of security about the permanence of culture. Most of the million details of a complex, living culture are transmitted neither in writing nor pictorially. Instead, cultures live through word of mouth and example. . . . Educators and mentors, whether they are parents, elders, or schoolmasters, use books and videos if they have them, but they also speak, and when they are most effective, as teachers, parents, or mentors, they also serve as examples." Jacobs goes on to say, "Even in a literate and archive-keeping society . . . time for corrective action is finite: culture resides mainly in people's heads and in the examples people set, and is subject therefore to natural mortality."

And yet, as promised, in the midst of her gloom she cites examples of tenacious survival. "Ireland," she writes, "is almost miraculous for not having sunk into a Dark Age. The conquering English, especially during their brutal invasions, massacres, and oppressions under Elizabeth I and Oliver Cromwell, treated the Roman Catholic Irish as an aboriginal people to be cleared from the land for benefit of the conquerors. Famine, Pestilence, War, and Death devastated Ireland for centuries . . . but the Four Horsemen of the Apocalypse were never joined by the fifth demonic horseman: Forgetfulness. The Irish stubbornly remembered who they were and what they valued and refused to lose their treasured culture. They accomplished this marvel largely through the fragile medium of song. Their songs prevented them and their progeny from forgetting what they had lost."

Well, I may not be much of a singer, but I sense Jacobs speaks the truth, and I know that story is a form of song. Story carries the same elements: it is folk wisdom at its best. It is cultural code. To serve our culture — our real cultural heritages, not current consumerism and the dumbing down of the human journey — we find our sources in story, poems, songs, dances, and art of all media. We preserve what we know, passing the code to our children and our communities. We honor the voice of the people and celebrate how unconquerable this voice has been, how it has devised ways to sing of revolution at the feet of kings, and to hold out models of cultural identity in the midst of attempted obliteration.

On February 15, 2003, an estimated 30 million people in 133 cities in thirty-eight countries and all seven continents protested the then U.S. administration's determination to invade Iraq. The protest was worldwide: from McMurdo Station in Antarctica to Stockholm, Sweden, from New Zealand to Malaysia to India to South Africa to Portugal to the United States and Canada. The protests didn't stop the war and the date could have disappeared enshrouded in disappointment, except for the voices that began to speak and sing out the significance of what had happened. One of these voices, Dr. Robert Muller, former assistant secretary of the United Nations and at eighty years of age, chancellor emeritus at the University for Peace in Costa Rica, set the day into context. He said at a speech in San Francisco, "I am so honored to be alive at such a miraculous time in history. I'm so moved by what is going on in our world today.... Never before in the history of the world has there been a global, visible, public, viable, open dialogue and conversation about the very legitimacy of war....

"The whole world is now having this critical and historic dialogue — listening to all kinds of views and positions about going to war or not going to war. In a huge, global, public conversation the world is asking: *Is war legitimate? Is it illegitimate? Is there enough evidence to warrant attack? What will be the consequences? The costs? What will happen after a war? How will this set off other conflicts? What might be peaceful alternatives? What kind of negotiations are we not thinking of? What are the real intentions for declaring war?...*

"We are not at war," Muller kept repeating. "We, the world community, are waging peace. It is difficult, hard work. It is constant and we must not let up. It is working and it is an historic milestone of immense proportions.... We are in the most significant and potent global conversation in the history of the world... the surging voice of the people of the world is the new superpower."

This new superpower has no shared government, religion, or currency, it has only a dream: that the lives of the people will matter more than the policies of the powerful. This superpower must behave differently than any power before it. Our guidance will be based on story. We — the people — cannot be kept from each other. Something bad goes down, something wonderful happens, someone is video streaming it through his or her cell phone onto the Internet and the world is watching in real time. Story is out of the box. And you and I have lived to see this day!

STORY SET LOOSE IN THE HUMAN COMMUNITY demands that we keep learning how to handle this phenomenon, both by going back to our roots around the campfire and forward into cyberspace. In the midst of overwhelming stimulation, when we turn off the technology, and turn to one another, story still has the potential to calm us, to call us back into ourselves, to remind us of the length and breadth of the journey from which we come.

The problems that exist in the world today cannot be solved by the level of thinking that created them.

— Albert Einstein

It is a dark and stormy night, just the right environment for leaning into the glow of a candle or a fire and gathering in story space, so we can find each other, awaken each other, welcome each other. We're not the first, you know. We can't hold it all, but we can hold more than we think we can.

What would you put in the earth as a treasure for the future to find?

Let's start there.

Tell me that story.

Becoming a Storycatcher

Significant events become woven into our ongoing stories as we decide how to gauge their impact on our lives. We remember where we were, what we felt like, how it sounded, how it smelled, and what our reactions were. We compare notes with other people affected by these events, sometimes altering our details and merging our stories. Used as teaching tools, the stories that emerge can help us avoid repeating the worst outcomes and reinforce the best outcomes.

Tell Me This Story...

These story beginnings can be used in writing or conversation to enhance storycatching in your life.

- Describe a typical family dinner while you were growing up. Use all of your senses to describe the scene. Do you have fond or painful memories of family dinners? How are you carrying this forward in your family?
- Describe a world event that changed you. How did the world look to you before it happened? How did the world look to you after it happened?
- Describe in detail what you would put in the earth as a treasure for the future to find. What items would depict the life you know today? What would your treasures tell the people of the future about people today?
- Describe a time when you felt afraid. How did you handle your fear? How do you wish you had handled your fear?
- Did you have a special place to which you ran or where you hid when you were afraid, sad, or angry as a child? Do you have such a place as an adult?

- Create a journal entry that begins with "It was a dark and stormy night..." Describe this night in detail.
- What would you like others to remember about you? Create a journal entry that contains information you would want to leave behind to be found when you are gone.

CHAPTER FIVE

Riding Experience to Wisdom

THE MAP OF A STORY-BASED LIFE

Every generation has a collective story that marks it. This marker story serves as a reference point that holds millions of personal stories. Where were you when?...

I was trying not to cry, my brother wasn't crying, and this was, after all, his farewell more than mine. The plane was loaded, and the instructions for takeoff had begun. He was in uniform, and so was I: his was the uniform of the U.S. Army, mine was the uniform of the American peacenik, both of us vintage 1968. In August, two months earlier, I had moved to San Francisco to work with the American Friends Service Committee, a Quaker-based social service organization, and my first job out of college. My brother, Carl, had just graduated from boot camp and was heading to Oakland to ship out for Viet Nam. We had both ended up in Minneapolis for a weekend's leave, and the remaining family — my parents, our younger sister and brother — had brought us to the airport to see us off.

But at the last moment Ric, then age twelve, had gotten separated from the rest of us and missed the final good-byes — hugs and tears, and awkward pools of accumulated silence. We were all full of emotion and not sure where to put it, how to speak it; not even able to touch each other with it. A common sight at the airports of America in those days, and again and again as we cycle through wars, as families let slip their handholds on sons and daughters, brothers and sisters, husbands and wives, fathers and mothers and we fall into the great abyss of warrioring, worrying, waiting. The most important moment our family had faced in years, and Ric had drifted off, distracted by a newsstand or a gaming arcade, perhaps the men's room: anyway, when we looked around to pull him into this final huddle, he wasn't with us.

Bailey was the greatest person in my world. And the fact that he was my brother . . . was such good fortune that it made me want to live a Christian life just to show God that I was grateful.

— Maya Angelou

"There he is." I leaned across the stranger in the window seat and saw through the porthole our little brother spread-eagled against the thick plate glass of the airport windows. He was pounding on the glass and waving. I thought I could see tears streaming down his face. I tried to wave back through the little glass, even though it wasn't my hand he wanted to see.

Carl had just stowed his dress military cap in the overhead bin next to the battered guitar I hoped to magically learn to play once I was hanging out in the hippyfied air of Golden Gate Park. He leaned over me, looked, sat down in the aisle seat. "What do you want me to do?" he asked.

Good question: no answer. *I want you to go AWOL. I want you to be driving north to Winnipeg pretending you're going duck hunting. I want you to turn back time, to stop playing pool in the student union and study harder — Freshman English, Economics 101, whatever they ask you to do — just not to lose that hockey scholarship, not to drop out of college, not to put yourself in line for the draft*. I squeeze his hand and feel the man-bones, strong under his skin, this nearly twin brother, my buddy in the tadpole collections and firefly jars and maker of forts and raker of oak leaves and adolescent conspirator. And I see our little brother, Ric, who is still heading into all these things, frantic and pounding on the glass.

This scene is a turning point in the story of my brother's life and mine. While we are *in* the scene, we cannot see the scene. We are living raw experience. In the moment, we haven't had time or distance enough to make story. Soon this capacity to turn experience into words will click in: we will begin to think in narrative. We will begin to link this scene to what has gone before and to what we anticipate coming next: we will put what's happening in context. We will decide the importance of the moment and what our choices are. We will do what human beings do: mix experience and story together in a swirl that is part reality and part what we are making out of reality while it's happening to us.

When we look back this moment becomes a teaching tale for how we live with experience and ride it down to wisdom.

The Spiral of Experience

The year 1968 was a watershed for the boomer generation. It has become an icon year, even for those older, younger, or not yet born — the year things happened. In her book *Do You Believe in Magic? The Second Coming of the Sixties Generation*, Annie Gottlieb intersperses interviews with hundreds of members of this generation with her own threads of perception — her own spiral of experience. She calls 1968 "the second great turning point of the Sixties."

Gottlieb goes on to say, "With the assassination of King and Robert Kennedy, we lost our last hope of combating racism or ending the war through the System, and the System lost our consent." The entire year is a marker story full of iconographic events that hold huge stories behind them: Tet Offensive, My Lai, King, Kennedy, Watts, Prague Spring.

"Vets and non-vets," writes Gottlieb, "did the same drugs, listened to the same music. They shared a culture — up to a point. Then we come to the unbridgeable gulf that divides the combat soldier in any war from the civilian — a gulf forced wider, in the sixties, by the homefront generation's noisy non-support for those in the field. And yet for those who fought in it and those who fought against it, the war made the sixties real.

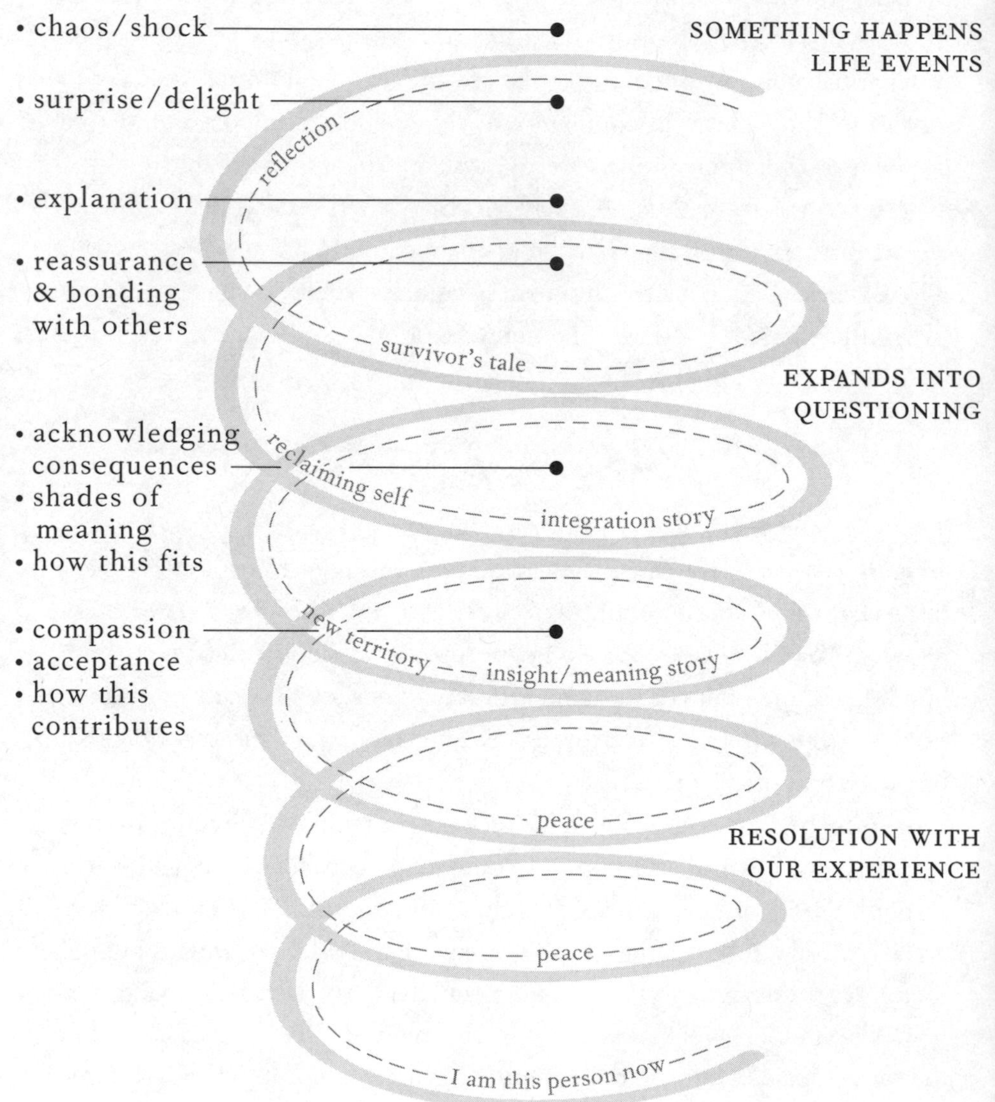
Spiral of Experience
• chaos/shock
• surprise/delight
• explanation
• reassurance & bonding with others
• acknowledging consequences
• shades of meaning
• how this fits
• compassion
• acceptance
• how this contributes
SOMETHING HAPPENS
LIFE EVENTS
EXPANDS INTO QUESTIONING
RESOLUTION WITH OUR EXPERIENCE
reflection
survivor's tale
reclaiming self
integration story
new territory
insight/meaning story
peace
peace
I am this person now

It forced our transformation, made it a matter of life and death. It left vets, non-vets, and women wounded and divided, holding different, jagged pieces of our puzzle: a new world."

This is helpful analysis, but it took her almost twenty years to articulate it. She, too, had to live her way through the spiral. In 1987 when I read Gottlieb's book, my biggest surprise was how generational things were: stories I had assumed were somehow personal were revealed in their universality. It was a lesson in context, in being marked by events happening in the Story.

In May 1968, I graduated from Macalester College in St. Paul, with a black armband on my sleeve, mourning Dr. King. I spent that summer driving foreign students around the country in a donated station wagon for an amazing program called Ambassadors for Friendship. The program was designed to give foreign students a broad experience of America and, of course, it provided *me* with a broad experience of my own country many Americans never have.

For to be free is not merely to cast off one's chains, but to live in a way that respects and enhances the freedom of others.
— Nelson Mandela

My brother Carl was at Fort Dix, New Jersey, and I was in New Orleans that June night Robert Kennedy was shot. Now it was October, and we were heading into our very different autumn jobs. During our two days with the family in Minneapolis before we both flew west, we walked the citified creek parkway that ran a few streets over from the house, smoked cigarettes — Marlboros/him and Tarrytons/me — and considered our war.

We engage the spiral of experience when *something happens* to shake up the status quo of our lives. We may not even fully know why, but our senses come alert, adrenaline rushes through our bodies. Depending on what's happening, we come fully present in delight, watchfulness, surprise, or trauma. We enter a long process, a learning curve.

Six months before our autumnal walk, Carl had called me out of the blue. The voice on the other end of the phone line was instantly familiar, "Hey Chris," that tone, and the fact that only a few people in my family call me Chris. We chatted a few sentences, but I was waiting for the real news because I could tell from my brother's voice that he had more to say. "I just heard from the army.... I've been drafted." So that was it.

"What are you going to do?"

"Go, I guess."

"There are options, you know. Counseling, Canada, resistance."

"Yeah, I know, but that's not my thing. That's your thing."

In the peculiarity of our family, Carl and I mirrored each other throughout our childhoods. I moved into the smart, verbal slot: Carl moved into the athletic, mathematic spot. I was decisive; he was thoughtful. On hot summer afternoons when we were both little and childhood was still just the two of us, mother would call from the kitchen door, offering us one Popsicle to share. "Grape or orange?"

"Orange! Orange!" I'd shout from the swing set.

Carl would be quiet until she handed him his half. "Grape," he'd finally say, "grape." I guess he did the same with the army. "Go or won't go?" they asked him. By the time he answered he was in Long Binh.

After the initiating event, we *begin responding*. Coping mechanisms set in: we may have the urge to tell somebody what's happening — like Carl calling me on the phone — trying to stake out some semblance of order by saying it out loud. Or we may head to the journal or write a letter. "Normalcy" continues on around us, but we are in a space apart: our world seems suddenly set on its end. Depending on the circumstances, we may be shocked, surprised, delighted; we may feel hypersensitive to emotions, or we may stop registering emotions.

In this first stage of reorientation, we need a mental rock to stand on, even if it's only a pebble. This first rock is often a question that helps us step into our changed reality. "Why me?" is probably not a helpful question, but "how do I be me in what is happening?" may offer the first inkling of stability.

When he'd gotten the draft notice, Carl had had only a few weeks to consider his options. He didn't want to kill anyone; he didn't want to go to jail. He adamantly refused to adopt anyone else's values, even if he hadn't fully formulated his own. This became his point of honor: he would let the army take him, but he would not let the army make him into anybody he was not.

"How's it going between you and the army?" I asked, talking loud enough to be heard as we crunched along over fallen leaves.

Carl looked pale. He'd lost weight, spent half his time in basic training struggling with pneumonia, and then recovered enough to attend radio school. He smiled with a little irony, "Well, the army has a pretty severe attitude problem," he said, coughed, dragged on his cigarette. "You know how patient I am," that smile again. "They try to break you down, Chris. They want to turn you all into the same dumb, stupid guy, the guy they have in mind makes the best soldier." I nod.

"Anyway, I wouldn't yell 'KILL' in bayonet practice and it made 'em mad. I wasn't turning into the right guy for them. So they decided to prove something to me, and I decided to prove something back."

"What did they do?"

"Made me eat a lotta shit." He laughs at the reference, which I don't understand yet. "Four in the morning, this sergeant gets me up, hands me a brush and bucket, and sets me to clean the latrines — spotless. Every day I do this. Then I stand at attention, miss breakfast. I don't much mind because the slop they serve you looks a lot like what I've just been cleaning. Later each day I have bayonet practice again. They're waiting for me to get it that this is all connected. I get it. They tried to keep me from graduating but they need my body in Nam more than they needed to win that round."

> *I knew growing up that at some point I was supposed to be the things I learned in the stories: compassionate, honorable, and brave. . . . I knew this because the storytellers lived the lessons they imparted in their stories. . . .*
>
> — Joseph M. Marshall III

I bummed a light and we walked in silence a while. His hair had grown out enough so he looked like my brother again, not like the military skinhead in the photograph the army sent home to families. Our parents had placed this anonymous face on their mantelpiece. Only Carl's deep brows, dark liquid eyes shadowed under the cap's brim, and our grandfather's nose gave hints that this was himself. In the slanted autumn light I warned him, "Be careful, they've got you now and they can make your life miserable."

"Yeah," he nodded. "That idea I did get."

Though we may feel isolated, we do not enter the spiral journey alone. Life events happen in a community of context and have repercussions both for the ones most directly involved and for the people surrounding them. We are tracking the catalytic change; people are tracking us. Every soldier has somebody wondering how they are.

1 November 1968

Dear Chris,

Well, what do I say now? I've only been here a week and things have settled into routine. I'm working the night shift 1830 to 0630, running radio for the commanding generals' command net. That's all I can say. Not strenuous duty. Only drawback, it's hard to sleep in the daytime when it's so damn hot. I don't know what the temperature is, but they say it's gonna get hotter. I won't have any trouble sleeping then — I'll just pass out.

I told a little white lie to the Minnesota family about the security of this area. Last night I pulled guard duty in the general area of the air base and we could see action. So there is VC. I'm a member of the Fifty-third Signal Battalion stationed in Bien Hoa at Long Binh. It's probably not on the map as it's just an army installation.

I haven't been able to get out and see much of the countryside or the people. From my contacts with them here on base they seem to be beautiful people, not only physically, but they are friendly and try to be helpful even when you can't make yourself well understood. This has been verified by some of the guys who have been here awhile and been out among them. So whom are we fighting? They're smaller in stature than I expected: the women's noses reach my navel and the men reach my shoulder. I want to roam around and see for myself, but unless there's some kind of truce, I'm restricted to base. And that, in a nutshell is my present situation.

It was good to spend those days with you in Flower Power City and to meet your friends and learn a little about what you're doing. Keep up the good work and we'll both get out of this alive.

Love, Carl

When he arrives at a momentary resting point, story clicks in to articulate the new status quo — Carl *begins to reflect*. He looks around with beginner's mind: questioning, noticing, wanting to have his own direct experience. Reflection is the first step in making sense; reflection elicits the first level of story. People stop there sometimes, but it is often not enough. We aren't deep enough into the spiral to have satisfactorily explained an experience to ourselves. I don't have the letters I sent back to Carl, but I know when we talk or write to others, people reflect back to us the points where our story is incomplete, or where their curiosity is piqued in response to what we're communicating, or how our experience reminds these listeners of something similar that happened to them. We find ourselves in a dialogue of learning from each other. We spiral deeper into story. And if we are writing, similar issues appear on the page: we notice the gaps in our narrative and these unexplored aspects of our thinking lead us into more reflection. We serve as our own listener, our own reader.

What emerges in these first layers of story is the *survivor's tale. In the survivor's tale, we work with an experience to a point where we can begin to reclaim our sense of self as one who now includes this changed circumstance.* We come up with two layers of explanation: one that is usually casual and social and another that is more intimate and honest. We look for reassurance that we are still part of the bigger story, that others have gone through this and left us their maps of story. We lay tracks for making our own way through. We may find support groups, formal and informal, and form meaningful bonds with others living through similar experiences. The survivor's tale proclaims a level of confi-dence: we're alive on this side of a major event, we are restabilizing, everything is going to be okay. We work to make our experience manageable.

Knowledge of the self is the mother of all knowledge. So it is incumbent on me to know my self, to know it completely, to know its minutiae, its characteristics, its subtleties, and its very atoms.

— Kahlil Gibran

6 January 1969

Dear Chris,

Well, I've either found the war, or it's found me. I'm now camping out with an Australian forward element providing communications. Could be out here two weeks or eight months. My new home is a pit, six by two feet, covered with sandbags and a slit at one end just big enough to crawl through. Last night the guy next to me slept with a tarantula; so far I haven't had company.

We have an armored cavalry detachment with us and so far Charlie hasn't tried to chase us out. We're expecting him, nightly, but I think the tanks make him leery. . . . I really don't know what's going on out here — the expressed purpose for this operation. I'm going to try and hitch a chopper ride and get some pictures. I bought a TL-Super Yashica camera. What do they cost stateside?

No change in address. They know where I am and put my mail on the chopper.

Love, Carl

Reflection helps establish a sense of mental order. Order is a relief, and sometimes we stop here, at least we stop and rest if life allows us that luxury. There are many reasons people don't take their story deeper than survival. Sometimes it provides adequate resolution. Sometimes we don't know how to move on. Sometimes we don't know that deeper layers of meaning are available.

At a social level, the survivor's tale is constantly reinforced as the BIG moment: miners pulled out of the mine shaft, sailors rescued from their overturned boats, the reappearing hiker, the lost and found child. Each of these stories is accorded a moment when the attention of the community or media is turned on them.

And then what happens? Mostly, we don't know. We see people in the high drama, the vulnerability and triumph of their survival. In the coming months, Carl takes his survival down layer by layer. In precarious moments he writes his survival in a stream of consciousness.

12 February 1969

Dear Chris,

I'm just sitting here listening to the war going on around me on the radio (43 this is 56) *and when I stick my head out the door I can see and hear it for real. This may be a short note. I just* (one KIA) *want to write someone.*

The action is all around us. (Two wounded in chest) *It's 8:10* PM *and Charlie is mortaring a village two miles from here* (one wounded in arm — almost severed) *and our 155 mm tanks are opening up on their positions. These tanks are* (three leg wounds) *so big that they use them for artillery. Don't think I'll be getting much sleep tonight.* (One casualty located 10 meters from enemy machine gun nest)

Situation as follows: North, village and small airstrip being mortared. (Unable to reach wounded man) *East, enemy bunkered in, air strike, heavy ground fighting. South — closest action — about one hundred VC holed up in town a half mile from here, may have to send some of our armor down there. I'd hate to see them pull off our perimeter. The only place left is West and no friendlies that direction. Perimeter radio operators are edgy, making commo checks. I suppose they want to be sure someone is close by if they need them. I would.*

9:40 PM *All stations report quiet. Going on listening watch. Just stepped outside. No moon. Black as hell. I think I saw the Big Dipper — unexpected. I didn't think it was floating around this part of the world, too.*

11:00 PM *I've been talking for the past hour with this Australian captain discussing America and the light in which other nations, particularly Australia, see us. I did my best explaining America, Americans, and the pros/cons of our foreign policy... anything to get mentally out of here. I didn't mean for this to turn out like it did. Don't start worrying. I'm still sitting inside a lot of firepower. I just felt I had to tell someone a little of what's going on and I don't dare send it to the home front.*

It's been a twenty-hour day and I'm ready to hit my dirt sacks. I'll probably be sorry I bothered you, but I love ya, Sis.

Carl

Our father, Leo, had been a conscientious objector in World War II. In the post–Pearl Harbor era, questioning American entry into the virtuous battle against fascism was considered nearly treasonable. A pre-seminary student at college, planning to follow his father into the ministry, Leo was the only objector ever registered in Cascade County during the 1940s. And though not one of his four older brothers ever enlisted (they enjoyed deferments accorded to men in their early thirties with families and jobs on the land or in education), they berated him as a coward. A schism was plowed into the family that

The ultimate measure of a man is not where he stands in moments of comfort and convenience, but where he stands at times of challenge and controversy.

— Martin Luther King Jr.

haunted the honey house of our childhood. We exiled ourselves to the Midwest, and Carl and I reached maturity just in time for Viet Nam. So in 1968, our little family held within it the schism of the larger family and of the society around us. What had *not* been integrated between our father and his brothers awaited integration between my brother and myself.

In her book *Hope in the Dark*, Rebecca Solnit writes, "What gets called 'the sixties' left a mixed legacy and a lot of divides. But it opened everything to question, and what seems the most fundamental and most pervasive in all the ensuing changes is the loss of faith in authority: the authority of government, of science, of patriarchy, of progress, of capitalism, of violence, of whiteness. The answers — the alternatives — haven't always been clear or easy, but the questions and the questioning are nevertheless significant."

There is a wound that lives in uncompleted stories. The wounding from the Viet Nam era says that we were a generation divided and polarized by this war, that the soldiers came home to discrimination and taunting, that the protestors separated themselves from their brothers instead of seeing our common entrapment. I have heard this story many times, and while I know it was true, it was not true between Carl and me. Somehow we lived out both sides of our war and stayed in relationship.

Our sister, Becky, commenting on the divisiveness elicited by the invasion of Iraq, wrote, "Because of how our family lived through the Viet Nam era, it never occurred to me that supporting the troops and working for peace would be perceived by others as a problem." Carl went to war and still, decades later, we are all riding the spiral to articulate *the story of integration*.

Wisdom is knowledge which has become a part of one's being.
— Orison Swett Marden

At Easter in 1968, I went over the bridge to Berkeley to visit my aunt and uncle, my mother's brother who had fought in World War II. They dragged out an old, old 8 mm clip of a movie taken of Carl and me in 1949. My aunt and uncle, then newly married, had been driving across country and stopped to see us at the little Methodist parsonage where we lived in Leaf River, Illinois. I was three; Carl was a year and a half.

In the old family movie I am riding my tricycle up and down the sidewalk, back and forth, going in and out of the frame. Carl toddles into view and wants a turn. I get off the trike and try to help him on. I heave my brother clumsily up on the seat and he rolls off on the other side. I run around and catch him, help him balance. Carl's short, chubby legs cannot reach the pedals. He begins to cry. Great fat tears roll down his cheeks into the camera's silent recording. We become more and more determined. Our aunt comes into the scene offering help. In unison, our arms push her away. We are a team of little people. We want to do this ourselves.

This is the only moving picture ever taken of our childhoods, but its gesture says something to me that bridges all gaps. We are still a team; we are still somehow working in unison. In 1968, and in all the decades since, we represent two choices made at the gateway moment into adulthood. In mirroring each other, we are the complement, the two parts needed to complete the whole. Orange — grape. San Francisco — Long Binh.

Working the Spiral

In working with the spiral of experience, significant moments come back around again and again, allowing us to harvest insight. Every time this cycle recurs, we have the opportunity to reflect and articulate the still unexplored territory of our stories. As we live inside the integration story, our experience becomes less urgent and more philosophical. We may speak of it less often, but it rises up in us when there is space and receptivity.

"My first year home from the war was full of confusion," my brother says from the safe vantage point of another October thirty-five years later. "When you're in a situation like that you don't have the advantage of 'view.' You can't see the war; you're just in it, tending to the business at hand. And the really bad stuff that is living hell is usually happening to the same 15 to 20 percent of the troops, over and over, and everybody else is in some kind of support position, and bored as hell.

"Soldiers rely on others, especially journalists, to tell us what's going on beyond the perimeters we can see from the foxhole or the base. When I came back home in '69 I began to see what the public was seeing. Three weeks after I got back to Minnesota, I went on a protest march in St. Paul. I wanted to see what the general flow was, see if I could join it. But My Lai was all over the front pages. Whatever sympathy there might have been for the soldier was gone in that moment. You could spot us in the crowd, though none of us were in uniform — the haircut, the way we bent over a match to light up. . . . The speakers were calling us baby killers. I didn't like being in that crowd, just drifted away, came home."

Falling leaves drift around us while we talk. We are seated at a picnic table in a county park. It's autumn 2004. Others in our family have gone off on a hike, made this space for us to have a conversation. My graying hair is the same length as it was in 1968; the mustache he grew in the war he's never shaved. "After that march, what did you decide to do with your experience?" I ask.

"I disavowed protesting. I am an information gatherer, though as you know, I don't disseminate everything I'm thinking about much. But I'm willing to consider things and shift my point of view. I like to learn from a number of viewpoints and pick my way through. So I had gone to the march to see what was available for me in the way of rejoining America. But I could not participate in anything that undermined the guys in the field. That crowd was undermining the soldier and his experience without understanding it. In any army, put under the pressure of war, some individuals will go off the deep end. I'm not excusing it; I'm just saying it happens and has happened forever. War does that to people: it brings out the best and the worst."

In all, 2.7 million American soldiers went to Viet Nam. Carl was one of the lucky ones. He lived. He wasn't injured. He did not spend months in jungle patrols. He has been able to make a good life: has a stable, loving marriage; has raised a daughter, managed a business, and is thinking about retirement. I worked with the Quakers, with draft resisters, went to Europe and the Middle East doing small, behind-the-scenes projects of peace and reconciliation. I became a writer, a teacher, a facilitator of conversations.

On May 4, 1970, the National Guard was called onto the campus of Kent State University in Kent, Ohio, to quell student protests over President Richard Nixon's decision to invade Cambodia. National Guardsmen fired into a crowd, killing four students and wounding nine others. This event became a closing signature to campus unrest.

I think of a hero as someone who understands the degree of responsibility that comes with his freedom.

— Bob Dylan

In 1991, I was invited to speak at the twenty-first anniversary of the Kent State shootings. My assigned topic was "What has the 1960s got to say to the 1990s?" I had forty-five minutes; it deserved a semester course. I began this speech by saying, "I was nobody in the 1960s — not Joan Baez, not Tom Hayden. I never went to prison; I did not lose a brother or a lover to the war. I applied to work at a refugee center in Quang Ngai and wasn't hired. I wasn't on the streets during the 1968 Democratic Convention in Chicago. I missed Woodstock. I was in Europe when the shootings happened here — trying to glean the story off of German television. I've never dropped acid. And all this was perhaps my most important contribution — the contribution of the nobody. The contribution of millions of people who threaded through the times while they were a-changin' and raised the questions that kept us awake and kept the story alive."

Now, sitting at a country picnic table, scrawling my diagram spiral on a pad of notepaper between us, I ask my brother a question that has often haunted me: "Did I ever do anything that made you feel disrespected? Did you ever think what I was doing undermined you in the field?" I hold my breath.

"I knew what you were doing, Chris. And I knew you wanted me to be doing something else. I just couldn't go to Canada." I've long ago quit, but Carl lights up a low-tar cigarette. The young, twenty-something woman in me wants to break the tension, join him in a long inhale. "I had no fear of not returning. Maybe it was that sense of invincibility that happens when you're young, but I just always believed I'd be safe, so signing up wasn't such a big deal, I thought I'd go and see firsthand what was going on. My own death wasn't a possibility." Carl smiles ruefully. "Do you suppose that's what they all thought — all those guys with their names etched on the wall? That movie *Platoon* has the most realistic fight scenes. I heard friendly fire killings go on within earshot. I drove down highways where all the roadkill was human. Truth is, stuff like that happens, you don't sleep for three days, you go crazy...and then you wait around weeks before the next action.

"As for what you were doing, the most popular insignia in Viet Nam was the peace symbol. People wore it on and under our uniforms, painted it on our helmets, on the sides of crates and buildings. Army didn't like it, but it was a small subversive action: You want to stop this fight and send me home tomorrow? Yes! Okay by me. No soldier starts a war. And once you're in one, you just want to live through it. Soldiers turned politicians will start a war, but no trooper on the ground wants to set something off where he might get killed. That's what the protestors didn't understand at the time, and I was affronted by that attitude when I came home...but you, naw, I knew what you were doing."

We become ourselves based on a combination of life events and how we respond to them and how we make story of them. There is one more spin to the spiral. Not every experience takes us there, but the most life-changing experiences eventually lead us to *the story of insight and meaning*. At this depth we are able to see our most significant experiences as transformers. They anoint us with a sense of completion and release.

"So what do you think now," I asked him, "how do you see Viet Nam influencing your life over the years?"

"As much as I bucked it, the army got me over the bridge from drifting along as a school dropout to coming home with a sense that life was something I should be taking care of. It made me a more tolerant person. After a year in Viet Nam I know I can put up with anything, that I can find a way to live with anybody, that there are good people in every situation, and that there are good people on every side of an issue. The war made me more skeptical and more faithful. I've never been deeply religious, but I have a kind of spirituality that is based on love for life.

"I'm tough to scare. Politicians and the things happening in America and the world right now are not as powerful as most people think they are. What you and I both prove, through the decisions we made then and the decisions we're still making, is that there is always a positive countervailing force. Nobody is pure, no situation is all good or all bad, but every situation is full of that counterbalance. We just have to see it and use it."

When the traveling version of the Memorial Wall came through Minnesota, Carl and his wife, Colleen, went to see it. "There was a map of the country and I was showing Colleen where Long Binh was, and where I thought I might have been up-country.... This passerby overheard us and reached out to shake my hand. 'Thanks for going,' he said.

"I told him, 'You're not looking at a volunteer here, I was drafted into that....'

"'Nevertheless,' he said, 'you served. And you guys never got properly thanked... so thank you.'

All suffering is bearable if it is seen as part of a story.
— Isak Dinesen

"I never asked for thanks. I don't think wars deserve it, though the young people who fight them do. That man needed to say thank you, and I looked him in the eye and took it from him. So maybe that can finish something. And maybe even the guys who used to ridicule our dad, now that they're old, have gained some perspective and could shake his hand and respect his pacifism. A war like that — Dad's or mine — it's a long story. It would take a long time to understand."

Over the rise of the hill, our families are returning. The space for one story ends and another space opens. For now, we have ridden this story down to the point of grace and let it go, drifting off in the swirl of autumn leaves. We wave a welcome and rise to join them. I am trying not to cry, my brother isn't crying, and this is, after all, his homecoming more than mine.

What event or experience in your life have you ridden to wisdom?

Let's start there.

Tell me that story.

Becoming a Storycatcher

We all have moments in our lives when we find our depth. Reflection on those times helps to create a story that defines how we live our lives. The responsibility of a Storycatcher is to use the spiral of story and experience to add insight and meaning to our life events. The more deeply we carry the story, the more we can recognize wisdom in our lives and the lives of those around us.

Tell Me This Story…

These story beginnings can be used in writing or conversation to enhance storycatching in your life.

- Write a dialogue between yourself and someone you love who took a different path. Talk about how you felt about this person's path — what it meant to you at the time, as well as what it means to you now. Write as though you would share it, even if you can't.
- Describe a lesson you learned the hard way. How did this lesson's cost affect its value for you?
- What are you willing to die for? What are you willing to live for? What could change your mind?
- Describe a time when you felt afraid. How did you handle your fear? How do you wish you had handled your fear?
- Describe a sacrifice you've made. How did it change you? Would you make the same sacrifice now, knowing what you know?
- Where were you at age twenty-two? What was going on around you?

CHAPTER SIX

A Story to Stand On

CREATING A STORY OF THE SELF

Our life story is our constant companion,
the litany that guides our every move and thought.
So we need to make our lives a story we can live with,
because we live the life our story makes possible.

Our own self-story contains so many details, nuances, emotions, and memories that it is often easier to notice the path that choice and influence create in someone else's story. This is part of our attraction to each other: what can I learn from your story that helps me see my own? We imagine ourselves in each other's stories. In the first half of this book, I invited you into my story in hope that you would find your own story mirrored there. For the second half of this book, I've invited other voices to carry the narrative: a young woman in Africa, an old woman in Arizona, a visionary Danish friend, two Episcopalian priests. Our story is contained in each of their narratives, and their stories are contained in our own: it's a treasure hunt.

Africa — let's start the treasure hunt there. It all starts there: learning to walk on two legs, learning to use our opposable thumbs, the brain mutating inside our skulls, making room for thought and consciousness, rolling the tongue around the mouth until our grunts mature into a thousand languages — each one holding the stories of the people.

Africa. To arrive here is to find the whole world contained in this continent, from snow-covered mountains to desert to jungle, to penguins surfing onto the beaches at the Cape of Good Hope. Mother Africa. To arrive here is to step into all five senses, and not step gingerly, but to be thrown into touch, sight, smell, taste, sound, up over our heads. No wonder pale people stumbling out of stone edifices and closed rooms and intellectual history and the accretion of class and propriety have come here and never looked north again, have come here and fallen in love through the body. Africa is the body naked, body draped in leather thongs, beads and shells, cloths of brilliant color dyed from plants that spurt out of the ground; hair shaved, hair nappy, hair rolled in braids of mud; torsos painted with whitewash and ochre, scarified, pierced, and tattooed. Africa is the red soil, the black soil, the desert, the grasslands, the green hills, the red skins, the brown skins, the black skins, the white skins. Bless our Mother, Africa.

There is always something new out of Africa.
— Pliny the Elder

We arrive in Harare, capital of Zimbabwe, after twenty hours en route and stumble into twenty-first century urban Africa. Harare is a modern city and it makes me wonder if we've really switched continents, until I look more deeply into its face with my travel-bleary eyes. It's all colonial buildings mixing with African-inspired architecture, cars, buses, pedestrians everywhere. Home to around one million people.

The airport keeps us outside the city, and after clearing customs we are heading directly into the country, the taxi driver going much faster than I wish he would, the common complaint of the stranger. Along the road's sandy shoulders, dusty, strolling men carry shovels or pickaxes, tools of their labor; they smoke and talk as they pass women carrying water jugs or firewood gracefully balanced on their heads. The men wear slacks and long-sleeve cotton shirts: formal dress is a white shirt, informal is plaid. The women bring out color in head scarves and bright dresses and wrapped sarongs. The land stretches undulating in all directions, veldt and savanna, acacia trees and underbrush, paths that cut across straw fields heading for the horizon. We come to a crossroad surrounded by flower farms, with the rounded backs of workers moving through fields of brilliant color. Then come the settlements, hundreds of small mud-brick huts with tin roofs laid out as close as honeycomb. The place must zing in the rain when water drops on tin, a phenomenon that looks as though it would be welcome in this high, dry veldt. After that, we are in the bush, no asphalt road, lots of birds and beauty. We are heading to Kufunda village and a conversation with its young founder, Marianne Knuth.

The Story as the Source of the Self

In the beginning is the baby, a little bundle of genetic predispositions and characteristics born into complex determining circumstances. Every child is born into a time and place, and into a social context, including nationality, economic status, race, religion, gender, familial size, stability, health, birth order. And beyond this context, additional conditions come into play: the quality of the parents' relationship, their desire for a boy or girl, the presence or absence of extended family, and everyone's dreams and desires for this baby. The self-story starts with the story we will be told about who we are: our personal version of "once upon a time...."

The self-story is the narrative voice in the stream of consciousness that runs babbling along the edge of our awareness. Minute by minute this narrative defines who we are and what we are capable, or not capable, of doing. It speaks a lot of nonsense, and it whispers our greatest truths — all jumbled together. One of our primary internal tasks is to work with this narrative until the self-story supports our abilities to grow, to fulfill our promise to the world, to keep our commitments to other people. The self-story is the story we stand on.

The self-story is the most influential story of our lives, yet it is often the one we are least aware of, because it speaks to us largely through influence. Influence is the capacity of something — a person, event, or remark — to act as a compelling force on our beliefs, behaviors, actions, and opinions of ourselves and others, whether or not we are aware of it. Influence is the lens that drops between our story and reality. Consequently, this is the story we are often unearthing in the therapeutic process.

The essence of parenting is to never lose faith in your child and the essence of adulthood is to assume that faith in yourself.

— Ann Linnea

The self-story is a universal aspect of human consciousness. Our awareness, reactions, and permission to change this story are influenced by all the conditions of our birth mentioned above, so the self-talk of our grandparents and the self-talk of our grandchildren, the self-talk of a midlife American and a midlife Chinese are all likely to be very different, but if we make the effort to observe, it's there. Every person carries a self-story.

How we look up and greet each other is a balance between the story happening in reality, and the story happening in the mind. Will we open the lens of influence and see who we are? How will the world change if we do? I'm in Africa. Will Africa let me in?

Marianne Knuth, Servant Leader and Shining Light

Starting in the 1950s, a Swiss doll maker named Sasha Morgenthaler decided to make a universal child's doll by pouring together all the skin colors of the world and making all her dolls one skin tone. Combining every pigmentation from the blue-black skin of African and Indian peoples to the alabaster paleness of Nordic Europe, and all the yellows and browns and freckles in between, the bodies of her dolls are a delicate coffee latte — and so is Marianne Knuth. She is the color of the world poured together, and the world is her home.

She's not famous, not published, not rich, but Marianne so fully inhabits herself I asked her if she'd share her story and allow me to listen through the ear in the heart for the ways she has — in just over thirty years — so thoroughly assembled an enduring sense of self. Shyly, bravely, she said yes.

Though often delightfully animated, Marianne can be quiet in a group, not one of the bold and loud, yet so thoroughly present that after a while you look around for the source of that lightness of being. And then you look into eyes that are chocolate brown with flecks of gold, like mica glittering in the dust of a bush country path. She smiles with such genuineness you know you are being truly greeted, whoever you are, neighbor or stranger.

She often twirls her hair as she speaks, her fingers meditating on the soft black coils that surround her face. She began to share her story. "When my mother was a young woman, she received a scholarship to travel to Kenya and study journalism," Marianne says, pouring two cups of roibush tea. "She was sponsored through the Danish embassy, and my father was a young Dane also working in Kenya. They both were invited to embassy functions and events. They met, fell in love, got married, and I was born. Zimbabwe was still Rhodesia then, and I think we lived that first year in Kenya and then we moved to Denmark. That was 1972 and Denmark is where I have my first memories."

Those who take committed stands develop different explanatory stories — new definitions of self — which encourage their impulses to shape a better world.

— Paul Rogat Loeb

Going to Europe was probably a wise choice: Rhodesia would have been a difficult place for a black woman, a white man, and a brown baby to start their lives. In 1965, in the fissuring of British control over Africa, European settlers who had come to Rhodesia during British rule and established economic control over farming, mining, and import/export markets unilaterally declared themselves an independent republic. Under the presidency of Ian Smith, an all-white colonialist government was imposed on the country until Britain, the United Nations, and insurgent African political unrest finally forced a general election. The struggle for independence took ten years of guerrilla warfare in a country where the average income for the black African family was $314 a year. Since Marianne's mother was raised in a Shona tribal village under these social conditions, her education speaks of profound family determination.

The determination to succeed in becoming ourselves in all the variations of the human condition becomes the stuff of memoirs, novels, and movies; gripping, often repeated survivor tales. We love to watch, read, and listen to each other's stories of triumph over the odds. We are fascinated by each other's abilities to work the raw mud of our lives into something wonderful. We are inspired by each other's determination to take what we were given and make the most of it.

While the primary image of Denmark is a country of fair-haired, blue-eyed Nordic people, the culture has an openness to hues of skin that made the young family's life easier; however, it didn't make the marriage easier. "My parents divorced when I was really young, and I don't remember my first father, I only remember my stepfather. He came into my life when I was about three. He became my dad, and he and my mother stayed together until he died in 1995. My family was middle class when we lived in Denmark, and also later in Africa. My stepfather came from an upper-class family, but he did not like the snobbery, and our family took on a more modest way of living. At the time in Denmark this meant we lived in a comfortable house in the suburbs with a big garden. My sister and I each had our own rooms. My favorite hobby was horse riding, and I shared a pony with another girl so I could ride three times a week. I loved the group Abba and John Travolta in the movie *Grease*. I think I was a pretty typical young girl growing up just outside Copenhagen. My mother worked for a shipping company and my father worked as a librarian.

Denmark — little country of cottage cheese and courage.
— Bette Midler

"My sister is six years younger than I am, which makes her the daughter of my stepfather and mother. At some time in middle childhood I realized that my father was not my biological father. I don't have a sense that this disturbed me; it was just a little fact I began to comprehend.

My dad and I loved each other and the bloodline didn't make a difference in how he treated my sister and me. *I remember being amused at my mother's discomfort and her sense that I needed to be protected from this information.*"

I have italicized the moments of insight that appear in Marianne's story to illustrate how naturally we speak (and write) about the points of choice in our life narratives. Even as a very small child, Marianne has her own idea of what this "story" about her father means and is not drawn into a sense that something is wrong. Mentioned in passing, this little incident doesn't look like much, but it has profound influence. It is a declaration: *I am my own self, with my own reactions and interpretations within the story of my family.*

Each of us begins the journey toward personal discovery because someone else gave us a vision that allows us to be more creative, more resourceful, more powerful than the child inside us ever thought possible.

Juan Williams

There is a point in all our lives when the self-story starts coming into self-awareness. We slip from the unselfconsciousness of early childhood into explorations of who we are and what our lives might be.

In her memoir *An American Childhood*, Annie Dillard sets out deliberately to explore this phenomenon. "A child wakes up over and over again, and notices that she's living. She dreams along, loving the exuberant life of the senses, in love with beauty and power, oblivious of herself — and then suddenly, bingo, she wakes up and feels herself alive.... She notices she is set down here, mysteriously, in a going world. The world is full of fascinating information that she can collect and enjoy. And the world is public; its issues are moral and historical."

With Marianne's gracious permission, we can watch her extraordinary ability to work with her self-story, and through empathy and vicariousness, we can transfer these lessons into our own life stories. My own career has brought me into intimate connection with thousands of personal histories. Drawing on that experience, I have identified four activities required to work with self-story: linking, editing, disorienting, and revisioning.

Linking

Somewhere in all our convoluted gray matter, brain researchers tell us, is the full rendition of everything that has ever happened to us. We don't begin to remember our lives in such detail; huge sorting and discarding is constantly going on in the mind. The self-story is composed of those events, relationships, and reactions that make the cut into conscious memory. We then link these memories together to create a coherent narrative. Linking makes the story: linking is the building block of what we choose to remember and how we make meaning out of recall.

For example, as Marianne realizes the quality of her father's love is the same for herself and her sister, she links memories of their relationship that provide evidence of equality, and she may unlink any little occurrences that don't affirm the self-story she has chosen. Linking reinforces the core assessment of ourselves that we embed in self-story. When we link evidence of inadequacy, our lives take on psychological pallor; when we link evidence of worth, our lives take on psychological vitality. Our stories are never all pallor or all vitality: we are a complex mix of self-perceptions, constantly linking, editing, disorienting, and revising our story of ourselves. We create these links, and we can unlink them: we call this changing our minds.

Starting early, Marianne links a story out of her experiences that reinforces positive choices about the nature of herself, her family, and her possibilities in the world. This resilience does not come any more easily for Marianne than for anyone else, but it is *in* her: a foundational story that grants her room to grow. We all need a story to stand on: a core belief that affirms who we are, which we won't relinquish no matter what. In every self-story of triumph, there is a foundational link toward self-affirmation. This link may even become lost to the conscious mind, but it still has an influence. We hear people say things like, "I just always continued to believe in myself," or, "I knew they/it couldn't break my spirit." When we find this link, it's the first page, the first paragraph of our own life story.

Marianne tells us: "In my early years, I think being a little brown girl among so many white children was actually a bonus. I received much positive attention. It's part of the Danish social view: if you are acculturated, if you speak Danish without an accent, you belong. I grew up totally fluent in Danish. My parents had a social group that consisted of Danish couples and mixed-race or international couples, and it all seemed quite fine to me.

Choose well: your choice is brief and yet endless.
— Ella Winter

"In my primary school years one incident stands out. We were learning about the slave trade in history. I was not a very well-behaved child at school. Not overly bad, just a little too chatty and energetic. At one point the exasperated teacher told me to behave myself, these were my ancestors we were studying. I guess because slaves had a negative connotation, this got me pretty mad. So I rushed out of the classroom, shouted something at the teacher, and walked home. And I think — though I may be constructing this in hindsight — *I decided I would let no one speak down to me because of my background and where I came from. I was as good as anyone*. It is funny to think now how upset that little scene made me and how clearly I still remember it."

THE SELF-STORY STARTS YOUNG and grows with us. As soon as we begin to put our experience into language, we bring ourselves into the story. Children are quite adept at developing a narrative about who they are. (This self-commentary is often a charming source of amusement to adults.) We understand the power of the self-story by listening to each other's stories. Other people's stories send us scrambling through our own story looking for correlations, similarities, or different possibilities. Sometimes we can hardly wait for a person to finish saying his or her piece because we want to share a piece of our own that's suddenly come to mind. The stories that rise in us while listening to and reading other people's narratives contain information and insight we can apply to our own choices.

We want to trade these nuggets of insight and offer each other gems of awareness. When I listen to Marianne tell me how she decided she was as good as anyone that day stomping home from school, I see her girl-self, and I also see my own girl-self; her story activates my memory of setting the table at my grandma Baldwin's house, the time my mother said I didn't count and I declared I did.

When someone else's story activates our own memory, we enter the editing process with our own story. One of the healing properties of sharing our stories is the potential to reinforce each other's positive choices and to model options that we may not have thought of on our own. We piggyback on each other's experiences: through listening and reading we change our relationship to our own histories so that our experiences keep sustaining us. We aren't changing our past: we are changing the links, changing the interpretation. We give each other permission and expand each other's ideas of how a situation can be survived.

This is the Spiral of Experience becoming an interactive tool. Life is all story, and it's our story, so we might as well empower ourselves to see that it serves us well. My mother was simply counting place settings; Marianne's teacher simply wanted her attention to return to the lesson: there was no intention for us to link a memory out of that moment, we just did. It's our memory, and ours to make serve us as a positive foundation in the story of the self.

Wherever she is in the world, when Marianne speaks of Africa, something subtle shifts in her: she drops her European reserve for her African ease. The light that rises in her eyes, her gestures and animation seem warmer. This warmth must mirror the transformation she underwent when she and her family moved back to Africa.

"I was twelve when we moved to Zimbabwe," she says, "and though I had been born in Africa, I was a Danish girl arriving in a foreign land. Independence had come four years earlier, and my mother was eager to get back home. In Zimbabwe, our money stretched a little further, so with the sale of our Danish house, we could buy a farm: 320 acres. Many other things were going on and the cultural shock was huge, but the deepest impression I have of those years is the land. Africa was color and texture, smells and heat, and learning a whole new landscape. I fell in love with the farm.

"Being a child who enjoyed being alone, I could spend hours walking across the land, getting to know the bush. We had two dogs, which made it even more pleasurable — and I suppose more safe — to roam around. There were lots of snakes — cobra, python, and black mamba — but I've never been bitten or particularly afraid. The farm has many trees, not Danish birches, but feathery acacia and thornbushes. The landscape is savanna interspersed with dense brush. Exotic birds wake up loudly with the first rays of sun, which is why sleeping in is not so easy, nor all that desirable. There are rocks as big as huts that balance at seemingly precarious angles. A central strip near our house had been turned over for tilling, and those years we raised maize and beans, groundnuts and cattle. The farm did not generate any real income, but my father tried. After a year he joined my mother in commuting to Harare, and they ran the farm more as a hobby. *I don't know that I had constructed my storyline yet, but the land was part of it; the farm grounded my soul and body in Zimbabwe.*

What one loves in childhood stays in the heart forever.

— Mary Jo Putney

"My mother's family ranged from several members who had gotten educated and become middle class to my grandparents and other uncles who lived in the rural area in thatched mud huts. I think the Shona people are the Italians of Africa. Many Africans are loud, at least by Danish standards, but the Shona are even a bit more so. I remember this huge family showing up around our kitchen table. The sound of their voices, their connection to my mother and each other, and the earthy smell they brought into the kitchen were so exotic. It made me realize that my mother wasn't just the color black, she was African; she belonged to this place. *She had another life beyond being my mother, a life of being Shona. To realize this about one's parents is always a mystery to children, I think. I hung out at the edges of her Africanness and longed to understand.* I spoke Danish and English and would later study French. I am still learning Shona."

The farm is where we are heading. I do not know if it has another name. Marianne just says, "You must come to Zimbabwe to the farm." Marianne's mother lives in the farmhouse that has been the family home since 1984. A few minutes' walk away is the original house, called the cottage, where Marianne herself lives. There is a garden in back and a large thatched hut sitting next to her vegetables.

We are not going to the farmhouse or the cottage. We are going to a corner of the land called Kufunda, to walk in the middle of Marianne's dream.

Editing

The self-story *requires* editing. Editing is a constant process of updating who we think we are and how we speak about our histories and ourselves. The choices in the self-story focus on survival and self-esteem, interpretation of the present, and anticipation of future direction. Because our view of the world is always changing, we are constantly editing our story to see if the choices still fit, or if they need revising. We hear this editing and revising process in each other's narrative through self-references and commentary. ("You know, my father always said I'd never...but look at me now.") Some people edit through therapy, while others allow successful experiences to overlay influences from less successful experiences. I've done most of my editing through journal writing.

Throughout my thirties, the decade Marianne is living now, I wrote and wrote and wrote about my childhood years. First I got the story down on paper, then I did pages of written dialogue between the child I had been and the woman I had become. To accomplish this, I wrote with both hands: the "child" wrote with my nondominant hand, the "adult" wrote with my dominant hand. The child wrote with a purple crayon, the adult wrote with a fountain pen. This form of dialogue can authentically connect us with the story of the child-self. Writing with the nondominant hand tends to be laborious and concentrated on forming legible letters, just as when we first learned to print. Meanwhile, the dominant hand, writing with its fine motor skills and penmanship, becomes the voice of the nurturing/structuring adult — not the reinforcer of flawed messages

I have always believed that I could help change the world, because I have been lucky to have adults around me who did.

— Marian Wright Edelman

but the editor, the one who can say exactly what we need to hear and support in us what needs to be supported. Page by page my two selves explored the territory of our decisions, and over time negotiated a self-affirming story.

Marianne's choices from her Danish childhood had laid an essentially self-affirming foundation in her, but Zimbabwe's intensified racial environment raised new challenges. "Racism is such a huge part of the history in Africa. If you took a helicopter and flew over my school, you would have seen little separate clusters of white children, black children, Indian children, and colored children. To say I am colored, in Africa, means very specifically that I am mixed race. Some of my friends had been colored for several generations, with mixed-race grandparents and parents marrying amongst themselves; I was, of course, the first generation.

"There were four little girls who were my friends, two colored, one black, one white. Something happened to us one day: we got in a big disagreement focused on the black girl, and one of my colored friends made the remark, 'This just proves my mother was right — you can never trust blacks.' I was totally shocked that she didn't see herself as part black, that she was prejudiced about her own bloodline.

"About the same time I was hanging out with a boy who was also colored. I don't know that we were old enough for him to be my boyfriend, just holding hands and being thirteen. I went with him to my father's office, where I was to catch a ride back out to the farm. I was all excited to show my dad I had a boyfriend. 'Dad, this is Vernon. Vernon, this is my dad.' I was really surprised when my father just ignored him and ordered me into the car. As soon as we were under way he told me sternly, 'Marianne, you are not to hang out with coloreds. They're not your kind of people.' I almost fell out of the car — how could he be saying that to his own colored daughter? I realize now that he was referring to the social conditions for many colored Africans: neither black nor white, they don't have a place in society. They are often poor and struggling, without a village system or tribe, and can be the group with the most social problems. I didn't have a way to think through the sociology; I was just shocked at the racism. So *I began to see that there was something significant about being biracial. Race was all around me. I could look in the mirror. I knew people wanted race to apply to me, but I chose to disregard color. I am who I am, regardless of my color. I will not allow myself to be placed in the same boxes that everyone places everyone else in.*"

This awareness is Marianne editing.

There is a summation point to childhood. We don't usually know it at the time, unless it's cataclysmic, but in retrospect we see an ending and a shift. For Marianne, the shift comes through her ability to stand as herself. In the context of two races, two countries, two families, two ways of life, she stepped out of the box and into a process of self-definition.

"In 1987, at age sixteen, I moved back to Denmark, alone. My father's mother invited me for a summer educational program, but through the ensuing conversations it got extended to finish high school there and go into university. My mother was ambivalent, but she always told me, 'Get an education. Get a good job. Be able to look after yourself. Then when you have your house and car and a career, you can drive down the street and choose any man you want. Leave the men alone until you have reached complete independence.'

The interior life is in constant vertical motion; consciousness runs up and down the scales every hour like a slide trombone.
— Annie Dillard

"When I landed back in the Danish school system I got reverse culture shock. I thought I was returning to familiarity, and yet things were so different. *I was imprinted with the notion that the West was better and more advanced than Zimbabwe and it was cool to be on this adventure*. But I returned as a child, very innocent and naive. My old friends were drinking and smoking. They seemed so sophisticated. During my time in Africa, I had joined a Pentecostal church. The church services were amazing, song and dance and people speaking in tongues and praying for salvation. I loved the energy and joined it enthusiastically. I had been boarding at school in Harare when I got involved in the church, and I remember every morning I'd wake up and before I got out of bed, I'd pray to make it through the day without sinning. Then the last thing at night I'd lie in bed again and pray for forgiveness because I knew I had sinned. I couldn't tell you then or now what I had done that was so bad. I brought my religious fervor inside me to Denmark to a society where the church is not a main part of life. First I saw my old friends as fallen sinners, then as I joined the boarding school crowd, I too fell into worldly ways and agonized about hell. I felt very guilty and very sad that I was going to burn in eternal damnation, but I couldn't resist the life of my peers.

"*There was so much that jarred me when I returned to Denmark, and I think inside this jarring is where the story that influences my life was shaped.* I saw my Danish grandparents as very reserved, almost afraid of showing emotion, and as a result of that, very lonely and focused on money and material things. Though she was wealthy, beautiful, and intelligent, I realized my Danish grandmother was not happy; while my poor, dusty Zimbabwean grandmother was full of energy, vitality, love, and joy. *The contrast between cultures, so evident in the contrast between grandmothers, made me question happiness, wealth, materialism, and religion.*"

Disorienting

The gate to any new period of growth or maturity in our lives requires a period of discomfort and disorientation. Out of this experience we eventually create a more deeply integrated story.

Whenever we find ourselves in a period of disorientation, we can gain perspective by viewing our crisis as though it is a key turning point in the plot of a novel — after all, our life is a story, and stories follow certain structures. In the beginning of a book or movie, we glimpse the stability that sets the stage: we see where each character is standing, how the scene is held in place. The camera swoops down on the farm in Africa, or along the street of a neighborhood, or to a family at supper... we are lulled into enjoyment of this intimate moment, but our pulses quicken because we know it's not going to last: something is coming....

Plot is set in motion by some detonating event that discombobulates us, shakes up the status quo, and sets us off on the journey. When this happens in real life, we may try to reestablish our former life, but eventually we realize that is impossible. Plot carries us forward into new territory; there is no going back. The only resolution is to reorient our lives so that we can integrate this experience into who we are.

"How does one grow up?" I asked a friend. She answered, "By thinking."
— May Sarton

Part of the creative tension in novels, movies, and reality is that this integration is not guaranteed. For many reasons people get stuck in these periods of discombobulation: maybe the drama is the most important thing that ever happened to them; maybe resolving the tension would require the betrayal of someone they love; maybe they don't have the resources, financial or otherwise; maybe they've waited too long and the options are closed. And, we don't like to talk about disorientation when we're in it: we're open to this discombobulation when it's a plot, but not when it's fallen through the roof of our own lives.

Jerome Bruner, in his book *Making Stories*, calls these periods of disorientation "a *peripeteia*, a sudden reversal in circumstances." Describing story as "the coin and currency of culture," Bruner says, "Everyone will agree that it requires a cast of characters who are free agents with minds of their own. Given a moment to think about it, they'll also agree that these characters have recognizable expectations about the ordinary state of the world, the story's world, though these expectations may be somewhat enigmatic. And... everybody agrees that a story begins with some breach in the expected state of things —*peripeteia*. Something goes awry, otherwise there's nothing to tell about. The story concerns efforts to cope or come to terms with the breach and its consequences. And finally there is an outcome, some sort of resolution."

In these moments, we truly become the narrator of our own life narrative. As with the survivor's tale, we begin to explore the territory of our *peripeteia*. *Where was the moment of status quo? What detonated it? And then what happened? And then?* If we can't see it clearly, writing in the third person always helps. Marianne did this when she wrote, "There was a young woman who started at the Business School of Copenhagen. She was eager to make a career. Her goals were simple: a fancy job, a big salary, a flashy car, a pretty house, and maybe one day even a boat. She worked hard at it. Though she was asleep." Ah, here is the recognition of status quo and the beginning of plot: how will this young woman awaken?

She continues: "Every summer I went home to Zimbabwe and became more and more aware of the discrepancy between what I was told to value and what I was told to pity. The social contrast played out very personally for me, but I didn't have any idea how to reconcile it. *I held my mother's advice close to heart*, graduated, and went straight into university, to business school. As a business major, I was learning about micro- and macroeconomics, statistics, accounting, and so on. In the best pedagogical style, I was taught to see humanity as *Homo economicus*, a species simply interested in maximizing his own profit and material wealth. The complex world of human organizing was summarized into people expressing their well-being through financial figures. *I never stopped questioning*: my Zimbabwean grandparents made it very clear that there were other definitions of wealth. *I was looking for something idealistic to emerge in my European world.*

"In 1992, I joined an international student organization called AIESEC (a French acronym for the International Association of Students in Economics and Commerce). At that time there was a move in AIESEC International to create a more critically thinking student network. Here I found a community of peers, idealistic graduate students who wanted to challenge *Homo economicus*, who wanted to infiltrate global corporations and bring them the gospel of sustainability. AIESEC Denmark, among the practical Danes, was quite against these developments, which gave me another contrast to live and a chance to stand up for my beliefs. The questions I couldn't ask about myself, I could ask by trying to reform AIESEC. *If I could integrate the materialistic, mechanistic view of mankind I was being taught in school with the humanistic, biologic living system that was Africa in my blood, I could make a world in which to hold myself.*"

Here comes Marianne's vision rising out of her period of disorientation.

Revisioning

Revising the self-story provides the foundation for doing our life work, and for seeing our lives, whatever we choose to do, as a never-ending story.

To make *a world* that can hold us is a universal longing. And we start by organizing *a story* that can hold us. In Marianne's life, she is living out this dilemma across two continents and in the convergence of three major life events: assumption of leadership, experience of loss, and search for spiritual foundation.

Just when she thought the plot was solidifying, when she had found her cohort group and was taking her first adult steps into leadership, her father was killed in a car accident.

"It took a long time for my father's death to become real. I had been gone from Zimbabwe for so long that I just continued to think of him as being there. I suspect that letting his death seep in was a way to try and manage the loss. I didn't know what else to do, so I returned to Denmark to finish my master's degree. And to keep myself even busier, I deepened my work in AIESEC.

When people . . . rethink their personal stories, they begin to build a sense of connection and responsibility. They recognize that their actions can matter. . . . They learn to view their personal stories as intertwined with history.

— Paul Rogat Loeb

"I ran for president of AIESEC International and in 1996 was elected the first female president in their history. Our idealistic team set about to dismantle a bureaucracy and to institute the creation of a living system — a network. However, we got stuck. Perhaps we tried to move too fast; perhaps we had seen something that we weren't able to convey. At the end of our one-year term, we were excited at the vision we had brought to the association, but the team that followed ours turned around and moved everything back toward structure. This disillusionment decided me against ever working in a large corporation. If I could not manage to change a student organization when I was its leader, how could I expect to change a multinational corporation coming in at a junior position? AIESEC taught me about inertia in large systems and resistance to change. *I made up my mind to work from the outside, to disturb the system, and to create new structures as part of my work in the world.*"

In her decision to make her own way, the alchemy of revisioning emerges out of the editing and disorientation and provides the foundation for her next steps in the journey. To complete her master's degree, Marianne changed the focus of her thesis to study the lives of nine mentors and peers around the question of "bringing the human spirit to work."

"These people saw their lives as a mission or calling. Things didn't just happen for them; they made things happen in response to selecting the best choice among many opportunities. They consciously and deliberately exercised their ability to choose. By studying their stories, I learned how to lay out my own story map and to step into it."

Making a world that can hold the self requires that we find a spiritual frame inside which we see our life story happening. The question arises: *what beyond human mind, human ego, or human design is at work here?* Even in stories that don't express revisioning as spiritual awakening, some revelation happens that changes the context.

That was the year she went to Sri Lanka for the AIESEC International Congress and some vacation time. She and her friends stayed next door to a Buddhist temple. She says, "I was attracted to the quiet energy that seemed to be emanating from this place. I had not given much thought to my soul since leaving the Pentecostal church; I just didn't know how to think about a spiritual life. I bought a number of books at the temple and took them with me down to the beach. I tried some of the simple meditation techniques.

"Having only known the Christian doctrine, which emphasized my sin, I was intrigued by a philosophy that placed responsibility with me to work at quieting and purifying my mind. I had to 'redeem' my own life. In 2000, I discovered Vipassana meditation and went on a ten-day silent retreat that was transformative in many ways and grounded me in a meditation practice that is core to me to this day.

"I am not a Buddhist — I don't think Buddha wanted people to become Buddhists — but the sitting keeps me open, receptive, and able to deal with the challenges that are a natural part of any life. I sit regularly, one hour in the morning and one hour in the evening. I am not sure how it fits in with my story; I simply know it increases my ability to stay balanced through whatever happens.

"Meditation is not all sweet and pretty, just sitting around on pillows — I need it. Sometimes I lose touch with the source of my inspiration and act like someone I don't even recognize. One time when we were physically building Kufunda village, before the programs started, we were working under time pressure and something went wrong with the building process. The workers — four big Zimbabwean builders — were trying to explain it to me. 'We thought this, that, and the other and da da da da.' I was standing there, just fuming, and I screamed at them, 'My word is law! Do you understand that?' And they stopped and just looked at me, and I thought, 'Did I just say that? What is happening to me? Where are my collaboration values?'" Marianne ducks her head with embarrassment at this confession and we both laugh. "And now, even though it is not part of Shona culture, we are doing meditation in the community at Kufunda, in my little garden house."

It is possible that the next Buddha will not take the form of an individual. The next Buddha may take the form of a community — a community practicing understanding and loving-kindness, a community practicing mindful living. This may be the most important thing we can do for the survival of the Earth.

— Thich Nhat Hanh

Kufunda

Kufunda is the Shona word for learning. Kufunda village is a small residential learning community built on a corner of the Knuth family farm. Of course there's a story to the coming of this dream. The idea for Kufunda occurred during Marianne's weeklong thirtieth birthday party in 2001. Her mother, now the director of state occasions for the Zimbabwean government, helped arrange for a traveling party of Marianne's

European and American friends to tour some of Zimbabwe's primary attractions: the game reserves, Victoria Falls, and the thousand-year-old ruins of Great Zimbabwe. The highlight turned out to be the visit to her grandmother's rural village in Mhondoro, where her extended family hosted the international group. There, in the midst of an all-night party, singing, dancing, drumming, drinking *chibuku*, and eating huge bowls of *sadzu* and *nyama*, Marianne had an epiphany that would lead her into the next chapter of her life story.

"I saw my Shona family, materially poor and uneducated though they may be, as beautiful and incredible people who have something to teach my middle-class, educated friends. People here have challenges, and they are struggling, but in the midst of that, they have a wealth of culture and community and approach to life that is critical for the rest of the world to understand. And the people also need to recognize themselves as treasures, for the colonial chapter deeply wounded their stories, so they disbelieve their own heritage and power. But that night, across barriers of language and strangeness, I watched my life come together. I watched people trading gifts and songs and dance steps. I watched my Western life laughing and hugging my African life. By bringing my world home, I was able to bring myself home. I began to dream of creating an African learning village, a place where some of the practices and skills that I had learned from studying in Europe could be tried out in the realism of a country in desperate need of developing community leaders.

"I returned to a country seemingly facing imminent collapse. We are now well into that process — political violence is rife, with the government, in my opinion, being the main aggressor. Zimbabwe has in many ways become a police state and dictatorship. Many NGOs (nonprofit organizations) are being shut down. During the presidential election in 2002, many rural communities were closed to the outside world, unable to receive visitors or host gatherings larger than a handful of people, even if the gatherings were not political. While those restrictions have loosened, the fear lingers. The economy is rapidly collapsing, which at one time left us with critical shortages of basic commodities, including maize meal, cooking oil, wheat and bread, salt, sugar, fuel, and more. After being the breadbasket of southern Africa for years, this is a hard blow. While the goods are back in the stores, the prices are much higher and many lower- and middle-class families are struggling.

"Nevertheless, with my return to Zimbabwe, I stepped into what the universe was asking of me. I announced to the world that this was what I was doing, and then I thought, *Oh my god, now I have to do it, and I don't even know exactly what it is.*

"I traveled to different places in Zimbabwe, I met people, I told them 'I'm starting a new kind of village. We're going to bring people together to explore how we can create sustainable communities.' I remember in one town the older women sat down with me and listened while I explained the plan for their young people. They said, 'Okay, we will support the young people to study at Kufunda because they will come home.' These wise women didn't want any more desertion to the city while the villages stayed in need.

"In July of 2002, our first fifteen students arrived for a three-month learning program on leadership and self-reliance. We cooked together, planted our food together, built the village together, explored the nature around us, and explored ourselves. After each training a few of the students have stayed on, so it looks like Kufunda will become a real ongoing community."

Marianne is pacing now, heading out of the kitchen, a round thatch-roofed building with walls only halfway up and the rest open to the air. We follow her to the teaching house, a large oval room in which all of Kufunda's classes, conversations, circles, and celebrations occur. The building is nestled between two very large rocks, which Marianne pats like the sides of an elephant as she walks by. The permaculture garden is growing eggplant, covo, and enough organic produce to feed the Kufundees and take to town. Beyond the garden are fields of sugar beans, peanuts, and maize. The village itself is a scattering of small huts: Silas's house, the dormitory, Sikhethiwe's house, compost toilets, a hut that serves as a common living room.

The people have high spirits and great respect for each other. There are young faces and older faces, black faces and brown faces and white faces: here is Marianne's schoolyard in another incarnation. "I am learning, alongside the students, that community teaches us how to move forward. I am learning through story, through listening. It's been a surprise that the story is more important than the training. But when the stories go deep, the training occurs. We are learning to work together again, and play, and learn, and simply be. So much power is available as we learn to be in community. When we recognize that we each have something of value to offer, our sense of self-worth grows and our process of unfolding is just like a flower.

"The more we trust the experiment, the more I realize that Kufunda and I are being spiritually held and supported by the universe. And the other Kufundees are waking up to that sense too: not simply that the universe may hold them, but also that the universe *needs* them. In a session, one of the students actually laughed out loud and said, '*What if the future is waiting for me?*' and his eyes sparkled with excitement at the possibility that his life was truly meaningful, in fact critical, for the future to be a better place than the present.

We are all meant to shine, as children do. As we let our own light shine, we unconsciously give other people permission to do the same. As we are liberated from our own fear, our presence automatically liberates others.

— Nelson Mandela

"It is a crazy and dark time here in Zimbabwe, and increasingly we find ourselves bringing into our circle prayers for those who are suffering in this beautiful country. Our infection rate for AIDS is the highest in Africa. I can't help but wonder how it will all end. *And yet, in the midst of a vicious downward spiral, we and others like us are walking in the opposite direction.* It feels good. We feel strong. And I hope we can look back one day and see that our simple experience of building a community of light in a time of darkness was part of turning things around. It is possible to walk against the grain, to open to another way, letting life flow through us in a spiral of experience.

"And I am so thoroughly enjoying the journey," she says and swallows the last of the tea. That evening she is walking back across the farm. Her dog, Jack, trots at her heels. Her mother comes out from the house and the two women watch the sunset. There is something about the light, the light in Africa, that sets them both aglow.

The Story from Here On

I am a long way from Africa as I write, but close to Marianne. Her story and the stories of the Kufundees remind me again that human beings can survive and grow through anything as long as we can wrap a story around our experience that fosters resilience. The more horrible the conditions we live through, the harder it often is to work our story into moments of confidence and resilience, but over and over again we inspire each other to see our lives differently. This mutual inspiration — how the story that gets one person through lays out a map to get another person through — remains essential. We need the mirror of each other's courage.

In the beginning is the baby: in the end is the life story. Days, weeks go by when the self-story is humming along underneath all the other stories and the world's noise and demands and we don't hear the narrative that shapes our lives. We are like a person who has grown accustomed to the ringing in his ears: it's just there, accommodated as background buzz until something starts to snap, crackle, and pop. It's midnight on our birthday, or New Year's Eve after everyone's gone home, or we can't sleep and are wandering the house looking in on the children, or a coworker our same age dies over the weekend while mowing the lawn, or a sunset stuns us with beauty while we're driving home from work and a moment of reflection sweeps over us. We check in with ourselves. We ask: *So, how am I really?* And then, like all good Storycatchers, we listen.

In those moments when you are listening to the story of yourself, what do you reclaim?

Let's start there.

Tell me that story.

Becoming a Storycatcher

We each create a story of the self that begins with our birth story and then continues with what we remember, speak, and write about our own lives. We decide throughout this process what we want our lives to include and what kind of a legacy we want to leave behind, and then we are challenged to act on this story — to become who we say we are.

Tell Me This Story...

These story beginnings can be used in writing or conversation to enhance storycatching in your life.

- Do you know your birth story? Who told you the story? Do you have artifacts from around the time of your birth that have been saved for you?
- Who are your real-life mentors? What have you learned from them?
- Do you have memories about the pivotal choices you made at ages six, twelve, sixteen, thirty, forty, and fifty? Write these in story form.
- Whether you are a peer or an elder, what is the hope you want to inspire in the young people around you? How are you facilitating this inspiration?
- Describe something you did that made you feel really proud. Where were you? How did this event come about? How did others react to this event? Did others' reactions change the way you felt about it?
- What do you see as your life's purpose? What do you need to set behind you to complete your particular life path?
- What would give you courage to continue your work in the midst of crisis in your country?

CHAPTER SEVEN

Writing and Talking in the Seven Generations

HOW STORY HEALS FAMILY HERITAGE

Making story of our family history doesn't mean we change the realities of our forebears' lives — we don't turn a thief into a pillar of virtue — but we learn to carry the story differently so the lineage can heal.

Respect for "the seven generations" is a gift from the Iroquois nation, a sophisticated and ancient tribal culture in the northeastern United States. Throughout their history they have understood in their councils that decisions made by the living tribe must take into consideration the impact on the next seven generations of the tribe. The decisions we make in our personal lives also have generational consequences. We have inherited these consequences and we will pass them along.

The heritage story gives people the opportunity to link, edit, disorient, and revision their lives in a generational context. The Spiral of Experience also addresses collective experience and the time it takes for a family to absorb, integrate, and release initiating events. In the larger scope of storycatching we are challenged to raise our attention from self-healing to explore how story might heal the families and communities and organizations we live within. In this chapter, we look at family lineage.

Over time, we can see how the life choices of our ancestors impacted the family, and how individuals in each succeeding generation made choices that accentuated or counterbalanced what had happened before. The grandson of a pioneer logger becomes a forester who pioneers old-growth preservation. The great-granddaughter of a slave owner and a kitchen maid works to increase racial understanding in both Anglo- and African-American communities. And the great-grandmother who hardly spoke raises a daughter who seldom touches who raises a daughter who overcompensates with talk and touching and whose daughter becomes a midwife, helping women and babies appropriately bond in the first interactions of their lifelong relationships.

The healing of family is not genetically dependent. We can do this work of story healing with any family system. Adopted children, sons- and daughters-in-law, stepparents and stepchildren, family friends who become "one of us," immigrants and refugees — all have significant roles in their families of choice. In my family, we call this the red line and the green line: the bloodline and the chosen line. My heart has two sisters, one red, one green: one I grew up with, one married my brother. The word *heritage* encompasses both bloodline and other ways we claim our belonging. Our belonging occurs in a generational spectrum that extends backward and forward from our lifetimes, and healing the heritage story influences both ancestors and progeny.

Most of the homes in the world have some kind of small shrine that honors this generational spectrum, from the elaborate rituals of Chinese ancestor worship to the collection of family photos parading down the hallway and over the mantel in many Western homes. In my living room is the small wooden chest marked with painted initials — *HRR* — and the date *1860*. This is the chest my Norwegian great-grandmother carried onto the boat on her way to America. When I touch it, I am reminded that these planks were milled of Norwegian pine and strapped together with iron bindings from a village forge. What did a nine-year-old farm girl bring to America? I use the chest to store photographs and other small family artifacts in my care. I am tending these things for a lifetime, waiting to see who will come forward in the next generations and pick up this responsibility.

The desire to honor our ancestors in some way, and to maintain connection to the lives and stories of those we come from, shows up in most families. My grandfather, Leo, had his Bible, with pages between the Testaments full of familial statistics. My Aunt Ruth kept a notebook on each branch of the eight Baldwin children and their descendants. In the 1990s, my cousin Frank and his wife, Jan, drove all over New England verifying the arrival of our clan in the 1700s and their influence in the settlement of New York and Massachusetts in the early 1800s. With the onset of computer software for building family trees, with archives online and websites buzzing with data, genealogical information is available as never before. For Storycatchers, such research also raises the question: *as we find the statistics, will we also find a way to heal the heritage?*

All of us carry within ourselves something that is waiting for the right moment when it can burst out and repair the particular separation that we are experiencing.

— Malidoma Somé

Angeles Arrien, a transcultural anthropologist raised in the Basque traditions of the original mountain people of Spain, teaches that our ancestors hover over the cradle of each new baby born into their lineage and ask — *Will this be the child to heal the line? Will this be the one to change our story?* In her teachings she proclaims, "What is not integrated repeats itself until it is integrated. I look at the personal story and the societal story as being one and the same, only in larger or smaller scale. In our families and in our nations, what we see is our dis/integration being played out. The journey needed now is the integration of ancestor wisdom into the living community — personally in each of our families, and globally in the human family."

The journey to address heritage begins with a willingness to consider one's personal story *in the context of* the family story — and the family story in the context of the ancestral story. When we attend to healing the self-story, we realize the interconnection of self-story and family story. If we change the self-story, we change the stories of those we relate to. It's like plucking one strand of a spider web: one thread moves all threads.

Kit Wilson, A Grandmother's Timely Voice

Sitting comfortably in her home in Phoenix, Arizona, a modest hacienda along one of the side streets of this sprawling desert metropolis, a wise and witty woman sips her daily indulgence of coffee and brings the perspective of seven decades to the question of family story. "I remember exactly the moment I realized I was taking on the work of healing my life and family," she says. "It's a scene of such pain that I would do anything to not repeat it — and that 'anything' has turned out to be committing the rest of my life to growth and healing. Which hasn't been easy either, but is still more tolerable than waking up that Thanksgiving Day in 1971."

The woman pushes back wispy gray hair, adjusts a shawl around her shoulders, and stares into the walled courtyard of her backyard. The surface of her swimming pool is adrift in puffs from the weeping acacia tree. There is a grapefruit tree and a lemon tree heavy with fruit, several splayed cacti, but she sees a different scene in her mind. In a raspy, well-used voice she begins to share her story. "I remember the snow had built up throughout the night. When I opened my eyes, the tree we had planted after the previous Christmas was almost covered. For a moment I felt that sudden little-girl spurt of joy, and then I remembered what I had committed myself to do. I closed my eyes, trying to block out the feelings, but the sobs came over me, uncontrollably. They went on, and on, and on, deeper than the snow.

Alcohol doesn't console; it doesn't fill up anyone's psychological gaps. All it replaces is the lack of God.

— Marguerite Duras

"Over the last twenty-five years, I have come to understand about the dark night of the soul, the process of death and rebirth that occurs within life. I have come to understand how these moments bring us, willingly or unwillingly, to the very core of life and to the very heart of our story. But that morning I did not have any wisdom or perspective. I threw the covers over my head, bit down hard on the pillow, and bellowed my pain into the feather ticking. I was married, a mother of two teenagers; soon I would have to go downstairs to the kitchen and try to pull off a family occasion that I hoped would fall this side of disastrous. I had no idea if I could summon the will to move and face the day. I had made a commitment that would change me. I had decided to begin an unstoppable process inside myself, and in the end I would not be the same. I had no concept of what I would become, no idea if I would lose my home, the people I loved, the rituals that brought meaning to my life. I only knew that life as I knew it was over, that there was no turning back.

"My name is Kit W. and I am an alcoholic. The day after Thanksgiving in 1971, I entered treatment, and more importantly, I entered recovery. I come from a family of longtime drinkers and longtime sufferers. My grandfather was an alcoholic. My father was an alcoholic. One of my grandsons is an alcoholic. This is only one aspect of our family lineage, but it's a defining intergenerational pattern for those of us who have taken directly to drink, and those who have watched, endured, and enabled. From where I sit, thirty-plus years sober, a woman in my late seventies, I can see three generations back and two generations forward: I am writing and talking my story midstream in the generations."

The story was the important thing and little changes here and there were really part of the story. There were even stories about the different versions of stories and how they imagined the differing versions came to be.

— Leslie Marmon Silko

Making Family Story Conscious

What Kit has done is to make her family story conscious. She has put herself into the cultural context of her lineage and evaluated what happened to her in light of what had already happened in the family line. She began linking behavior that had never been talked about, at least not effectively talked about, and is now making these links and their accompanying awareness part of her lineage story. Whenever someone does this work on behalf of a family, it gives everyone in the family the opportunity to perceive themselves and their inherited characteristics differently. As we all know, not everyone in a family will accept this invitation, at least not when we would want them to, but even if temporarily rejected, the insight starts to exist within the line; someone will find it and value it.

When something exists in a family that is not discussed, it goes into what Carl Jung termed "the shadow," the unacknowledged aspects of the self. This is true individually, and also collectively — whether the collective is the family or society. In the vernacular of Alcoholics Anonymous, the shadow is called "the elephant in the living room." Everyone knows that something is wrong, but no one speaks it. Everyone accommodates the presence of what is unspoken and verbally talks around that territory, avoiding it as though there really is an elephant in the living room. Everyone knows better than to cut directly from point A to B because he or she would bump into a huge obstacle. That obstacle is silence; that obstacle is fear; that obstacle is facing the unknown. These were the obstacles Kit faced on Thanksgiving morning 1971, and instead of drinking, she found the courage to experience her terror and head into a new life of building consciousness.

Fear and I don't get along very well. I throw fear behind myself and keep on going, but sometimes I ought to stop and listen. That's the spiritual practice of my seventies; knowing when I should not let fear stop me, and knowing when I should.

— Harriet Ost

Every family I know well enough to glimpse its story has developed family behaviors that perpetuate themselves from one generation to the next. Many of these behaviors are supportive: the determination to increase education, to improve economically, to take care of less fortunate family members, to celebrate holidays and family traditions, to serve in certain professions. Part of what sustains these supportive behaviors is the stories that develop around them. Families reinforce their sense of identity by making family myths about the kind of people they are. In 1990, one of my father's older brothers wrote and self-published a little book grandly titled *The Montana Baldwins: Saga of a Century*. It is a celebration of the pioneering and Protestant ethic that sustains our family myth. It articulates a social story that makes us look pretty good and avoids a dozen darker tales that even I, a generation younger and several states removed, am aware live in our spiritual bones. The book is a contribution to intergenerational storycatching and contains many hints (should a future reader want to explore that territory) at what was unspoken during that time in our history.

For there are, in every family, corresponding behaviors that thrive in the family shadow. In the midst of whatever else is going on that is held in the light of story, people also come to expect certain negative or unacknowledged behaviors to mysteriously recur. They may even regard these things as a family curse. While families often cannot, or do not, "talk about such things," other people perceive our familial flaws and do talk about them. Want to know the shadow in your family? Ask your neighbors or a child under five.

So what is the shadow that's traveling in your family: Addiction? Unmanaged anger coupled with timidity? Fear of risk? Women who marry the wrong men; men who marry the wrong women? People who set up disaster just at the brink of success? Acceptance of oppression or abuse? Religious intolerance or avoidance of spiritual tradition? Stereotyping and projection onto other racial, ethnic, sexual, or religious minorities? If you can't see how the unconscious and unspoken show up in your own family, just look into one of the world's famous families and notice the myth and the shadow in, for example, the Windsor family, the Kennedy family, the bin Laden family, the Gandhi family. They live their lives on a larger scale than the rest of us, but what perpetuates who they are, and the urgency with which their ancestral line whispers over the cradle, are no different from our own.

The balance of light and dark is ultimately possible and bearable.
— Robert A. Johnson

Kit is a psychotherapist, transplanted to the desert after spending the first half of her life growing up in Pennsylvania, going to college in Massachusetts, and living in Connecticut during her marriage and child-raising years. In the years after that fateful Thanksgiving, she decided to work with others who were addicted and moved to Phoenix to study psychodrama. She found work in an outpatient chemical dependency clinic, a psychiatric hospital, and finally in private practice. She is a pioneer in the work of healing through story. After all this experience, what still fascinates her is evidence that the work of healing has a collective impact beyond the single person who comes in the door.

Although some use stories as entertainment alone, tales are, in their oldest sense, a healing art. Some are called to this healing art; and the best, to my lights, are those who have lain with the story and found all its matching parts inside themselves and at depth. In the best tellers I know, the stories grow out of their lives like roots grow a tree. The stories have grown them, grown them into who they are.

— Clarissa Pinkola Estés

"People come into therapy on behalf of others as well as on their own behalf," she says. "They may not know this for a long time and may even be resistant to the idea. Often people come to see me because they are mad at somebody. They feel wronged or misunderstood. They want someone to listen to their view about, say, their relationship with a partner or parent. They don't want me to immediately take that person's side. Part of my job as an educated and empathetic listener is to encourage their story to emerge and emerge until they can begin to see it in a multifaceted way. *The day I can ask, 'What do you think was going on for so-and-so in that moment?' and they follow the question without defensiveness, is the day I begin to see the family heal*. I would not have understood this about my clients if I had not already done that work in myself."

If we step up to the challenge of healing the family story, we need to be grounded in the healing of our personal story. We start there, standing firm in our own life experience and the person we have become through linking, editing, disorienting, and revisioning our personal story. This is the psychological and spiritual foundation required to head into family history. When, as Kit says, we get to the point where we can wonder about other peoples' perspectives in the turning-point events of our lives, we begin to heal laterally across the relationships of the living family. When we get to the point where we can wonder what influences and assumptions were at play in these situations, we begin to heal intergenerationally.

This intergenerational insight occurred for Kit around the emerging story of alcoholism in her lineage. "I was the only child of my generation in my mother's entire family — an oddity among grown-ups, indulged by childless aunts and uncles and my grandparents. They talked over my head as though their words didn't filter down to where I was playing or reading, so I garnered a lot of family information, even if I didn't understand it all. From a young age I was thinking about coming from a line of people.

"All the years of my childhood in York, Pennsylvania, we went to my maternal grandparents' house every Sunday afternoon and evening for dinner. We had the same meal every week: pot roast and mashed potatoes, hot slaw, and creamed corn. Our weekly reunions were a set family pattern and everybody was expected to be there. One aunt came from Baltimore, another aunt and uncle came from Harrisburg. My father never attended. He considered my grandfather a crook and didn't want anything to do with my mother's family. So this whole rich family experience was only on my mother's side, without my father.

To own one's own shadow is to reach a holy place — an inner center — not attainable in any other way.

— Robert A. Johnson

"I don't remember ever seeing Pop, my mother's father, drinking, or being aware that he was drunk. But he only gave up drinking when he was 89 and then after twelve years of sobriety, started up again at 101 — and died six months later. So, he must have been drinking all that while. As a child, I never thought of either my grandfather or father as being alcoholics; we didn't even know the word. What I remember about those Sundays are Pop's arms around me helping me push the old-fashioned lawn mower and teaching me how to graft apples onto a tree trunk so skillfully that we had one tree that produced six different varieties of fruit. I remember walking up to his lock and gun shop, which was set on acreage like a little farm in the heart of the city, and he would sit me on his grinder and let me pedal while he sharpened knives. To me, he was quite wonderful, but the adult stories of him are terrifying. I overheard my mother and aunt talking about how he'd take a gun and shoot over the heads of anyone who approached his fence, that he had a violent temper and hit my grandmother. But I only know those things from overhearing them — to me, he was gentle. My mother and aunt always referred to him as the devil and to my grandmother as a saint. Grandma had slipped on a boardwalk when I was two weeks old and broken her hip. This accident put her on crutches and in a wheelchair the rest of her life, and that's the only way I knew her. Maybe part of the equation was: the devil drank and the saint did not.

"What my father did alone on all those Sundays, when we were with my mother's family, I have no idea. Maybe he drank. *My father's alcoholism was pretty invisible to me.* He didn't drink at home because my mother wouldn't let him. He may have drunk when we weren't there, but during the week he would stay out late, miss supper and come home drunk, have a terrible fight with my mother, and go to bed. I didn't understand the role booze played in this. And I had no one to talk to, not even a cousin with whom to compare notes. *Like most kids, whatever was happening to me, well, I thought that was the norm.*

"My father was the first alcoholic in his family to ever stop drinking. Though I don't have much specific information, I suspect the thread of alcoholism trickled back goodness knows how many generations. He came from a long line of hardworking, hard-drinking laborers who emigrated from England to America. He was the first one in his family to graduate from college, was an avid reader — and a loner. A lot of what I love about my own sense of aesthetics and cultural understanding I got from him. He used to buy me big books on art history and literature, and we'd spend hours poring over those volumes together. Or he'd make up assignments for me to seek out something in these books. Beyond the standard American education I was getting at school, through him I felt like I was getting a European education as well. For several decades after my father's death, my husband and I led student groups on cultural tours of Europe. *His legacy ran deep in me.* On my father's side I was only one generation American, and going to Europe felt like going home."

The particulars of Kit's tale have a universal quality when we see her story as illustrative of how any repetitive pattern inserts itself into a family heritage. A young woman grows up with a father who drinks and rages; she marries a man to escape this scene but discovers that he also drinks and rages, so she inserts a corrective action: he cannot drink at home. Surely he will choose her, surely he will choose their child, surely he will choose to stay home. But the man stays away from home to assert his independence — and to drink. The woman grows depressed, bitter, projects her sense of entrapment onto their only child. The child grows swiftly independent and withdraws from the family as quickly as possible, determined to make her own way in the world. She marries a man to escape the situation. She misses and loves her father. She starts to drink.

All this corrective action, which takes decades to occur within the family, occurs outside the healing story. Story would have made these actions conscious behavior instead of unconscious behavior. Story would have shifted these generational decisions out of shadow. As Angeles Arrien taught Kit, and as Kit taught me, "in order to change something, we need to be able to name it, to speak about it. We cannot respond to what has not yet been brought into form through story. Story is the liberator from shadow to transformation." I think of story as a corral fence: we round up the unnamed experiences and behaviors that have run wild through our families and bring them into the hoop of saying. We need to be seasoned Storycatchers to do this work.

Though family stories have been passed along for generations, only in recent decades has the influence of psychology, therapy, and other self-help tools fostered increasing consciousness among large numbers of people. Consciousness is the ability in the human mind to be simultaneously aware of our feelings, our thoughts, and our actions. There have always been thought leaders who have developed and cultivated consciousness, but the phenomenon of entire populations of literate, educated people holding tools for increased self-awareness is a new human experiment. Because we are new at this, our understanding of what we are capable of shifts constantly.

Action is the antidote to despair.
— Joan Baez

Working with our lineage begins with questioning: *What exists in my family that I want to celebrate? What exists in my family that I want to change?* My own family lineage is the story that filters through chapter 1. I see the interaction of story and silence, of consciousness and shadow. I make choices to use the silence for listening, to use the stories for truth telling. These are choices that Kit is also making in her family.

"My father died when I was in my early thirties," she says, "about four years after my grandfather. He had a massive heart attack while traveling in Baltimore and none of us got to say good-bye. My father had stopped drinking and started going to Alcoholics Anonymous about six years earlier, but by that time I was so into drinking myself that I was angry with him for stopping. He came to Connecticut to make his amends and tell me he was sorry for the way he had been, but his contrition only confused me. I felt that all the good things I knew about life, and all the bits of culture — my appreciation for art and music — were things he had taught me during his years drinking. So all I said was, 'I never thought you drank too much.' I worshipped my father, but I didn't know him.

"When I began to study with Angeles Arrien and heard her statement about the ancestors, I realized that not only myself but my lineage needed healing. I could picture my grandparents and my parents and their struggles with their own personal lives, and I wanted to help them in some way. I wanted to articulate their lives more deeply than they had been able to. They were very concrete people. They talked about money, cooking, crops, and politics, politics, politics! But they didn't talk about psychological or spiritual insights. They didn't seem to have interior lives, at least not that they could put into words. *I didn't want to erase or diminish the reality of who they were and what they lived through, and I don't know if I could have undertaken this work while they were still living, but I wanted to add my experience to what they handed me. Otherwise, what is evolution for?*"

Here is a point where Kit gives herself permission to bring the family stories into the corral of consciousness. Kit begins the task of reframing the role of alcohol in her family line. She shifts it from shadow to questioning. "Did you know a lot of people in our family have been alcoholic?" changes the awareness. Alcoholism becomes a proclivity to be informed about, an occasion to take increasing responsibility for one's actions. Her father and grandfather are both dead, yet as Kit holds the story of their lives in the context of her own experience, she affects the capacity of succeeding generations to learn. She does not change the realities, but she changes how those realities are understood, and therefore, what quality of story is passed along.

"In AA, telling the story is required as part of recovery. Drinking is a disease fueled by shame that we are drinking. The shame spreads silence. When you sober up you have to say everything. You have to speak the truth to yourself, no matter what you've done. And you need to have your story heard by people who don't condemn you — but who also hold you to the full telling as a way of getting free. And then you have to make amends to everyone who has suffered because of your actions — no excuses for being drunk, just genuine apology... and listening to their pain. Boy, that was the hard part, looking at my children and understanding what my father had been trying to do, and how I would not let him do it. I wouldn't listen, and so I suspect he died with things still in him he wished he had been able to say to me. *My kids were able to listen to me, and I could listen to them, and that itself is part of healing our lineage.*"

Here is another point where Kit makes an evolutionary shift from one generation to the next. She chooses to honor her children's readiness to go through the process of making amends rather than to dwell on her own lack of readiness. She shifts the focus, not the reality. She acknowledges her own lack of readiness in the past and the incompletion left in her relationship to her father, but she brings the story of her children's readiness to the forefront. She shifts the focus from herself to the next generation. She sees progress. She sees events in relationship to each other, and sees these relationships maturing from one generation to the next.

In an essay in *Parabola* magazine, Colin Berg writes: "Forgiveness is simply returning energy: returning and receiving energy until any warp in the circle is healed, balance restored.... There is no real effort because forgiveness is the natural flow of life. There is no real loss because the flow is circular, it always returns. There is a sacrifice, a giving back that makes whole, makes holy.... To remember our roundness is our first great healing, forgiving act." It may take a long time to reach this understanding. It may take a lot of sorting through our stories and opening to new perspectives, but it is essential work in the human family, and always has been.

Since I know Kit is a journal writer, I know she has written dialogues between herself and her father that allow their relationship to come to completion in her mind, even though they couldn't complete the conversation while he was alive. In many circumstances, writing dialogues in which we play both voices provides direct access to helpful and healing insights. These dialogues serve as soul-to-soul conversations that bypass whatever obstacles exist (or existed) on a personality level or physical plane.

"It took my grandfather his whole life to sober up, and I'm clear that if my father had not gotten sober and shown me the way, I might not have been able to do it when I was forty-three. Even without being able to talk about it, my grandfather and my father and I created a track of recovery in the family. Based on this track, addiction became the catalyst that took me into the dark night and brought me to a new life. When my grandson turned up alcohol and drug addicted at age twenty, he not only had a mom and an uncle ready to intervene, he had his grandma who was carrying as best I could everything I had learned from his grandfather and great-grandfather. We helped Cholla rescue himself after only a year. He's got a good life. He knows where and how he's vulnerable. He knows something of the lineage he carries, and a whole lot about the pattern. *He's says I'm a model for him and the two of us talk about addiction and recovery and how to lead a whole life without drinking. He's heading into a good story*."

Genuine forgiveness is participation, reunion overcoming the powers of estrangement.... We cannot love unless we have accepted forgiveness, and the deeper our experience of forgiveness is, the greater is our love.

— Paul Tillich

The Spiral of Experience is not only personal, it is familial and intergenerational. Kit's articulation of her history shifts the family out of the survival tale into the story of integration. Now, as she and her grandson talk, her story will become his story, a story that extends deep into the twenty-first century and lives on after Kit is gone. Buddhist writer Pema Chödrön says, "*There are no true stories. We are making up every one of them.*" In my classes I sometimes say, "*There are only true stories. We are discovering the truth in them.*" As Storycatchers, we live with this paradox. We are not handed the truth; we are handed the story. It's already an alchemical stew of fact and fantasy.

"I know the work of family story is a delicate balance. I know I am seeing my parents through the lens of my own life choices and the influences of my times. My grandsons and their children will see me through the lens of their choices and their times. We can't control what future generations do with the family story, but it's still worth contributing to it as deeply as we can. I think it's part of the human task. When I'm done being me, they can have my story. It's my gift to them: a story about forgiveness, about compassion, about questioning. *I am contributing to my lineage backwards and forwards, through the personal work I've done to heal myself.*"

That's the point: Kit does the work of finding the story and then gives it away. When she went in search of herself in the context of family, she had two generations to work with. When Cholla or his brothers or cousin take up this search, they will have four generations of story available. When their children take up the story, they'll have five generations to work with, and each person and each generation will change the story. Just as physical characteristics are changed in the gene pool, so is story. It's not exactly Grandpa's nose coming down the line because other genes are added, and yet a baby bears a resemblance to the folks he or she comes from. And it's not exactly Grandpa's story coming down the line either, because other experiences are added, and what we believe about ourselves shifts; yet our story bears a resemblance to the stories that were handed to us, and we take them in, mix them up, work them through, and pass them on in the best shape we know how.

Storycatching in the family line requires

- *commitment to the integrity of different people's experience;*
- *staying within the frame of reality;*
- *ability to acknowledge multiple perspectives;*
- *saying what is without drama;*
- *following what has heart and meaning;*
- *being open to surprise;*
- *being ready to forgive.*

Healing the lineage through story is not about adhering to someone else's version of historical truth, but letting the story be what *we* need it to be. This worries people who think there is empirical truth at stake in family tales. There is no such truth: there is *authenticity of voice and exploration of intention*. Authentic means genuine, original, trustworthy, real. We don't knowingly lie about who we are. Standing with our commitment to authenticity, we can explore the family story through speculation, imagination, myth, and mysticism.

One of the profound healings in Kit's family story comes through an experience of mysticism. For as much work as she did and all the insights she had with the memories of her father and grandfather, Kit's relationship with her mother remained difficult over the years. Healing that part of Kit's lineage could not occur until after her mother's death.

"After my mother died in 1994," says Kit, "I went to my cabin in Oak Creek in the Arizona canyon lands to grieve her death. I had taken my journal with me and was writing and meditating and being with myself and trying to put the long difficulties with her in some kind of framework where I could be content. I did a lot of writing, listening to music, crying, and walking. There's a trail that runs through the woods along the creek for several miles, and I always hiked that trail in the morning with my dog, Charcoal. As was my habit, I took the trail during this time as well. One day, a week and a half after my mother died, I got to a certain place and felt this whoosh of energy. Charcoal was acting very strange, as though he'd felt it, too. I had no idea what it was, and after a minute of puzzlement, we walked on. Then on the way back, when I got back to the same spot, I looked up in this tall fir tree, and though I couldn't actually 'see' her, I knew my mother's spirit was sitting up there. My first reaction was to be really angry — and very blown away. She'd never been to this cabin. What was she doing in my space while I was trying to grieve her?

"I assumed it was a onetime experience, but three days later it happened again. Once again, I realized that her energy was still up in the tree. I went home and resumed my busy life. But regularly, whenever I went to the cabin, this experience of energy occurred. One day I decided I needed to pay attention to this, so I sat down and began talking to the energy of my mother. At first I just told her she didn't need to be up there and was generally encouraging her to leave. All my years with my mother had been very, very difficult, and I just wanted her to leave me in peace. But then I began to realize that she wasn't going to go away. It was sporadic, this whoosh and sense of her in this same tree. I wouldn't be thinking about her; it just happened when I went walking by the cabin. So after a while I would sit down and talk and tell her about stuff I was doing, stuff I could never have told her while she was living. And I would ask her questions about my growing up, and something would come back into my mind — like bits of story — and I began to appreciate more what it was like for her being the next to youngest sister in this very chaotic Pennsylvania Dutch family. And how come she felt so bad about herself most of those years, and where her rage came from. *I began to have compassion for her. And one day I was walking up the creek and realized she was completely gone. And I was completely at peace.*

> *In the photograph by my bed my mother is perpetually smiling on me. I guess I have forgiven us both, although sometimes in the night my dreams will take me back to the sadness and I have to wake up and forgive us again.*
>
> — Sue Monk Kidd

"The story I tell myself is that her spirit and I began to heal our relationship through these conversations and that the reason she hovered so close to this plane was that she needed healing from me as much as I needed it from her before she could get on with wherever she was going. We did our work finally."

Writing as Legacy

One of the ways Kit and I have come to know each other over the years is through her participation in a seminar I teach called "The Self as the Source of the Story." Starting in the late 1990s, Kit began to write her life and family story as though she is leaving a letter to be found by the seventh generation. "I'm already in the middle," she says, "so the seventh generation is my great-great-grandchildren. I'll never live to see them, but it's not impossible to imagine they will exist. What I cannot imagine is what the life around them will be like. So in writing to the unknown future, I get to explain things that we take for granted, like a car or cell phone or even the way the desert shimmers in the morning light, and see it through new eyes myself as I pass it on. I want these unborn children to remember me as the one who started tending the story. If I don't write something before I die, my kids and grandsons will lose two generations of story.

"So for a decade now I've been writing my story. Not just journal writing, I've done that for years, where I just write something down and keep going. In this story I'm crafting what might be called memoir — if it was ever published. At first I was driven to write. Being in my own life story was like reading a really good book. I'd set it aside and go to other things, but I'd always be wondering how my story was doing and what was going to happen next. I healed some very major pieces of myself by writing those stories. I could be sitting at the computer wailing one moment and laughing the next. I'm glad my clients couldn't see me! It felt good, and in a family of so many men, the writing helped me feel connected to my daughter in a new way.

"*Now, I don't know what I'm going to do with my long story*. It's not finished, but I don't feel so driven to complete it because healing has occurred around most of what I had to say. The parts that remain are more personal, reflective, and spiritual. They are harder to write about, harder to believe anyone will be interested in reading. When I look over these pages, I realize that while I'm writing to the seventh generation, there are parts of my own history I've never shared with my grandsons. They are busy young men, and it's not a time in their lives when they are particularly reflective, except for Cholla, who has had to become more self-aware to manage his sobriety. But *now that my personal healing is pretty much done, I want to pass it on*, if only to sit in the living room and read some of my story to them on a series of winter nights. That's not an impossible idea. We all live in the same city, and though we don't get together every Sunday, we do see each other quite a lot. I guess we're living a little less constricting version of my mother's family — at least we change the menu."

Within and around earth, within and around the hills, within and around the mountains, your authority returns to you.
— Alfonso Ortiz

Kit's dilemma will show up in many of our lives as we chronicle family stories, in writing, on tape, or other media: the work is important to us but may not appear to be important to others around us, even those for whom we think we have been writing. Our stories are a legacy that will become important, however, even if we don't currently see how or to whom. Maybe the person for whom you write is not yet born, not yet married into the family, not yet adopted, not yet working on a thesis documenting the impact of experiences you carry. Trust. You have not done this work in vain; when a story is sent authentically into the world it is received. Just as when we speak, it is received; your listener/your reader will show up.

I often suggest that people get manuscripts edited and formatted so that they take on the appearance of a book. Maybe ask a grandchild — so many of them seem to be technical wizards these days — to help insert photos or make design suggestions. It will get them curious and involved. It is affordable to self-publish a small print run for families and friends, to give copies as gifts, to tuck a copy in with other important papers in the safe-deposit box.

With a little help from their friends, stories survive. The safest way to preserve your life and family legacy is to look for longevity in the medium. "Digital storage is easy; digital preservation is hard," says

Stuart Brand in his book *The Clock of the Long Now*. In my own office I have floppy disks no longer readable by any computer I own, and they're only twenty years old. Paper lasts, papyrus lasts, stones last. If humanity is lucky enough to survive its current crises, the coming generations will need our knowledge — and the best way to help them retrieve it is through story. Your story, my story, have a place in this archive.

Depending on the intimacy in your writing, and the integration and grace you have achieved in the process, you may want to donate a copy of your "book" to a local, county, or state historical society and ask them if there is other material they would like to have accompany the story. Contact your college and see if they have an alumni archive collection. When I first began teaching journal writing, I went to the Minnesota Historical Society and was allowed to view some of their collection of letters, diaries, and journals. Here were the voices of ordinary people preserved. I felt as though I had come into a family reunion — and found my ancestors of the story.

Writing as legacy is a gift that grows out of a life of reflection and story. As a generation ages that has had permission to deal with the story of the self and has contributed to a social environment where personal story is valued, legacy writing is becoming increasingly popular. Not every woman or man Kit's age has reclaimed the story of their lives, or taken time to write it down, but midlife sons and daughters are reaching for their parents' stories, and the market is full of books, formatted journals, and other tools for eliciting life material from the older generation.

In his book *Ethical Wills*, Barry K. Baines encourages readers to write a letter articulating in "the voice of the heart" the things they want future generations to know about them. He suggests writing these values statements at any point of life transition: at the birth of a baby; at the time of marriage or divorce; when sending children off into young adulthood; when faced with danger, like men and women in the armed forces; or when facing an illness. If we are paying attention, we will notice these moments rise up in our lives. Maybe for no discernible reason, some winter night when we cannot sleep, we make our way to the sofa, sit in the circle of lamp glow, and find the stillness in the house and in ourselves to say again who we are, how our life matters, and what we hope others will someday understand.

I know a grandmother who has committed herself to writing a reflective letter to each of her twelve grandchildren. And, having learned from the pain of Viet Nam era veterans, a quiet national movement is developing to pair soldiers from different wars to help those returning from recent conflict to speak and write about what they have experienced.

When a colleague of my father's was dying of cancer, a group of men who had pioneered in the same profession gathered at his house and spent a weekend reflecting to each other the contributions they had made throughout their careers. When my sister-in-law found a box of old photographs while closing her parents' estate, she drove with the treasure to her only surviving aunt. With a magnifying glass, a tape recorder, and an archival pen, they identified and annotated every photo they could.

These are impulses that live in the human heart: story invites us to self-organize, to acknowledge in those quiet moments what we really want to do, and to carve out the time to do it. Nobody assigned the grandmother her task. Nobody assigned the soldier to listen. Nobody assigned Kit her memoir writing. Story calls us to be Storycatchers.

Kit has taken her storycatching seriously. "My Zen teacher says, 'When you sit in meditation you sit for everybody.' and I believe when you tell your story, you tell it for everybody. I hang out with a lively group of women my own age who have designed an annual storytelling and story-listening gathering we call the Council of Grandmothers. So if the younger generation isn't ready to hear us, we are ready to hear each other. Maybe it doesn't matter if the healing of story goes down the generations or if it moves laterally among a generation. In the grandmothers council we strengthen ourselves for the work we are doing in our families and communities, and for the place we still want to hold in the world. We are not going to die with our wisdom unspoken, our stories unwritten, or our opinions unheard. We proclaim this with the humility of perspective, understanding what it takes to create a life year after year. Mary Diamond, one of the founding grandmothers who is gone

Story is a sacred visualization, a way of echoing experience.

— Terry Tempest Williams

now, used to say, 'A life lived well by any mindful individual has the power to change the world.' That is a story I hope my lineage will remember about me — that I lived my life well, that I moved our family, and perhaps our world, a little further along in our process of evolution."

We are living in times of continuous turmoil. Just when we begin to think we have something coherent to say that helps us make sense out of life's current conditions, planes fly into skyscrapers, cars blow up, wars start in yet another country, earthquake and tsunami and famine and disease break out. Our first child is born, or our first grandchild; we get a job or lose one; we get cancer and recover — or not. The drama of life goes on and on and on. It seems as though experiences catapult us along with less and less time for integration, even for reflection. We are no longer approaching a destiny point for humankind: we are in it. However we are tracking this destiny point, we are aware that something huge is happening. Whatever this is, it is longer than one human life span: the event itself is multigenerational.

Every one of us gets through the tough times because somebody is there, standing in the gap to close it for us.

— Oprah Winfrey

We were far from the beginning of this story when we entered the world, and it will be far from over when we leave. This has always been true, but ordinary people have not always had to be aware of the immensity of life in the ways we are made aware today. Noticing where we stand in the middle of the generations gives us a sense of continuum and a way to recognize how time proceeded before we were born and will proceed after we die. Noticing that we stand in the middle of the generations gives us a way to make story out of how we got here — both in a small life and a big life sense — and to lay out tracks of story for where we might go. We who become the Storycatchers, who become the chroniclers, the journal writers, the interviewers, the listeners, the gatherers of tales contribute to our families and to the human family through the work of healing story.

What do you hope your family will remember about you?

Let's start there.

Tell me that story.

Becoming a Storycatcher

Story can help us understand, forgive, and heal family heritage. Storycatchers have a responsibility to make family stories conscious, creating a space in which family truth can be spoken and heard with compassion and a commitment to preservation.

Tell Me This Story...

These story beginnings can be used in writing or conversation to enhance storycatching in your life.

- How far back can you name the people in your father's line? In your mother's line? Do you have any stories that go with these people?
- What are some of the things about your family that you want to celebrate? How do you celebrate them?
- What are the unsolved mysteries that show up at the edge of your family tale?
- Create a legacy letter that describes in detail the things you wish to leave behind for those you love. Are there letters you want to write for specific friends or family members? Have you written them?
- Write down one thing you will forgive someone for today. Explain why you are willing to forgive them and what you will do. What action will you take to make peace and allow change?
- What decisions made in the last three generations are you grateful for? What decisions are you making now that you hope your grandchildren will be grateful for?

CHAPTER EIGHT

We Are the Ones

THE POWER OF STORY IN ORGANIZATIONS

Bringing story to work introduces elements of wisdom and creativity that release the essential spirit of our organizations.

Every human endeavor is grounded in story. Story is how we call each other together and explain what we are doing in each other's company. "Come on over to my house, or office, or cubicle..." immediately raises the question, "Why?" We see the question in each other's faces and fill in the gaps as creatively as we can, working to convey our excitement, wanting to bring people "on board," to gather energy and collaboration around whatever has excited us to put out the call. Nowadays, the call may appear in the email in-box, but the energy behind it is that of the runner who dashes into the heart of the village, or the rider who gallops into camp with news. We look up expectantly. Shift is in the air; routine is broken open to possibility. At least that is how it should be. We blow a new invitation into each other's lives on the winds of story.

Toke Paludan Møller, A Spiritual Warrior for Story Space

One of the masters in this art of blowing on the winds of story is a man named Toke Paludan Møller. A citizen of Denmark, Toke travels throughout Europe, Africa, and North America practicing what he calls "the martial art of story space." Tall and still lean in midlife, with eyes like sea-blue marbles, Toke speaks with a resonant baritone voice in Danish, English, German, and Swedish. Folding up his long legs like someone tucking away his height, he composes himself in a chair at the rim of a circle, but he always seems ready to spring into action, to leap toward the flip chart and sketch his latest insight, or record what he sees emerging from the speaking of a group. He is a spiritual warrior for what it takes to hold the space for story.

Gesturing broadly with an aikido stance, he says, "To me, the martial art of story means to crack open the unconscious space. The space that can shift our awareness is already present in the room, but we are most of the time asleep to it. To wake us up requires martial strength for just a few moments. So there is this warrior in me who likes to crack unconsciousness like an eggshell and hold open a conscious space for people to jump in and find the story. People try to explain me as a consultant, but I am a student of space, a codesigner of energy fields, and a practitioner of what happens when we join each other there.

"When I am invited into an organization, someone calls me because they want to amplify something — to make something stronger, to increase the signal. The first thing I ask myself is whether or not I want to contribute to what they want amplified. I make choices. I'm not for sale. I work with human beings, not institutions, and I work through story because story is the human part of the organization." He smiles and sits down.

Because it is the human part of the organization, story is mutable and constantly unfolding. In every organization we belong to, whether it is a church, a community group, a volunteer or nonprofit board, a business, a hospital, a government agency, a school board, or a huge corporation, the story is ever changing within that group. This mutable nature of story opens new possibilities but also creates tension. The foundations of an organization, the mission, the business or strategic plan, the vision and values statements create an expectation of consistency. A strong organization reinforces these structural elements with a mythic or heroic story of its origins and/or founders (*note the running examples of Hewlett-Packard throughout this chapter*).

Yet we also expect organizational story to allow for and support change, innovation, and effective response to the market. Founders retire and eventually even those who knew them retire. People join in and feel entitled to influence direction. Leadership changes, society changes, the marketplace changes, and story is made out of all these things. In the actual ongoing organizational story, contradictory elements vie for attention, power, resources, and loyalty. So when entering a new situation, the first question is: *what was the founding story and what has happened to the story so far?*

In 1939, Stanford University friends Bill Hewlett and Dave Packard started their company with $538 in capital in the garage behind a little house Packard was renting in Palo Alto, California. Forbes Magazine columnist Michael S. Malone dubbed the site "the most famous garage in history." The garage became the symbolic source for the purpose story that has held HP together throughout its evolution. Malone writes, "As it turned out, Bill and Dave proved to be among the greatest and most influential businessmen of the twentieth century. Their innovations as managers — profit sharing, flex-time, management by objective, the 'HP Way'— transformed modern industry. . . . It's not surprising then, that by the mid-1960s the old Addison Avenue garage began to take on a mythic glow. I remember as an HP employee in the late 1970s, taking a lunch hour drive by the place as if it were Lourdes."

The work of storycatching in organizations starts with the search to discover how this original groundwork has survived within the swirl of influences that have shaped the organization so far. We look for the interplay between the founding values of purpose story and the innovative mutations of organizational life. Toke and I call this the dance of the *now* and the *purpose*. The *now* consists of real people working together in real time. The *purpose* is the basis for the now; it is the initiating energy that set the organization into being.

Attributes of the Purpose	Attributes of the Now
Foundational and traditional	*Quixotic, innovative*
Evolutionary, slow to change	*Adaptable, quick to respond*
Centering, stable, deliberate	*Reactive, interactive*
Thoughtful	*Emotional*
Written, recorded, lasting	*Verbal, ephemeral*
Objective, open-minded	*Subjective, opinionated*
Vision-based	*Relationship-based*
Expansive	*Territorial*
Long-term	*Short-term*
Focused on the context	*Focused on the organization*
Service- or constituent- or market-involved	*Self-involved, task oriented*

Toke tells the story of a long-respected Danish union that had fallen into a pattern of infighting that was damaging the quality of its work and inhibiting the staff's ability to function. When a union representative telephoned Toke and asked if he and Monica Nissen (Toke's wife and cofacilitation partner) would offer a two-day seminar to help the staff address their problems, Toke assessed the situation by listening for what had happened to the *purpose* and the *now*. "Nobody was telling the purpose story anymore," he noticed, "because nobody was remembering it. Their source was lost. People were working for their own egotistical needs and making up stories that supported partisan thinking rather than unifying around the purpose of the union. The loss of the purpose story had ruined the environment of the *now* to the point where people were in open conflict and resigning. But I knew we couldn't work with them if they were going to stay focused on their 'problems.' Solution is not in the problems; solution is in the story."

People in organizations tell stories all the time. We gather around the coffee service or the copy machine, on the assembly line; we lean into each other's work spaces and pass along bits of news, information, and hearsay in conversation and email. These day-to-day stories constitute the network of relationships that makes the *now* of the organization function. When we apply storycatching skills to the conversations going on around us in organizations and listen to these stories consciously, we can tell whether the *purpose* is being reinforced, shifted, changed, sustained, ignored, or undermined. When the purpose story is tended, people's day-to-day stories reinforce how successfully the organization is fulfilling its purpose under current conditions. If the purpose story is lost, misrepresented, or hoarded by leadership, the day-to-day stories speak of frustration, abandonment, and fragmentation.

In 1957, when HP had grown to 1,200 employees and the two founders found it increasingly difficult to maintain personal knowledge and management of everything going on in this constantly innovating company, they called the first off-site meeting for about twenty senior managers. In his book, The HP Way, *Packard writes, ". . . we felt it essential that despite HP's growth, we try to maintain a small company atmosphere . . . Bill and I often thought about how a company like ours should be organized and managed. We thought that if we could get everybody to agree on what our objectives were and to understand what we were trying to do, then we could turn them loose and they would move in a common direction." This is a perfect statement of the* purpose *and the* now.

Every year, millions of consulting dollars are spent trying to figure out what's happening in organizations and how to harness people's energy and talent in ways that benefit profitability or outcome. Theories abound, and new tools, methodologies, team-building games, and personality assessment profiles are invented week after week in an ever-expanding industry. But what if human beings simply do not function well when the *purpose* is lost, when the *now* is confused, when they have forgotten what gathered them and are not trusted to productively fulfill an organization's primary purpose?

Creativity is piercing the mundane to find the marvelous.
— Bill Moyers

"Story is like Sleeping Beauty," says Toke, "snoring in her castle under a hundred years of tangled-up branches. Along comes the prince, and he wants to get at the story, so he begins to hack away at all the complicatedness that has grown over everything. He starts to look through what is hiding the original purpose, peering in every window. In my work, 'the prince' is a good question. If you have the right question, the story starts to wake up. And when you keep talking and listening and don't give up, eventually the right question kisses the original purpose and the whole collective comes to life again."

BEFORE TOKE AND MONICA AGREED to work with the union, they asked to meet with everybody on the staff who would be coming to this seminar. They requested only a one-hour meeting, but with the condition that everybody would be in the room. So the union set the time and place and everyone gathered. "We wanted to see," said Toke, "whether or not people would come out from behind their problems and participate in remembering the purpose."

I come indoors reluctantly, but with a clear purpose in mind: the survival of the natural world depends on humans getting our act together. Every conversation toward clarity is overheard by those just outside the window: trees, birds, animals, weather all encourage us toward stories and actions that include their well-being.

— Ann Linnea

Toke and Monica asked the union staff to interview each other, to choose people they had not talked to in a while, or even people they weren't sure they liked. A great squeaking of chairs and calling out of voices filled the room as people shifted into pairs facing each other knee to knee. The first interview question: *What are you proud of and what do you really appreciate about working in this organization?* They had ten minutes, five to talk and five to listen. The second question: *What do you dream is still possible for this organization if we decide to go for the next level?* Again they had ten minutes. And the third question: *What do you personally feel should be the purpose of these two days?* And in the babble of voices that filled the space, through these interviews, people began to remember the forgotten story of the *purpose* and the unconscious story of the *now*.

In just these few moments of conversation, the alienation between coworkers began to lift. "These people had been wobbling in their problems for four years," said Toke. "We asked for very little time because we wanted to show them how swiftly a shift could occur. Not because we *made* the shift occur — but because they *allowed* it to occur. They allowed the possibility for their real story to come back into the room."

Leadership is the art of invoking wisdom and right action out of the people needed to accomplish the goal.

— Sandy Smith

After the interviews, people were invited at random to stand up and speak about some of those things they were proud of, what they appreciated, what they still dreamed for. Toke wrote it on flip-chart paper. "It was obvious they loved their institution, they were proud of it, they had just forgotten." Monica asked each person to write two, maximum three, ideas for the purpose of the seminar on sheets of paper and set them out on the floor in a cleared space for everyone to see. Silently, in reflective time, the ideas were laid out like scattered white puzzle pieces in the center of the room. People walked around to read what was there and then began to make a pattern out of it. Anyone who saw a pattern could clump ideas together, and then someone else could interact and further refine the connection, and soon the ideas came together in a series of topics. Four topics were gathered as the focus for the seminar.

What happened here was that the purpose story was glimpsed again by a group of people who had wandered away from the core meaning of their work. No one intended this; it just happened. In the busyness and demands of the job, they forgot why they were doing it. They forgot to keep telling their story. And once the purpose story had been lost, day-to-day stories began to dismantle rather than support organizational functioning. If these day-to-day stories are not connected to the purpose story, they have no organizing principle. They become stories without context, and telling them or listening to them sets people adrift. The purpose without the now is history: the now without the purpose is chaos.

When the cohesion of the purpose story is lost, people start to scatter like meteorites freed from gravitational pull. This can be a slow process in which one piece of cohesiveness goes missing, and then another and another: the founders move on or retire, the board experiences turnover, a new leader is hired who takes the organization in a significantly different direction. Or the loss of cohesiveness can be cataclysmic: a whole division of people is handed a severance package and a box to clean out their cubicles, a board uncovers embezzlement, a competing company introduces a new product that makes their product obsolete. As chaos occupies territory previously held together by shared story, small-group alliances form around divisive stories as people seek to protect territory, exert influence, or simply take care of the aspects of the endeavor they most cherish.

The story is something that comes from the outside. But the meaning is something that emerges from within. When a story reaches our hearts with deep meaning, it takes hold of us.

— Stephen Denning

When the cohesion of the purpose story is restored, people tend to respond like meteorites coming *into* gravitational pull. This can be a slow process in which one piece of cohesiveness at a time is brought back into play, reconnecting the now and the purpose like puzzle pieces brought back together: a leader emerges who bridges the gap between original vision and current conditions, management institutes a series of listening councils and asks questions such as the ones Toke brought to the union organizers. Or the recovery of story may be catalytic: a crisis that rallies the organization and its people around a cause, pulling all of them together for their own survival or an altruistic vision. The dedication and sacrifice of such events create a new story to stand on; they provide renewed belief in the ability of purpose to help people function in the now, to act as their best collective self.

A FEW YEARS AGO Toke was asked to become chair of an entrepreneurial network in Denmark. Toke had refused this position several times before. "This was an organization that had lost its original purpose. People were just there for name and fame and it was creating debt nobody wanted. And when I finally agreed to become the chair, I was given the freedom to revive the story. So the first thing I did was to find the man who ten years earlier had founded the association and I invited him to dinner. I made us a good feast and poured a bottle of wine and we sat on the deck of my house in Silkeborg and looked out over the lake together. In our conversation I found that the fire he had had at the time he set out his purpose was similar to the fire I had for the association now. I connected to that fire and it gave me subtle but powerful strength. It was as if I entered the DNA of the association's story. It gave me enough insight so that I could join with a few other people to shift the way things were going and bring back the fire for the full membership."

Revisioning the Story

One of the most empowering aspects of how story functions in organizations is that *anyone* can initiate shift and realignment. Remember the fairy tale of *The Emperor's New Clothes*? It is not the emperor who realizes the folly of his ways, nor the fawning courtiers, but a child. It is the person lacking social power or status: perhaps an hourly wage employee, a floor nurse, a line worker, an administrative assistant, a new recruit. The ability to crack open what Toke calls "the unconscious awareness that is already in the room" is not dependent on position or rank. This ability is something else: courage to trust one's own perception, willingness to break the spell and challenge people to test reality for themselves.

In the climax of the fairy tale, all the inhabitants of the city are lined up along the streets to applaud the emperor as he parades by wearing his new set of magic clothes. They have been told that all good and loyal citizens of the realm will be able to see this finery, and that only disloyal ne'er-do-wells will see anything wrong. So everybody sees what they are supposed to see and hides from others — and perhaps even from themselves — the suspicion that they are participating in a fraud. But somewhere in the crowd is one who stands with a free mind in the middle of group unconscious. Somewhere the voice of the disenfranchised, the one who is willing to lose approval, calls out, "Hey, the emperor has no clothes!" Dang. Now we have to wake up.

We want meaning. We want purpose. We want the story to be noble, to be worthy of our loyalty and to serve the common good. Sometimes this longing gets us in great trouble and we put on blinders to the truth for a long, long time.

This is where the Storycatcher shows up, or is invited in. When I go into a setting like this, I listen to the territory of confusion and ask the question: *how far back into the history of the organization do we have to go to understand the choices that brought people here?* Now that the organization has experienced the consequences of its choices, we work to reconstruct that moment where the defining choice was made. Just as we learned in the self-story, we are seeking the links that began to pull the organizational story down a self-reinforcing path of decisions. I call this exercise "The Clearing in the Forest." We seek the way back to that point where many options were still obviously available and people were able to entertain the possibilities and consequences of going down various paths.

Writing is another way to practice storycatching in an organization. Writing, especially writing the myth or the fairy tale, can collect the story and mirror back what has happened in the dance of the purpose and the now. The myth that comes forward may be the story of disruption, like "The Emperor's New Clothes," or it may be a description of the current state of affairs in the organization told through metaphor. We can often speak more intimately and truthfully in metaphor and by using archetypal characters to represent real people — the wizard, the dragon, the naive seeker — than by speaking directly about our bosses and coworkers or the chair of the board or the school principal. We can articulate the underlying values and threats to values. We can give ourselves a magic lamp to see our way through, or a magic sword to cut through injustice. We can exaggerate and embellish and let characters speak the unspoken, speak the shadow, speak our hope. And once we understand the story we have been living, we can band together and change the parts that don't serve the good of the whole and reinforce those parts that do.

We all know the elements of a good story: there's a protagonist, whom we cheer and identify with, and an antagonist, whom we boo and don't want to identify with. There is an initial status quo, the idyllic moment between changes, and there is interruption of this moment. This interruption sets the story in motion and releases the mythic elements that reside in our story-entrained minds. We know there are challenges to be faced and lessons to be learned and seemingly impossible tasks to be creatively handled as the protagonist makes his/her way through chaos in search of a new resting point and triumph. In the mythic story we trace the maturation of the protagonist from the lone hero to the one who knows how to ask for help and collaboration. And we squirm with tension, hoping the hero will discern in time who is really an ally and how charmingly deceiving corrupting influences can be.

In an organizational story workshop a participant wrote the following tale about a small manufacturing company that had held on to its success but gone through some very hard relationship issues:

> *Once upon a time there was a girl named Priscilla whose father was a needle and whose mother was thread. With parents like this, of course she loved to sew. When she was little she sewed dresses for her dolls. And then as a teenager she sewed her clothes for school. When her girlfriends realized what she was doing, they asked her to sew them dresses for the prom. The night of the big dance they had their picture taken: seven good friends all wearing Cilla's fashions. Now the young girls graduated and four went on to college, two stayed home, and one had a baby, but they never lost touch with each other.*
>
> *One day Priscilla got a message that her mother had cancer, and she came home from the big city to care for her. In the sad and happy months that followed, the seven women gathered round Cilla, and to cheer her during that dark winter they decided to join together to start their own company. Priscilla would design clothes, and Eleanor would travel and buy marvelous cloth, and Joan would market, and Hettie and Ashley would sew and teach others to sew, and Anna would keep the books, and Thea would set up the systems for taking and fulfilling orders. In the sunny corner of an old warehouse the beautiful bald-headed mother sat wrapped in a warm robe and watched over these proceedings and played with Thea's curly-haired child. And the line of Seven Sisters Clothing began.*
>
> *The mother lived and the baby grew and the clothing sold. Everyone knows a fairy tale also carries the dark and the dark comes in as a big*

surprise. For one day Cilla's prince came from the city to visit. He looked around and saw how happy the women were working together and jealousy coiled his heart into a snake. He began to whisper that they were doing everything wrong, he began to show them all the ways they might fail. One by one he told each woman that she was not getting her fair share. He made the mother sigh and he made the little girl cry. And soon the only color of their clothing was black.

In the midst of its charm, a fairy tale reveals the complexities of the organizational journey. The story challenges us to consider what we are donating our life to, and whether or not this donation aligns with our values and respects the dreams that started us. The writer of this story was the baby, now age fifteen, who had grown up under the feet of and sitting alongside the determined sisterhood. At a time when the company was in danger of fissuring, she set this story in a notebook in the middle of the original cutting table that served as the board table in company headquarters. She decorated the book with purple velvet and gold trim, and the first page was a picture of the girlfriends at the prom. After the last line of this preamble, she wrote: "*to be continued... by you. I've left you lots of pages.... Love, Lacey.*" She called the founders back to purpose and cracked open the story.

It is one of the great ironies of our age that we created organizations to constrain our problematic human natures, and now the only thing that can save these organizations is the full appreciation and application of our human natures.

— Margaret J. Wheatley

The story is always residing in our organizations. There is no organization without a story, but we may not be quiet or reflective enough to hear it. If we know the story we are living in our organizations, we can shape it more fully. We can dedicate ourselves to behaving as the kind of character we want to be, in a story we want to have turn out for the better.

And if the story driving an organization is heading into patterns that seem destructive, counterproductive, or against the values of the people involved, we can edit the outcome and behave differently. If we behave differently every day and speak the day-to-day story in ways that support our renewed vision, our speech and action will actively shift the consciousness in the company. Options will open up; we will see possibilities differently. We will find our allies and discover our collective courage. Sometimes, this storycatching work will reveal blocks and limitations that thwart change, but by then, we have the confidence and clarity to move to another story if necessary.

Several decades ago, five engineers were working for a highly diversified corporation whose core technology could be applied to a number of different products. Though they sat in bright offices at big desks making good money, the men could not deny that the tiny little parts they were helping to design were being used in nuclear weapons. As they got to know each other, they found the courage to admit that the thought of "spending their lives improving the delivery of death" was killing their souls. They longed to find another way to sustain themselves and they made a pact: one man would resign and the other four would continue working and support his basic necessities while he found another job. Then he would join four in supporting the next and so on until all had found jobs that were based on stories they wanted to live. They thought it would take them several years, but their story was strong and all the men were in new jobs in six months. This is not a fairy tale. This is the power of telling each other the truth about our situation and banding together to do something about it. Story leads to action: first we say it and then we do it.

> *They always say time changes things, but you actually have to change them yourself.*
>
> — Andy Warhol

Toke sees it this way: "So if you want to really shift something, you need to allow everyone, or at least a cross section of the people, access to the story on equal terms. And that, I think, is the work of hosting meaningful conversations. The willingness to release story calls the bluff of the leaders. A real leader allows people to become part of the story and then she or he leads as a conscious storyteller in the unfolding. Of course this requires the leader to let go of the superficial control of people's actions, to foster autonomy in how people contribute, and hold the confidence that they are dedicated to collective fulfillment and to understanding their role in the story.

"Now, in every country, we are being called into the real story."

Toke's expressive hands spin an invisible orb between his palms as he talks. "In every country there are courageous new eyes that see how naked the emperors are. And when they call out the truth, more interesting questions arise. The power of questions is important to releasing story. People are not particularly accustomed to being asked to think in narrative in organizational settings. Most of the time they are asked for information or data and for the ability to defend or explain their data. A good question releases a good story. This is the door into design. If the story is being called forth in an organization, the timing is built in; the readiness is there or the call for the story would not have been sent out. Then we warriors of the story can arrive and create the space where the story can speak itself."

Toke's Favorite Questions

- *Who calls the story to be awakened?*
- *Where does the story-caller come from?*
- *What is the quality and context of that call?*
- *What is the question that cracks the space?*
- *And what needs to be in place to hold people in the chaos of coming awake?*

Toke continues: "In the late 1990s I met Lew Platt, who was then CEO of Hewlett Packard. He said something about leadership I've never forgotten. He called himself the gardener of the original values of this company and told me, 'Even though I was hired years ago as an electrical engineer, I don't know how to produce what we are producing today. The young people do that and their skills have surpassed me. But I am leading by keeping those values alive. I am the gardener and practitioner of our culture.' This is a very important role for a leader. Those young people in the passion of their productivity, they aren't thinking of culture, they are just enjoying it. But culture is a story that requires tending, and the role of the leader and the elder is to see that this piece is not lost."

Throughout his life, Dave Packard seemed to understand that his contribution to HP and to the larger sphere of modern business required that he tell the contextual story that he held in his mind. "Any organization, any group of people who have worked together for some time, develops a philosophy, a set of values, a series of traditions and customs. These, in total, are unique to the organization. So it is with Hewlett-Packard. We have a set of values — deeply held beliefs that guide us in meeting our objectives, in working with one another, and in dealing with customers, shareholders, and others. Our corporate objectives are built upon these values. The objectives serve as a day-to-day guide for decision making." He wanted to transmit the DNA of his thinking and actions, to make sure the purpose story was not lost.

Democracy Is Story

A woman named Merete, who served as the development consultant in the Department of Education in Copenhagen, saw the need to sustain an important piece of Danish culture through intentionally designing a legacy story. She called on Toke and Monica to facilitate a conversation addressing the need to teach democratic principles and practices to Denmark's schoolchildren. In the purpose statement she wrote as an invitation, she said: "Democracy is an attitude, a worldview. Democracy cannot be put on the agenda once a year, or taught in a weeklong curriculum and studied theoretically without being practiced in the present. Democratic processes happen and are taught in the relationship between grown-ups and young people in the field where they meet. When children are treated as human beings with the right and ability to appropriately negotiate their place in the adult world, they experience democracy. The purpose of this meeting is to assess how this happens in ways that support Danish children to

Democracy is when everybody is part of deciding what is important.

— Nicolaj, third grade student, Denmark

become good Danish citizens, and to design the continuance of those practices."

"I love the word *democracy*," says Toke. "It comes directly from the Greek word *demokratia*." He leaps toward a flip chart and starts diagramming his points: "*Demo*/ meaning people, and *kratia*/ meaning purpose: democracy is people gathered around a purpose. So a country is founded on purpose and lived in the now. For our meeting, we asked children to codesign the day with us and be part of the hosting team. They hosted the opening frame of the day, and then the whole pupils' council led everyone outside for an hour of breaking-the-ice games. Their design and their hosting— and it was wonderful.

"There were ninety kids and ninety adults in this dialogue: teachers, parents, school administrators, and elected officials. The goal of the conference was to gather a new starting point for the democratic work between children and young people and adults in Copenhagen. *How could we create space for development and reflection on democracy so that the children of the twenty-first century would be able to carry on the story of our country?*

Democracy is when we do things together and make it work.

— Louise, seventh grade student, Denmark

"We asked people to find a partner, someone they didn't know, and to take some minutes and first tell a story about a time in their own childhood when they were respected and experienced a good democratic process with an adult. Then we asked them to speak about the influence this experience has had on who they are today. After this exchange, we asked the partners to join one other set of partners and in this group of four to listen to the stories and the awareness of their impact, and then have a table conversation addressing the question, *Now that you are the grown-up, how would you like to create opportunities and possibilities for today's children to have their own experiences of democracy?*

"There was wonderful excitement arising from all these conversation groups sitting on the floor of the sport hall. To complete the gathering of insight, we invited each person to take a piece of paper, to settle into reflective space and imagine a child they know now, and to write a brief letter to that child, describing the kind of opportunity they would desire for them. There was a microphone in the center of the room and we witnessed a sampling of these letters. The love and commitment were very heartfelt. Only then, with a fresh reminder of what created the foundation of our own personal sense of democracy, did we go into an afternoon time of open-space technology, and circles, and project planning that is more typical of these sessions.

A democratic form of government, a democratic way of life, presupposes free public education over a long period; it presupposes also an education for personal responsibility that is too often neglected.

— Eleanor Roosevelt

"Democracy comes down to the dance between being allowed to speak and being listened to at the same time. Speaking from the heart is dependent on being listened to with respect. However that can be arranged between people, the quality of the listening pulls the story down to its truth. And when these processes are hosted with consciousness and love, you are actually entering the collective story in real time. The quality of listening is like a magnet that pulls the story out of you; you say things that are more honest, more intimate, more visionary than you had any intention of saying. Suddenly it's as though the listening makes you speak. When listening reaches quality, when it actually *becomes listening*, then the collective story surfaces. It is unstoppable. So even though people come into the room with their consciousness fragmented, when listening arises, the story being told reconnects us to the collective. We remember."

Allowing Story to Self-Organize

The story is already there: any group of people has the ability to self-organize and find the best way to do anything. This is the human genius: we are constantly innovating, redesigning our tasks. This skill doesn't have to be created, but it can be temporarily controlled. Inside any organization, inside every country, are people asking for the real story. These are the "callers," who long to bring back the real remembrance of the story. They want to be able to make sense. And much of the time all they get back are fragments and explanations that either simplify or complicate things, but hide the truth. Eventually, many of the callers get discouraged and give up and settle into what has been presented them. But not all of them, and not forever. Story is out of the box.

Key elements of story:

- *A protagonist the listener cares about*
- *A catalyst compelling the protagonist to take action*
- *Trials and tribulations*
- *A turning point*
- *A resolution*

This is the classic beginning-middle-end story structure defined by Aristotle more than 2,300 years ago and used by countless others since. It seems to reflect how the human mind wants to organize reality.

— Herminia Ibarra and Kent Lineback

Toke says, "You can slow down the arising of human genius by hiding the story; you can put people in disjointed spaces and remove their sense of connection to purpose. They will produce something, but the joy of work will be taken away and the best will not come out of them."

People are incredibly resilient. We are willing to work hard; we are eager to contribute; we are able to use many forms of recognition as fuel for continuing our loyalty to a purpose. We call this the work ethic and are proud of our ability to labor. We will make great sacrifices, even risk our lives, in the belief we are serving the common good. The firefighter runs into the burning building, the teacher shields the child, the coworker donates a kidney, the boss takes the pay cut instead of the employees, the politician admits he was wrong.

"There is a natural flow in this work," Toke reminds me. "We are connecting our lives to the larger story. Wherever I am, whatever I am doing with a group of people, I am thinking about three levels of story: the individual story, the organizational story, and the species story. These three stories are inseparable. We have entered an age where the story of the human species is breaking through in everything we do. We are in so much danger we *must* bring the story of the human species into individual consciousness. I have heard several very high-status people at top-level global leadership positions speak of this, and it excites me to more courageous action."

In October 2003, Toke led a small team of facilitators at the Forum 2000 Bridging Global Gaps Conference in Prague, the Czech Republic. In the opening plenary, Jean-François Rischard, the vice president for Europe of the World Bank, took the lectern and challenged the gathered dignitaries and academics. Rischard's words are emblazoned in Toke's memory. "This man began his talk by saying, 'I'm not speaking here for the World Bank but as a concerned global citizen, as a human being in this world. I'm not here to argue whether you think I'm right or wrong. We have no time for that. There are twenty global problems in the world right now — water, food, disease, depleting the oceans, global warming, population, leadership corruption, and so on. We don't need to list them; every person in this room knows what they are. What I believe is important about these twenty issues is that we have twenty years to solve them. If we don't, the human species will become extinct....'

"Such a strong announcement electrified the room," says Toke. "Many people wanted to jump into intellectual argument, but Rischard ran his PowerPoint lecture so effectively there was no arguing with his analysis. He just laid out for us the whole story. And he offered his thinking that solutions are possible, but the human species must understand the urgency. Urgency actually raises my love and strength in

What we need is what the ancient Israelites called hochma *— the science of the heart... the capacity to see, to feel, and then to act as if the future depended on you. Believe me, it does.*

— Bill Moyers

a way that I have never experienced before. It makes me scared on one hand, but inside of my fear is the survival instinct unleashed with consciousness.

"More and more fully I comprehend that the story of my life and the story of the human species are one and the same. It is not what nation I happen to be part of or what political turmoil is going on, or labeling each other and saying these are terrorists and these are not. It is not do we come from apes or do we come from fish, but what are we about *now*? And I see that our twenty crises, instead of being overwhelming, may be of great help because suddenly I am in a more real context. I want to take this warrior energy for story and use it to unite people faster than we ever thought possible.

"Look at what happened after the planes flew into the World Trade Center, or the worldwide peace protests in February 2003, or the tsunami disaster in Southeast Asia. These events become huge markers for us in the now. They are moments of great sacrifice and possibility. When things seem the darkest, we reach out to each other with stories and actions that reconnect us. The Netherlands sent three thousand tulip bulbs to be planted in New York City. A man and woman who lost all their children in the tsunami adopted children who had lost their parents. The individual becomes the universal. Some of the problems we think are unsolvable can be shifted if we spend our energy thinking of the connection between these three levels of story."

Story Spaces in the Real World

I met Toke in December 2000, in the first seminar of an international conversation called From the Four Directions. Initiated by American societal visionary Margaret J. Wheatley and cofounded with my small educational company, PeerSpirit, we set out to introduce circles of conversation as a cross-cultural forum for gathering life-affirming leaders.

At Hazelwood House, a rural retreat center in the Devon countryside of southwestern England, thirty-two people from twenty nations gathered to explore the possibilities of forming local, interconnected circles of community leaders. The call had gone out for diversity, and people flew in from Africa, Latin America, eastern and western Europe, the United States, and Canada. Many people arrived at Heathrow airport flying on faith and determination that this meeting would allow them to share their stories, to listen to others, and connect through conversation. Africans in borrowed woolens shivered in the English winter; people translated for each other, lent each other clothes and notebooks and blankets. Outside the old Victorian farmhouse, it rained, it snowed; the river Avon overflowed its banks at the bottom of the meadow. We banked the fire in the old ballroom and tucked in with the essential tools for changing the world: "each other, a good question, and a willingness to be present." And the world showed up.

The Art of Hosting is a social technology and spiritual practice in one, because it opens up the real meaning of our own presence and our mutual relationships.

— Monica Nissen

Out of this work has grown the conversational hearth where Toke and I and a growing cadre of Storycatchers call in the story. This vision is called the Art of Hosting. Toke says, "The Art of Hosting is a calling. And the calling has always been within me. We support conversations that are meaningful, generative, and deeply honoring of the wisdom each person carries into the room. Hosting is an evolutionary tool for humanity. The talking together is the healing together."

Someone puts a staff in the ground and calls for a team of hosts to volunteer to hold the space for the three levels of story: the individual, the organizational, and the species. We bring people together of diverse nations and backgrounds, both those who call and those who answer the call. And what we create is a community of people who are practicing the power of conversation to change the world.

Invitational Questions to the Art of Hosting

- *What if the solutions for our future are hiding in our collective intelligence and wisdom?*
- *What if hosting conversations is the kind of leadership that allows learning to take place?*
- *What would our societies be like if we based them on our collective awareness and the courage to exercise our understanding daily and without ceasing?*
- *What comes into the world when we talk about what matters and act on what inspires us?*
- *How can we contribute to a culture of conversation that will reknit the human community?*
- *How is nature the ultimate host?*

Toke is a fire starter. He believes in the human spirit and believes that spirit is accessible in everyone he meets. He tells this tale of his recent encounter with a Danish taxi driver: "I believe the urgency and essence of this work are graspable by any human being in the right moment. So one morning when I was leaving for Africa I was riding in a taxi between my house and the airport. Of course the driver and I got in conversation about my destination. 'Kufunda Village,' I told him, and he looked me in the eye through the rearview mirror. His soul said tell me everything — so I did. For half an hour I spoke my world to him and asked him questions, and when he accepted his money at the end of the ride he shook my hand. 'You are a wild man,' he said. 'You have given me things to think about for many weeks to come. The next time you go to the airport, ask for me and we will continue.'

"So I see the work is to keep looking for the right moment and to support that moment coming alive in every person, in every way I can. I am happy to dedicate the rest of my life to asking the questions that can crack the trance — 'Hey everybody, the emperor has no clothes and he's not even an emperor, just another confused fellow, so let's see if we can imagine a new story, right here on the street corner, in the taxi, and meeting in our organizations.' And then we will sit down and build a little fire, and heat some water for tea, and tell each other stories that change the world."

Once upon a time somebody started this endeavor in which you work today.

Tell me that story.

Let's start there.

Becoming a Storycatcher

Storycatchers can be valuable assets to any organization trying to move forward in a thoughtful and ethical way. The organization might be a multimillion-dollar corporation, a school PTA, a neighborhood watch group, or your own family business. The Storycatcher can help to preserve the original purpose of the organization while helping to shape the current environment.

Tell Me This Story...

These story beginnings can be used in writing or conversation to enhance storycatching in your life.

- What gives you a sense of satisfaction at the end of the day?
- Describe your current community or organization. What makes you proud of it?
- Choose an accomplishment and write about it putting yourself in the story in the third person as a character.
- What do you wish to carry to the future from your community or organization? How can this be accomplished? Who needs to be involved?
- Put yourself six years into the future. Describe the community or organization you really want as if it exists now. What is life like? What relationships exist among people? What are you contributing?
- If all the people you work with were characters from a fairy tale, who would they be? Who would you be?
- Is there a founding symbol like the HP garage in your organization? Are you using it or ignoring it?

- Set aside a place in your journal where you note world events. Include press clippings, photos, commentaries — whatever seems important to you. Write brief responses to headlines.
- Write letters of condolence, concern, and celebration about world events. You may decide to send these letters to local newspapers or share your thoughts online, or just take time to honor the species story as it occurs.

CHAPTER NINE

The Possible God

HOW STORY SHAPES THE SPIRITUAL DIMENSIONS OF OUR LIVES

I don't know what God is, but I believe God is, and I believe our devotion to story is divinely inspired.

Spirituality is story. Since consciousness and language first claimed us, human beings have made up sacred stories to explain how something larger than ourselves created us and the world. Spirituality seems to be innate to human beings. If children are not told a spiritual story, they will quite confidently make up their own explanations. And just as society develops language, so society develops a spiritual story of its creation. The story of creation is the universal first story.

Since humans are born out of the body of woman, our ancestors naturally imagined the Creator must also be female. As each child comes from a mother, so all people must come from the Mother. Women received their spiritual role through gender identification with the Mother goddess. Able to bear life, able to bleed without wounding, their bodies contained unsolvable mystery and their power mirrored the power of the Creatrix. In Europe, clay statues and carvings of the female body representing the body of the goddess have been found that date back to the Paleolithic era twenty-five thousand years ago.

Grounded in Great Mother, humans looked around creation and extended their story to include animals as allies and teachers who were willing to sacrifice their flesh to our flesh (and sometimes the other way around!) through the ritual of the hunt. Men received their spiritual role through association with animals. Willing to risk their lives in the hunt, in war, in games of strength, their power mirrored the strength of wolves, birds of prey, mastodons, saber-toothed tigers, aurochs, buffalo, and bear. Paintings of the male body representing the hunter/shaman, figures half human, half animal, began appearing on European cave walls twenty thousand years ago.

i found god in
myself
& i loved her
i loved her fiercely
— Ntozake Shange

The world was experienced as a familial relationship: God is Mother, people are brothers and sisters, animals are cousins, rocks and mountains, plants and trees, rivers and seas are all extended family. A huge body of teaching tales comes out of this worldview that has been passed down the uncountable generations and continues to contribute to humanity's spiritual legacy.

During this early Age of Spirituality, the story of creation was still making its way through the Spiral of Experience. Interpretations of spiritual intervention were dynamic and constantly changing. Wisdom was received from many sources and voices. A child, an elder, a contrary, an ordinary woman or man could contribute to a people's understanding of the world and add to the story they carried. I can imagine humanity's ancestors coming to the fire, exchanging dreams, insights, metaphoric teaching tales, piecing together the story of the world and their place within it. While we cannot overhear the stories of prehistoric tribal societies, we can observe how creation story and spirituality still function in the remnants of aboriginal cultures today. And we can experience our own spirituality, moments of awe at the natural world and our spontaneous responses to it.

Spirituality has several characteristics: it is eclectic, diverse, local, mutable, and directly experienced. Because it is innate in human beings, spirituality possesses a kind of egalitarian quality. Spirituality can't be controlled: unless it's schooled or frightened out of us, it just happens. We, too, like our ancestors, are capable of dreams, insights, and metaphoric teaching tales. Spirituality is in constant evolution. Many people design personal spiritual practices into their lives, but few people would believe they could design a new religion.

Religion is also story. Religion grows out of our innate spiritual base, but it takes spirituality and systematizes it to foster uniformity, universality, and immutability. Religion develops a priest class that serves to interpret religious teachings to ordinary people. It develops a hierarchy, becomes a landowner, becomes protective of its wisdom, centralizes its sacred places and texts. And each religion believes it holds the correct interpretation of the Divine, of human nature, and of the world before, during, and after life. Religion developed in human history at a time when people began to organize beyond locale into larger identifying groups. Before, and even after, the rise of nation-states, people see religion and race as the primary definition of where, and with whom, they belong.

> *All of the larger than life questions about our presence here on earth and what gifts we have to offer are spiritual questions. To seek answers to these questions is to seek a sacred path.*
>
> — Lauren Artress

Starting five thousand years ago in India, Hinduism began to consolidate hundreds of local gods and goddesses into a complex pantheon of deities to interface between the spiritual world and human society. Just as Krishna brought order to heaven, the priests of Krishna brought order to the continent. Born into this system in 1029 BCE, Siddhartha Gautama Buddha introduced new elements of thought and insight that became codified as Buddhism. In the Middle East, Abraham, born around 1800 BCE, discovered monotheism and founded Judaism for the twelve tribes of Israel. When Jesus was born into this system, he introduced theological shifts that became Christianity, and around 600 CE, Muhammad introduced another shift in monotheism that became Islam. Back in Asia, Shintoism developed out of indigenous Japanese nature worship, and the world as we know it — a world arbitrarily divided into five great religions — was set into place.

Though intended to serve as a stabilizing spiritual force to support development of larger societal systems and cultures, religion tends to proclaim itself *the* culminating and ultimate revelation of humanity's spiritual story. This seems especially problematic for the three monotheistic religions of Judaism, Christianity, and Islam — each proclaiming there is only one God, and founded on shared soil.

The world in which you were born is just one model of reality. Other cultures are not failed attempts at being you: they are unique manifestations of the human spirit.

— Wade Davis

When she was about nine years old and visiting my apartment for a weekend ritual we called "going to Auntie Camp," my niece Erin asked me, "So what is religion anyway?"

"Religion is a language for God," I responded. "What God actually is remains a mystery as big as the stars, but people need a story that helps us think about it. So religion talks to us about what God might be, and how to be a good person, and what to do with our lives. Around the world people have many ways they imagine God. Some of that imagination has become religion, with its own language and stories. Some people think of God the Father and Jesus the son; some think of Allah and Muhammad the son; some think of Buddha; some think of the Great Mother; some people believe in many gods and some people believe in only one."

"Cool," she said, her question more than answered. And we went back to reading *The Lion, the Witch and the Wardrobe*.

The Crisis in Christianity's Story

Spiritual story is in crisis. In the West, in Christianity, in America, the delicate balance of power between the secular and the religious is tilting wildly. This is true in other cultures and in other religions as well, but in this chapter I focus on the crisis occurring inside American Christianity because this argument affects my life, my family, my community and country and poses danger to the earth itself.

As Storycatchers interested in consciously carrying stories to inspire, inform, and activate our lives, we may be able to play an essential role in helping reestablish communication and cooperation during this crisis. Stories make bridges where opinions make walls. In an atmosphere where the bridges are falling down and the walls are going up, Storycatchers may help keep a sense of expansive spiritual story in the conversation.

There is an Episcopal church in the Potrero Hill section of south San Francisco that invites people to engage in expansive spiritual conversations. The church building itself is an aesthetic blend of cedar shingles and octagonal cupolas adorned with ornate crosses in an architecture that combines a touch of Frank Lloyd Wright, a brush of Byzantine, a hint of yurt, and a little Shinto shrine at the corners. It seems to say: "Come on in, whoever you are and be ready for surprise." The main entrance leads into an open octagonal room with a simple raised table often covered with heavily embroidered African cloth. This is the altar. At various moments it holds name tags and liturgical songbooks, it holds communion, it holds coffee and tea and a potluck buffet of noontime snacks, it holds a toy picked up off the floor, it holds a child's drawing brought up from Sunday school. It is rimmed with the sticky fingerprints of toddlers and polished with reverence before the laying out of the cup and bread.

"Everything that happens on God's table is holy," says Father Donald Schell, one of two priests who co-pastor this parish. "The central message of our theology here at St. Gregory's is that God brings us into community with Himself and then entrusts us to take care of each other. The altar is the center of what holds us together, not the edge. The baptismal font is at the back in a garden alcove, it's not a ticket to the table. We feed each other in body and soul first, and then as people are ready to make a commitment to Christianity, we meet them at the holy well. We baptize as many adults as children, I think because we frame that sacrament as a signal — I am coming up God's mountain by this route — not a demarcation line between the accepted and the forsaken."

Father Rick Fabian joins in. "God is having *one* conversation with humankind," he says, "but in a thousand voices. Religious people all over the world need to be in conversation with each other so that we understand the fullness of God's conversation with us. The complete story of God is discovered in how the sacred manifests in every religion, in every gesture a person makes toward the Divine. Whether kneeling, standing, dancing, chanting, meditating, crying, laughing — I'm listening to the conversation between God and the human heart. When we understand that every one of us is sending and receiving part of the message, then we can embrace each other with that knowledge."

For god is nothing other than the eternally creative source of our relational power, our common strength, a god whose movement is to empower, bringing us into our own together, a god whose name in history is love.

— Carter Heyward

The two men might be brothers. Graying, balding, trim, one on each side of sixty, they are friends who met in seminary in the 1960s. Fr. Donald grew up in California; Fr. Rick grew up in Texas. They both went to General Theological Seminary in New York, interned together in Spanish Harlem, were chaplains together at Yale in 1972, and then briefly took parishes in different parts of the country. They never lost touch with each other, or with the rich experiments in worship they had developed together.

This church has been their common dream since seminary days when they rode the subway to and from Spanish Harlem, reimagining Christianity all the way there and back. On his way to the Yale chaplaincy appointment, Rick phoned Donald and told him he thought the time was right for the experiment to begin. Come join. Donald says now, "I had finished seminary, gotten ordained, gotten married, and was living in Louisiana, looking for work in the church. When Rick called I got in the car and started driving. Later he told me he had second thoughts and tried to call me back, but I was already on the road."

Since founding their church on Potrero Hill in 1978, the two priests have been bringing their distinctive and complementary gifts to this shared ministry. They move around each other with a comfort derived from deep acquaintance. When asked how it has been to be "brothered" in this long career, Rick answers, "It's been absolutely marvelous for me, and somehow Donald has survived." Both men laugh. The third brother here is the church's patron, St. Gregory Nyssen, Bishop of Nyssa in the Roman province of Cappodocia, now in central Turkey.

Living in the fourth century, Bishop Gregory was one of the most original early scholars of Christian theology. He was a Greek humanist, a Universalist, a mystic, and married, all of which later disqualified him for much sanctified attention by the Roman Catholic Church, though his writings have survived and are coming back into print and translation. His last book, *The Life of Moses*, ends with the words which are now inscribed in the octagonal skylight above the church's altar: "The one thing truly worthwhile is becoming God's friend." This sentence is the watchword of the congregation and the invitation it extends.

AMERICA IS NOT A CHRISTIAN-ONLY COUNTRY. In 1492, when Columbus accidentally — and disastrously — bumped into the Bahamas, several million Arawaks were living in a sophisticated social and spiritual society. When the first English settlers landed in Virginia and Massachusetts, they invaded the territory of the Powhatans and Pequots with no comprehension of the cultural story going on, and certainly no way to value their spiritual traditions. They set out to convert the heathens and destroy their "useless" way of life.

To emphasize the heroism of Columbus and his successors as navigators and discoverers, and to de-emphasize their genocide, is not a technical necessity but an ideological choice. It serves — unwittingly — to justify what was done.

— Howard Zinn

Through immigration and conversion the United States remains a religiously pluralistic nation. In the 2001 American Religious Identity Survey, the numbers come up 76 percent Christian, with the next highest category being 13 percent nonreligious (people who don't identify with any category); then 1.3 percent Jewish, 0.5 percent Islamic, and 0.5 percent Buddhist. It's interesting to note the pluralism within the Christian category: 24 percent Catholic, 54 percent Protestant, which includes (descending by size) Baptist, Methodist, Lutheran, Presbyterian, Episcopalian and dozens of smaller denominations. We are a nation with as many Mormons as Jews, as many Mosques as Assemblies of God. With this diversity, there ought to be abundant dialogue going on: dialogue, not diatribe. And so the role of the Storycatcher becomes clear.

Storycatchers, with our ability to entertain curiosity rather than judgment and our practice in listening, speaking, and writing, may find ourselves serving as a bridge between polarized groups and theologies. To be present in these difficult conversations will require us to be grounded in our own spiritual stories and journeys.

In the faith of my childhood, I was taught not to make a show of my religion or beliefs. In a family of five ordained men, we practiced our faith, but we didn't much talk about it. "A good Methodist," said my grandfather, "does not 'pray like the Pharisees,' standing on the street corner where everyone can see them." This is the opposite injunction from the evangelicals who are taught to see "testifying for the Lord" as a command and obligation. However, if people like me keep silent, our part of the story is missing from the dialogue.

When the Jehovah's Witnesses come to the door, when the Hare Krishnas try to stop me on the sidewalk, when a call comes into the office wanting to know if our little company, PeerSpirit, offers "faith-based consulting," I am often unsure how to respond. It's not that I don't know what I believe, it's that I'm not sure how to say it in a way that holds open the door of inquiry.

Because I have seen my faith as private, I haven't articulated this part of my story as thoroughly as other aspects of my life narrative. But if I'm willing to talk to people in a coffee line, a grocery line, or an airport security line, I need to be ready to talk and listen and bring story to the diverse questions and convictions we are currently holding about the possible God. This may not resolve our global crisis, but it can create little islands of open-mindedness in the polarization swirling around us.

A few years ago, one of my neighbors drove a Cadillac with a bumper sticker that read *Pray for America*. At first, making many assumptions, I felt put off by this slogan. But over time, I realized that I, too, pray for America. I pray for my country to espouse the values I hold dear — which I am sure include values my neighbor holds dear. Over time, as we established an acquaintanceship based on gardening tips and love of dogs, I found the courage to say, "I really appreciate your bumper sticker." He looked a bit surprised. "It reminds me what a vulnerable time this is for our country, and for many countries in the world. What are your prayers?" I asked, and then I listened. And when he was done, I told him my prayers. And then we petted each other's dogs and went on about our days.

I've started a track in my journal that I write only in purple ink. The purple paragraphs are notes to myself about what I believe. I have made a list of questions I ask myself in the course of this writing, and sometimes I pick a question from this list to start a conversation.

Questions for Exploring the Spiritual Journey

- *What moments stand out in childhood concerning religious faith and choices?*
- *How did you discover a direct connection to the mystery of God, inside or outside the buildings, the traditions, the holidays — or the lack of these things?*
- *How and when did you discover an innate linking to the Divine?*
- *What happened in adolescence, in your young adult years?*
- *When you partnered or married, did you choose someone with similar faith and/or values?*
- *What did you decide to observe, or not, in this partnership? What do you want your children — or the children around you — to understand about the spiritual journey?*

(A note from my heart to yours: if you have painful memories, or experiences of abuse or betrayal, please find the support to deal with them, and guidance to separate what might have been done in God's name from your birthright of spiritual connection.)

Back in their comfortable weekday studies at the side of St. Gregory's great hall, Rick and Donald are aware of the invitation the church sends to those who cross its threshold. "The gospel doesn't promise either stability or monism," says Rick. "Quite the opposite, the gospel is about instability and pluralism. St. Gregory informs us: 'Forget about rewards and punishments, forget about certainty, all that matters is becoming God's friend.' People come into our church, look up and read this inscription, and think: *these folks are not going to tell me I'm bad and going to hell.* And while there is relief from judgmentalism, there is not relief from dynamic encounter. Because for Gregory, everything hangs in the word *becoming* — how we shall *become* closer to God changes constantly. His invitation — to notice what connects or disconnects us from God's love — is a strenuous discipline."

Donald slides in on the end of Rick's sentence: "The heart of our theology is focused on God's friendship, God's compassion to humankind, rather than on judgment. But we are not just a bunch of Californians saying — oh, let's take the groovy parts of Christianity and withdraw from the rest of it. We're saying, the message of the New Testament has been skewed; let's correct it. What we practice and preach is rooted in the teachings of Jesus. It is the theology Gregory of Nyssa taught; it is what Julian of Norwich taught. These were thinkers close to the source, still in the epiphany of the New Testament revelation that God is essentially love."

God is love and those who abide in love abide in God, and God abides in them.
— 1 John 4:16

Rick leans in again: "There is a whole tradition of Christian scholars who have taught a much more forgiving and accepting version of the word of God than the theology of 'Christ died for your sins and if you take him as your Lord and Savior you'll be okay, otherwise you are out of the kingdom.' What we intend at St. Gregory's is an opening to that scholarship. Come into the place where God is working. Come into the story of God's conversation."

More Questions for the Spiritual Journey

- *What aspects of faith do you talk about with other people?*
- *Are you able to have conversations about values and religion inside your family?*
- *With whom are you most likely to share stories of your spiritual life and insights?*
- *Do you practice asking throughout the day: where is spirit in what I am doing right now?*
- *How might you express your own love of God in the world?*
- *What kind of support would you need in order to take conversational risks or actions in your daily life?*
- *What spiritual values motivate your actions?*

St. Gregory's echoes in midweek emptiness, but it comes to life on Sunday mornings, when an eclectic gathering of several hundred people — the fullest range of humanity that south San Francisco and a commuting range of over an hour can offer up — arrive for worship. People come here because the theology and the community help them live with uncertainty *and* hold a spiritual core. They are not rescued from the trials of the world; they are offered community, communion, and conversation so they know their experience is held within the larger story. The people stand around the altar and sing. They sit together around a seated homilist, listen, and dialogue. They dance to the communion table to the beat of drums, the sound of their own feet gently slapping the wooden floors, the chants of their own voices filling the room. This is radical Christianity — radical as in *root* — third-century Eucharist in a twenty-first-century church.

> *The miracles of the church seem to me to rest not so much on faces or voices or healing power coming suddenly near to us from afar off, but upon our perceptions being made finer so that for a moment our eyes can see and our ears can hear what is there around us always.*
>
> — Willa Cather

Ambiguity as Spiritual Practice

The deepest kinship I feel with the Gregorians of Potrero Hill is around the issue of uncertainty. I am relieved to hear the depth to which they call forth the tension of the times as part of the spiritual journey. "How are you doing with all the tension?" I ask in the churches, boardrooms, educational institutions, health care systems, and conferences where I talk and listen. "I mean the unrelenting tension that won't go away, that cannot be resolved by ruling party elections, or by switching jobs, or partners, or financial planners, or churches — that tension."

One of the promises of fundamentalism is to relieve believers of this tension. If a person focuses on hope of permanent relief from uncertainty, he or she will be drawn to fundamentalism. This is a significant attraction, because living with the level of tension alive in these times is not that much fun. Uncertainty and ambiguity are interesting elements when they occur in someone else's story, or good plot devices in books or movies, but not elements we relish in our real lives.

Yet as Storycatchers, we find ourselves living in the tension of the unfinished tale. Unarticulated story lives in us like electricity. We are bursting with the need to speak and write our questions, concerns, hopes, and fears in the face of the world. We can't hold it all in, and so we find ourselves trying to think it through in the middle of the night, or alone in the car, or numbing out in the noise of television, or wandering in a trance through the mall. What *does* this all mean? If we want to support religious and spiritual pluralism, we need to admit the stress of trying to live an open-ended story and bring ambiguity into our conversations so that we can relieve some of the tension by talking openly about it.

I have set before you life and death, blessing and cursing; therefore choose life, that both thou and thy kind may live.

— Deuteronomy 30:19

More and more often, I find myself thinking that the people with whom I most deeply belong are those who are willing to carry the ambiguity of the age, those who are learning how to manage tension in a heartfelt, spiritually imbued manner. I call us the Tribe of the Ambiguous — anyone can join, just start noticing.

Ambiguity is when things can be understood more than one way, when no one meaning is intended, or possible. Ambiguity is when a situation is doubtful, uncertain, difficult to comprehend, and where no outcome is obvious. This certainly sums up how the world seems to me these days. I expect this ambiguity to last the rest of my lifetime and way beyond.

I am basically a joyful person. I take delight in life, in nature, in the subtle magnificence of ordinary people. And to sustain this outlook, I find joy must include, not deny, ambiguity.

"I'm not sure I want to talk about it," said my sister, pushing an article on the growing schism in the Methodist church back across the kitchen table, "because I don't know how to fix it and it just makes me feel helpless."

"What if talking about it *is* the way to discover how the problem might be addressed?"

"That I could do. But how do I bring it up?"

"Ask a question," I say. "My friend Toke says if he has only one tool when he enters a room full of people, it's a good question. What's your question?"

"I could ask the women in my study circle to tell each other a story: *what is a moment in our church when you knew you loved this community?*...Like that Sunday when a little girl got away from her mom and crawled onto the organist's lap and he just took her hand in his and had her playing out the bass line with one finger while he went on with the postlude. They got a standing ovation....And then I could ask something like...*what action are you willing to take to preserve this kind of atmosphere in our congregation?* Is that what you mean?"

"Welcome to storycatching," I say.

It is very possible that the fate of the world may hang on our ability to help each other hold and release the tension of the times.

Judgment and Grace

It is very possible that the fate of the world may hang on the story we make of God. For we act based on who we say we are, and when the story we are acting on is our belief that we are doing what "God is telling us to do," powerful suprarational forces are set loose — for good and ill.

Social theorist George Lakoff has defined two religious worldviews that he sees as the foundation of the current divide in American Christianity and politics. In his book of essays *Don't Think of an Elephant*, he characterizes the divide as split between a view of God as a strict father, or a view of God as a nurturing parent: judgment and grace.

"Conservative Christianity is a strict father religion," Lakoff writes. "God is understood as punitive — that is, if you sin you are going to go to hell, and if you don't sin you are going to be rewarded. But since people tend to sin...how is it possible for them to ever get to heaven? The answer in conservative Christianity is Christ...."

All of us have a God in us, and that God is the spirit that unites all life.... It must be this voice that is telling me to do something, and I am sure it's the same voice that is speaking to everybody on this planet — at least everybody who seems to be concerned about the fate of the world.

— Wangari Maathai

For the strict father model to succeed people are required to see themselves as obedient or disobedient "children." In the fundamentalist interpretation of Christ's sacrifice, Jesus intercedes between a punishing God and children who deserve punishment. The believer hands over the tensions of uncertainty and imperfection, accepts Jesus as savior, and in exchange agrees to follow the moral authority of the minister and church. Obedience and discipline become the most valued characteristics of conservative faith.

On the other side of the religious divide, Lakoff says, "The central idea in liberal Christianity is grace,... you are given grace unconditionally by God... grace is metaphorical nurturance.... In a nurturant form of religion, your spiritual experience has to do with your connection to other people and the world, and your spiritual practice has to do with your service to other people and to your community."

In the nurturant parent model of Christianity people are still required to see themselves as "children," but the Divine parent is the source of love, forgiveness, and understanding. The emphasis in liberal Christianity is on the teachings of Jesus and the redefinition of relationship he brings forward. Don't be so afraid of God, Jesus seems to say, get close, cooperate, seek to love each other as you are loved by God.

The people who believe in God's judgment and the people who believe in God's grace stand with a chasm between them. Can the power of story make a bridge? I don't know, but it's what I have to offer.

And Still More Spiritual Questions

- *How do you stay joyful and grateful and keep your heart open to the world's suffering?*
- *How do you move confidently into action in a world that is always changing? In a world where you never have the whole story?*
- *How do you talk about tension and schism and put it on the table like a candle in the center of the circle?*
- *What do you want to say to young adults as they face their first griefs in the world?*
- *What do you want to elicit from elders?*

Religion has always swung back and forth between an emphasis on judgment and an emphasis on grace. In these times, religion seems to be going through a period where instead of holding either concept in balance, or even in creative tension, we are in a global struggle for one interpretation of God to "win." Whose children are we, anyway? And how will we act, depending on the lineage we claim?

Religion means to be gripped by story. Faith is the willingness to stay in conversation with this story.
— W. Craig Gilliam

Fundamentalism in its broadest context is a religious or political movement based on literal interpretation of doctrine. If the Bible says God created the world in seven days, it means seven days — Monday through Sunday, just like this week, just like last week. Fundamentalism stakes its security on literalism and fights to implement religious or political doctrine literally, without interpretation or adaptation. Seen through this framework, science is a lie. The earth did not evolve over billions of years: it was created in seven days. I don't care what the fossil records seem to indicate: I believe what the Bible says. There is no room for compromise on this issue because if one thing that has been taken literally is not true, then the whole belief system is threatened. I followed a car down the freeway whose bumper sticker proclaimed: *Read the Book. Believe the Book. No further questions.*

In an Internet interview, Karen Armstrong, author of *The Battle for God*, says, "Fundamentalism represents a kind of revolt or rebellion against the secular hegemony of the modern world.... The fact that it has erupted in almost every place where a modern, secular-style society has tried to establish itself tells us something important about modernity: it suggests a great disenchantment that we must take seriously or ignore at our peril. The great changes of modernity mean that none of us can be religious in the same way as our ancestors. We are, all of us, having to develop different forms of seeing our faiths."

Now that's a challenge to create a new story. I, too, am disenchanted by many aspects of modern life; I am frightened, offended, and outraged by how modernity behaves when it is cut off from spiritual values. I can't resolve my tension by choosing fundamentalism, but I do understand its appeal, and I feel aligned with some of the corrections of course that we both want to make in the modern world. Maybe we can start there: *what are the values we have in common?*

On a cross-country flight during which I was squeezed into a seat next to a devout young man who was reading his Bible while I was writing in my journal, I looked for a way to open some conversation between us. I ascertained that he was on his way back to college and was taking a literature course. "I used to be an English major," I said, in my best I-am-not-your-mother-just-an-interesting-middle-aged-lady voice. "So, what are you reading at school... Shakespeare?"

"Oh, not Shakespeare," he responded, "he wasn't a Christian. We only read books written by Christians." Except for the *Left Behind* novels, I wasn't familiar with any of the titles or authors he listed, and while I may be missing something, it broke my heart to think of all he was missing: the stories he wouldn't know because the authors didn't fit his criterion.

In the face of this young man's certainty, I suddenly wanted to save copies of all the "godless" books that are the foundation of a literary culture that has informed and shaped my life; books that wrestle with spiritual issues, questions of good and evil, right and wrong, heroism and sacrifice, the fallibility of all our choices, and how over and over again we muddle through to doing the right thing. Trying to think of a title that might intrigue him, I recommended *East of Eden*, John Steinbeck's retelling of the Cain and Abel story through three generations of a California family.

I keep praying we will find ways to talk and listen to what is underneath these choices, for there I believe we might find a common root. Aren't most of us afraid at some level of what's happening in the world? Remember the story about the child soldiers and the campfire set to welcome them and hold them accountable for their actions? Story is capable of holding all of human experience if we are capable of holding the story. I just want the chance for us to go there, to get into that depth. Moving around the country looking for ways to open up spiritual conversation is like twirling the dial on a combination lock, carefully listening for the tumblers that might unlock our hearts and minds in ways we cannot imagine until it happens.

Preserving the Story

In his book *Storytelling: Imagination and Faith*, William J. Bausch tells the story of a group of Oxford-educated intellectuals in Britain who decided in the decades between 1920 and the late 1940s to keep the tradition of Christian allegory alive in the secular culture. Dorothy Sayers, a respected author of theological texts, decided to write the Lord Peter Wimsey mystery novels "to promote a Christian value system through intrigue and entertainment"; C. S. Lewis, who had been an intellectual atheist as a younger man, wrote *The Chronicles of Narnia*; and the most famous among them, linguistics professor J. R. R. Tolkien, wrote *The Lord of the Rings*.

I realize I have learned much of my own theology from listening to and reading moral stories. Coming out of the theater after the first of the *Lord of the Rings* film trilogy, I trailed behind two young boys while one said to the other, "I hear this is based on a book...." I wanted to grab them, dash off for cocoa at the corner café, pull my old worn volume out of my purse, and begin reading: "When Mr. Bilbo Baggins of Bag End announced that he would shortly be celebrating his eleventy-first birthday with a party of special magnificence, there was much talk and excitement in Hobbiton...." It would give me an excuse to go back there myself, to reread stories that set deep roots in me; that have shaped how I love the world and view the universe.

One thing I do as a Storycatcher is to keep a library. My house is full of books that I show people and talk about and quote and lend. In the corner of my living room is a glass-fronted bookcase I call my "cornerstone." It contains an eclectic collection of books that have influenced my life. On a three-by-five card tucked in the front pages of each volume I have written a little statement explaining why the book is important to me. The statement is contextual: it places the book within my sense of the larger story. About William Bausch's book I wrote: "This book illustrates the integration of storytelling into Christian tradition in a way I had not considered before. I lived this tradition growing up, but he made it visible and valuable to me."

The preservation of books has many historical precedents. Perhaps the most famous example in terms of religious texts is a collection called the Dead Sea Scrolls. Discovered in 1947 by a Bedouin shepherd passing time chunking rocks into a hole in the ruins of Qumran, the scrolls turned out to be over a hundred additional gospels possibly considered too confusing to retain in the theological lineage during the fledgling years of Pagan-Judeo-Christian transition about 400 CE. Like unwanted cousins, they were no longer invited to the feast. But instead of using the papyrus for kindling, somebody sealed them in pottery jars and buried them in the desert outside Jericho.

You may in the privacy of the heart take out the albums of your own life and search them for the people and places you have loved and learned from... and for those moments in the past — many of them half-forgotten — through which you glimpsed, however dimly and fleetingly, the sacredness of your own journey.

— Frederick Buechner

Imagine that. Imagine that impulse to save the story. Imagine believing that the stories you value, even though discarded by learned authorities, disdained by emperors and popes, are so important you will take the risk to preserve them. There are real human beings in this story and we don't know who they were: perhaps a theological scholar, potters and gravediggers, and a community of faith. All their names and details are lost, but imagine their faith that someone would later value what they strove to hide away. It puts my foray into the woods with my journal into context: we want the fullness of the tale to survive. That's what I want, right now in the twenty-first century — to know the fullness of the tale will survive beyond me.

In European history, during what is called the Dark Ages, a gap between the dissolution of the Roman Empire and the reestablishment of order under Charlemagne, educated and visionary monastic theologians pulled the foundational manuscripts of Western culture and religious thought back within their walls. Society was falling into chaos: violence, looting, and cities under siege. Barbarian armies poured across the Roman-held lands. While some of these competing tribes had flourishing cultures, they brought in their own gods and had little use for Christian scholarship (like the writings of Gregory of Nyssa) that had been thriving under Roman rule since the conversion of Constantine in 340. For six hundred years, passing this responsibility from generation to generation, the monasteries at the edge of chaos hid manuscripts, such as the famous *Book of Kells*.

There are real human beings in this story. Imagine the lives of monks dedicated to hand transcribing texts. Imagine spending your whole life in a stone cell wrapping ink-stained fingers around a candle's light for warmth, going half-blind from meticulously copying and illustrating pages. Imagine the isolation, the cold, the meager food, the bitter weather. Imagine hardly remembering or caring anymore why this is so important, but doing it anyway. Imagine training the next generation, the young monk who watches your handwriting and learns to carry on when your fingers are too shaky to hold the quill. Imagine dying and not knowing if what you have loved with your whole life will ever again be valued.

Living in the moment, no one can see the fullness of the story or the full importance of these gestures. In the moment we cannot see the fullness of our own story or the importance of the gestures we make with our lives. In retrospect we can say what a good plan that was, to hide the wisdom until the reader was ready again. The truth is, men and women lived their whole lives based on the wager that a time was coming when what they saved would be valued. And they died keeping faith with that wager — and not knowing — and to a large extent, so do we all live and die with the grand scheme of things whirling unfinished around us.

We are real human beings living in a story that we think of in terms of our own lifetimes. But our lives are just a collection of decades in the middle of a much longer story, a much longer and far more complicated shift in human consciousness than most of us can imagine. It took three thousand years for the diverse spirituality of the Great Mother to give way to the monolithic religions. Nobody lives for three thousand years. Our perspective is limited: we *have* to trust. We have to speak as wide and broad a story with our lives as we are able and let that be enough.

I WAS WRITING when the doorbell rang and I opened the door to see a woman with a little girl about six years old. It was the child who held out a copy of the *Watchtower*, who asked if I would let her in so her mommy could talk about Jesus. The look in her eyes was trusting, and I wondered how many times in the next few hours a door would be slammed in her face. I slid into a sitting position so I could be at her height. "What's your name, sweetie?" I asked.

"Hannah."

"That's a beautiful name. Do you know that it means 'the grace of God'?" She nodded solemnly. "It's a good name for you." Her mother was looking puzzled but hopeful that she would soon be in my living room. "I am busy right now," I said directly to this child, "and I don't want to talk about Jesus — but that has nothing to do with you. If people slam their doors, it's not about you. Are you thirsty? Are you hungry?" She shakes her head no. "Well, Hannah, grace of God, I hope you have a nice day and that you get a special treat for helping your mother with her testifying." Then I rose up and looked at the mother. "You have a nice day, too," I said. And then, very gently, I closed the door and waved from the window. That was over twenty years ago. I wish I had let them in.

We have twenty years and twenty global problems, the experts say: one of these problems is that some religious leaders are making religious followers terrified of and full of hate for other ordinary people who are a lot like themselves. I am ready to invite this schism into my living room and see where it goes. I am ready to explore the story of the possible God.

I know arguing literalism versus interpretation doesn't work, but could we both get back behind our religious training to that six-year-old place where we knew we were the grace of God and could connect to direct experience of the Divine? Next time, I will let them in, and pray they will let me in.

Grace Happens

Everybody is on a learning curve in this conversation. God is mystery. We may stake our lives on one definition or another, but that doesn't resolve the mystery. And where there is mystery, the plot is still active; the insight is still in shift.

In the course of my explorations, a remarkable little book, *If Grace Is True*, educated me into the language of fundamentalism and allowed me to walk through the minds of two pastors as they made their way toward a change of heart from judgment to grace. Like Rick and Donald, Rev. Philip Gulley and Rev. James Mulholland have been friends since seminary and worked closely together over many years of ministry. They now pastor two churches near each other in Indiana. Though coauthors, they chose to tell their story in one combined voice. Their book reexamines the conservative Christian worldview based on the revelation that came to them in seven words: "I believe God will save every person."

Having grown up in a Pentecostal church and listened to years of hell and damnation sermons, they accepted Jesus at age fourteen and headed into seminary right after college. They say, "As a child I was taught only Christians would be saved. Billions of non-Christians would crowd hell. The thought of non-Christians in eternal torment didn't disturb me because I'd been told Christians were good people and non-Christians were bad people. Since I grew up in a Midwestern American town where nearly everyone belonged to a Christian church, I had little opportunity to test this assumption....

Celie, tell the truth, have you ever found God in church? I never did. I just found a bunch of folks hoping for him to show. Any God I ever felt in church I brought in with me. And I think all the other folks did too. They come to church to share God, not find him.

— Alice Walker

"The first time I did question this worldview," they write, "I was in college and saw the movie *Gandhi*. While he never acknowledged Jesus as Savior, he lived the way Jesus commanded us to live.... The more I read about Gandhi, the more I admired him, and his words and actions reminded me of Jesus again and again.

"One day I shared my admiration for Gandhi with a friend. He responded, 'Isn't it sad that he's burning in hell?' His statement shocked me, but I quickly recognized how traditional Christian formulas work...."

The book led me clearly through their thought process, until I could see in them the brother mirror of Donald and Rick. This is what I had been looking for: a story to expand my own understanding of these two worldviews. I have listened to Rick and Donald; I have read Phil and Jim: if these four ministers of faith and heart can reach across the crisis in Christianity's story with insights and theological understanding, I have hope for many spiritual stories.

At the end of the book, Phil and Jim talk about the transformation of their view of heaven that occurred in the course of their awakening: "I have often heard heaven described as a grand courtroom. God sits on the throne of judgment. We stand before him with head bowed and knees shaking. The scenes of our life are replayed before us with every sad and sorry act revealed for all to see.... Those who've repented of their sins and accepted Jesus Christ as personal Lord and Savior will be pardoned. Everyone else is thrown, begging for mercy, into the pits of hell.... Fortunately, this is not the only image of heaven in scripture. Jesus seems partial to another description. He likened the kingdom of heaven to a banquet and told us the parable of the prodigal son...."

The prodigal son is a widely known story in the Christian tradition: it tells how the younger of two sons leaves his father for many years, makes bad choices, descends into sin, and eventually comes home, where the father (a stand-in for the Father) welcomes him and calls for a great celebration. Well, the stable, law-abiding, obedient older son is pretty upset at this situation. Jim and Phil speak to this moment: "[The older son] stomped home to discover a party when he had hoped for a trial.... He turned his back on his brother and on his father. In the end, the son with his back to the father resisting grace is the elder son. He becomes the prodigal." And a few paragraphs later Phil and Jim have the courage to say, "I think one of the reasons I resisted the idea of God's saving everyone was that I wanted heaven to be a party for me and a few select friends.... Yet this is the way of grace. Forgive as you are forgiven. Be merciful as you receive mercy. Love as you have been loved." In their epiphany, they sound a lot like Rick and Donald: they see a nurturing God.

Late at night, propped up among pillows and soft lamplight, I finish reading their book. I am thinking how it gives me words to enter a conversation the next time someone asks me if I am saved. I am thinking about the reassurance this book can provide for those who anguish over the fate of their unsaved friends and family.

A global awakening can only happen from a spiritual awakening that is of global dimensions.

— Matthew Fox

Reluctant to put the little book down, I glance through the appendix where Phil and Jim trace the sources of their thought throughout scripture and Christian theological texts: Genesis, Psalms, Gospels, and the teaching of the early church — and there he is quoted, their common brother — St. Gregory of Nyssa.

I pull a three-by-five card out of the nightstand: this book is going in my cornerstone. Here is the bridge, here is the crossing, another step in becoming God's friend. May we yet heal the rift that tears our culture in half. May both sides rejoice, and grieve, and discover ways to live our grace.

Who is your brother/your sister in the spiritual journey of your life?

Tell me that story.

Let's start there.

Becoming a Storycatcher

Religion is a story. Not just one story, but many stories brought forth to explain the world and our place in it. Throughout our history, the political — the structure that governs human society — and the religious — the structure that governs the creation story — have often been in an uneasy dialogue and struggle for power. Every human life and every human society is commissioned to create a workable story between the secular and the spiritual. Storycatchers accept a responsibility to preserve all of the stories, to ensure that generations to come can choose their own religious story.

Tell Me This Story...

These story beginnings can be used in writing or conversation to enhance storycatching in your life.

- How did your religious attitudes change in adolescence? Youth? Midlife? Old age? What religious or spiritual rituals do you now observe? Why?
- What are the most meaningful spiritual experiences you ever had outside a religious setting? Describe a place that felt or feels holy to you. How has nature been a spiritual home for you?
- Describe or make a list of your greatest blessings. Think of ten ways you say thank you during the day.
- Think of a time in your life that was particularly painful. Did your spirituality or religious faith help you deal with the pain? How? If there was an absence of spirituality or faith in your life at that time, do you think that contributed to the pain?
- What are some of the mysteries of life that you continue to contemplate? What form(s) does your contemplation take? Do

you discuss your feelings about the mysteries of life with others?

- How would you explain religion to a child?
- What secular books help shape your theology?
- What one gift would you take from the universe? What one gift would you give in return?
- Is prayer a part of your daily life? Write your own prayer.

CHAPTER TEN

Storycatcher

TAKING OUR PLACE IN THE ORDER OF THINGS

Story is a search for community. As we tell each other who we really are, we find the people with whom we really belong. Story brings us home.

I live in a little neighborhood of three cul-de-sacs, two miles out of town on a cliff overlooking Puget Sound. Our house is a comfortable rambler, a modest home by American standards that we have been updating as we could afford it since the kids left home in 2001. I love to play with colors, and room by room the house has shifted from the all-white walls left us by its former owners to beach stone, olive smoke, cupola yellow, summer sky, and fir dream. When the words come hard in writing, I want to get a job just naming colors on paint chips, or wandering off into poetry that starts each line conjuring color imagery. In the autumn of 2004, it was time to do the kitchen. The old countertops were delaminating, the cupboards needed painting, and the 1970s track lights cast a harsh light over my cooking. We hired a local carpenter, talked our way through the job, picked out new Formica, and let him tear the place apart. One night after he left for the day, I noticed a four-inch gap between the wall of the lower cabinet and the actual wall of the house. I peered down into it: dark, dry, empty. The next day, when the carpenter fitted the countertops back over this gap, it would disappear and no one would know it was even there. For the second time in my life I decided to make a time capsule.

In a sealable plastic baggie I placed a current copy of the local paper, a *Newsweek* magazine, some photos of the house and its occupants, a business card, some sprigs of dried lavender from the garden, and the following letter:

> *28 September 2004: foggy morning that promises to burn off into sunshine this afternoon.*
>
> *This cubbyhole will be resealed by new countertop and is not likely to see the light of day again for a long time. Certainly we do not intend to redo the kitchen again while we live here and the carpenter is doing a very fine job that will be long lasting. So, I have decided to put in some memorabilia of the current times to be discovered — whenever, by whomever. Hello.*
>
> *At this writing, we have lived here exactly ten years, having bought this house in September 1994. The former owner did all the wood finishing — window and door trim, and the ceiling in the living room — out of a woodworking shop in the backyard. He took care with the things he loved and jerry-rigged the other parts, which, luckily for you, we have been fixing throughout our tenure. Enclosed is a photo of how the house looks at this time. We are now operating a small educational company out of the converted shed: PeerSpirit, Inc. (See business cards and photos.) We are writers and teachers, group facilitators and wilderness guides, creating eclectic and satisfying professional lives.*
>
> *On our minds this day: we have ongoing concerns for the state of the world. The country is in crisis, polarized politically, in a misguided war over oil in the Middle East (currently we are occupying Iraq). Corporate greed is bankrupting us, social services are being undercut, civil liberties are being eroded, and environmental protections are being reversed. It's not an easy time to be alive when we look very far beyond these kitchen windows, but we are trying to live our lives with a sense of service.*
>
> *Most every morning we spend a few minutes in prayer: one of us sits under the big Douglas fir in back of the house, one of us sits on the front steps. We pray for goodness to prevail, for humans to learn our lessons in time to save ourselves and the biosphere on which we depend. We give deep thanks for the beauty and peace that surround us and know it may not always be so beautiful or peaceful. We are glad to be alive.*

Headlines:

- *The presidential election this coming November is between George W. Bush, Republican, and John Kerry, Democrat. It's a very close race, excessively acrimonious and costing U.S. taxpayers four billion dollars. We hope there will have been significant reform in all of this by the time these words are read.*
- *We are voting for Kerry; the carpenter is voting for Bush. We are talking about our political views and differences as he works.*
- *The waters of Puget Sound still support salmon, seals, Orca whales, with gray whales and humpbacks coming through seasonally on their way to Alaska.*
- *Gasoline is currently $2.07 a gallon and 99 percent of the cars and trucks are still using this fuel. The first models of hybrid engines are available.*
- *Mount St. Helens, a volcano one hundred miles south of here, is experiencing mini-earthquakes and they predict a moderately sized eruption within the next few days. Four major hurricanes have slammed Florida in less than a month. Weather and planetary reactions seem to be getting more extreme, and there is scientific proof of global warming that the current U.S. government chooses to ignore.*

And yet, we are learning how to carry the bad news and still have happy lives — not out of denial but putting all that is happening in a spiritual frame and believing in the whole web of life of which humans are only a part.

We hope this note finds you also able to enjoy this place, that the work of many has preserved its beauty, that the neighbors are friendly and this island is still a vibrant community.

I ZIPPED THE BAG SHUT and dropped it into the cubbyhole. By noon the next day it had become history. It had become an irretrievable artifact; it had become story. As I have shared word of my little impulse, others have adopted the idea and set about leaving stories and messages in mysterious places in their own homes. Notes from life in action: a blessing scrawled on the plywood subflooring before laying new carpet, the scroll of a child's drawing and a list of her favorite things slipped into the wall of her bedroom, a poem dropped between the desk and the wall of an office cubicle. Story is an act of faith that our kind will continue, that our messages for each other will someday be received, that when you read this you will recognize the offer of kinship.

STORY HAS A WILL TO SURVIVE that seems almost independent of the storyteller, as though it has a life of its own. Oral story is a singing bird: when we let it out of the cage of the mind, it loves freedom! The song of the self will light on our shoulder as long as we don't try to capture it. Then it will flutter away and fly places we cannot imagine. It will nest and mate and raise other versions of itself that take on the color and hue and dialect of new territory. And some spring morning when we most need to hear it, our story will return outside our window and sing us back into ourself.

Written story also has a will to survive. It loves to trick fate, to slip out of the hands of carelessness or destruction, to curl at the edge of darkness waiting and watching for the flicker of welcome: Anne Frank's checkered notebook kicked aside by the Gestapo's boot; Sacagawea pulling the journals of Lewis and Clark out of the Missouri River after their canoe capsized; the ancient poetry of Sappho tweezered out of the mouths of mummified crocodiles in the excavation of Egyptian tombs; the Bedouins chancing upon the Dead Sea Scrolls; my great-grandfather's letters tucked in his Bible; recipes in my mother's handwriting; a bundle of old love letters left in a shoe box — and a message to the future hidden under the kitchen cabinet.

What are we willing to give our lives to if not the perpetuation of the sacred?

— Terry Tempest Williams

Adding Our Voices

These little acts are a profound declaration of belonging. We are putting our individual voices into the never-ending story. In *An American Requiem*, James Carroll writes, "The very act of storytelling, of arranging memory and invention according to the structure of narrative, is by definition holy. . . . Telling our stories is what saves us; the story is enough."

Story is enough when we honor narrative as the universal treasure that it is. Story is ours; story belongs equally to every human being. Telling our stories is what saves us, when we add our tiny piece of what we have learned in a lifetime into the great stewpot of collective wisdom. Whatever happens to us now, story is still our guiding star. And this guidance resides inside us, resides inside the hearts and minds of the human community. We cannot see or hear or read this guidance unless we bring it forth and make it accessible to each other through story. We do not know where to turn until our stories lay out a track, give us a word to stand on while we get our bearings, and then make the next word to stand on. What we need is in us, and around us in each other — we bring it to voice.

It is the work of the Storycatcher to revere the power and presence of story in all its ordinary magnificence. It is the work of the Storycatcher to retrieve story from the blur of background noise and reinstate its place of honor in our lives. It is the work of the Storycatcher to make sense out of nonsense, to put our stories in context so that we can see the connectedness in all that is happening.

It is not given to us to know who is lost in the darkness that surrounds us or even if our light is seen. We can only know that against even the smallest of lights, darkness cannot stand.

— Kent Nerburn

We don't ultimately know which of our stories is destined to serve someone else's need. We don't know our story's full impact — we just speak and write and let it go. We guess how to respond, hoping to help, to comfort, to call to accountability, to explain how something feels, to make connection, or to break it cleanly. The art of storycatching is powerful work: we are using archetypal forces to pass the time of day. It's a little like standing around the water cooler gesturing with a lightning bolt in our hands: we hope all of those present are being careful in how they make their points. Words are power.

We know what negative and positive narrative is capable of doing in our own minds. We know that story is so powerful it can drive us mad, send us spiraling down in depression, send us reeling into anguish — and that the world can change on a word. We know that story is so powerful it can redeem us, reconnect us, pull us back from the brink, and send us into bliss. Even if we have done those things we ought not to have done, even if we have betrayed and hurt one another, story is how we start to make amends, start to see each other again, work to understand. Story is how we come home.

Story is a search for community. Open your mouth, grab a pen, type on the keyboard — sing out who you are, for I need you. I am looking for you; you are looking for me. We are tribe. Something is happening to me: I am thrown into the spiral of my experience. I've never been here before. I am disoriented. But I know I cannot possibly be the first human being to experience this — where are the stories? Not that I'm going to live through something exactly the way anyone else has, but the purpose of the map is to show us how. And then I take my own steps.

A sailor lost at sea can be guided home by a single candle. A person lost in a wood can be led to safety by a flickering flame. It is not an issue of quality or intensity or purity. It is simply an issue of the presence of light.

— Kent Nerburn

None of us can judge exactly what is needed: we don't know; we just set out the stories because someday, somebody will need these clues. You may have entered this book alone; you leave this book held in a network of storycatching. It will save your life: for the story that gets one person through makes a map for getting the next person through. Storycatching is really the art of story releasing, of putting good stories out in the world, holding them high and tossing them onto the wind like a hawk taking flight into freedom.

The Storycatchers Network

Story moves through the world in a living network. No longer restrained by face-to-face transmission or limited by place of origin, story is a self-organizing force on the planet that works through us. Stories and people cocreate. Stories and people coevolve.

In their book *A Simpler Way*, Margaret J. Wheatley and Myron Kellner-Rogers talk of the world as "tinkering itself into existence." They write: "But life's tinkering has direction. It tinkers toward order —

toward systems that are more complex and more effective. The process used is exploratory and messy, but the movement is toward order.... What begins in randomness ends in stability. Life seeks solutions, tends toward support and stability, generates systems that sustain diverse individuals.... But how it gets there violates all our rules of good process.... Life seeks order in a disorderly way. Life uses processes we find hard to tolerate and hard to believe in — mess upon mess until something workable emerges."

That's where we are now, living in the repeated messes. But when we are messing *with* life, not against it — attempting to contribute, even in our human ignorance of the whole picture — we are tinkering toward wholeness. We are contributing toward order. We are part of the living system, the network.

This network animates the Storycatcher in us and connects us to each other and to the wholeness of story, even though we only have part of the story to share. The Storycatchers network seeds us with ideas, shares what works and what we learn when something doesn't work; this network reassures us that we belong to a community of human aspiration almost beyond imagining.

In trying to explain how sensitively and intricately life is networked, metaphysical scientists use the example, "When a butterfly flaps its wings in California, the weather changes in New York." I don't know much about butterflies, but I know story. I know that butterflies seem fragile and inconsequential and yet one hundred million monarchs fly thousands of miles in the nine months of their lives. Our stories may also seem fragile and inconsequential, and yet they fly beyond the perimeters of the speaker's or writer's lives and provide succor, challenge, and inspiration that cast an influence of nearly unlimited potential.

Random Acts of Story

In the first several decades of journal writing, I was so busy with the story of myself that the story of the world could hardly get into my journal.

Now I can't keep the world out. I live with an ever-deepening comprehension of how my story and the Story are connected. For decades, I have heard people say that to heal the self is to heal the world. While self-healing, like healing self-story, is a necessary foundation, the leap must be made to extend our healing into our actions in the world around us.

Story told to inform — inspire — activate — becomes an act of citizenship. If I make a little contribution to the common good and don't tell the story, it's good for my soul, but my silence creates a closed loop that starts and stops with me: nobody but me learns. If I make a little contribution and brag about my virtuousness or rant and rave about all the thoughtless people in the world, my story may reach out a ring or two, but my opinionating creates another kind of closure. But if I make my little contribution and share it through a story that speaks of beauty, love, and commitment, then the story and action invite the listener or reader to reflect and act in their own creative ways. The proper use of story creates community; communities create story.

Once there was a circle of journal-writing women who met in a fancy home along a little suburban creek. The creek ran through the backyard and into the city, where it was pushed underground in a large culvert until it discreetly disappeared into the swirling brown eddies of an industrialized river. Sitting in the solarium, month after month, the women wrote and read and noticed how often the creek appeared in their writing as a contemplative focus or a metaphor for their own life journeys. They began to think of the creek as a member of the group, and as they looked more closely, they realized she wasn't in very good health. As the water babbled around boulders, she churned up yellowish suds, and sometimes the water turned green with algae and smelled funny.

Ecology teaches us that the world is co-created through complex networks of relationships, no one of which is dominant.

— Frances Moore Lappé

The women talked to an old man who stood on a pond's edge near this home and listened to him speak of the fish he caught here as a boy, and how now the creek was nothing but carp. "It gives me peace to just spend an hour throwing my line in the water," he told them, "but I'd never eat anything that came out." They followed the creek into town and talked to the Hmong families who relied on those carp for food, whether or not they were healthy, and who plucked watercress out of the babbling places near the golf course and sold it at the farmers' markets. And they began to understand: the creek held a very large story that reached out into issues of farm-field runoff, storm-water management, industrial pollution, gaps in social services, cultural differences, and class privilege. And the women, sitting in the sunroom sipping tea and eating watercress sandwiches, were writing within the circle of the story.

In their book *Hope's Edge*, Frances Moore Lappé and Anna Lappé were puzzled by the amount of apathy and disempowerment they encountered while exploring issues central to our survival. Frances writes: "I realized that we humans can't do what we can't imagine, and we can't imagine ourselves playing real, satisfying roles in creating life-serving communities — what I came to call 'living democracy' — unless we see regular people like ourselves developing their power, their capacity to create." In media that focus on bad news, it may take some searching, but we can find these stories of regular people like ourselves developing our powers; and sometimes, we have to *be* the one of these regular people willing to take action and then willing to communicate our action so that others can use our stories as sources of inspiration and action.

Another world is not only possible, she is on her way. And on a quiet day, if you really listen, you can hear her breathing.

— Arundhati Roy

Here is a choice: *What will the women writing beside the creek do with their growing awareness? What would you do?* At different times in our lives we choose avenues of escape or engagement. This time these women chose engagement. They saw the creek as an issue that was the right size for them to develop their power. The women traced the creek back to the lake it flowed out of and contacted the Department of Natural Resources. They found that the DNR could provide them with water-quality data over the past twenty years, and they put this information into letters to the city council, the county government, and a flyer they were writing. They investigated how lawn fertilizer affects algae blooms. The next summer, when the water level was low, they walked the creek in one-mile segments, pulling garbage out of the muck and conversing with creek-side landowners about their lawn fertilizers. They carried their flyer: one side held information and phone numbers and websites outlining corrective practices. On the other side was a brief story about their writing circle and an invitation for others to do something about something they cared for.

So the journal writers pulled tires and scrap metal and plastic and slimy bottles and rusted cans out of the creek. They chipped their nails and got sunburned and got radicalized, step by sloshing step. They cried to find the lifeless bodies of ducks and buried a litter of drowned kittens. They cheered when landowners volunteered to join them and jumped in the creek to help them haul junk to shore, or agreed to inform others to become creek tenders and to pass along the word. And at the end of the day, nearly as dirty as the creek itself, they celebrated their transformation and proudly took a photograph of themselves dressed in their husbands' waders or old muck boots and rain suits, sweaty and bedraggled warrioresses of the creek standing in front of a mountain of garbage bags on their way to the dump. It was just the beginning.

Here is what they learned:

- *that working together is fun, even in moments when the immediate task itself is not fun;*
- *that there are many more allies and much more support than one originally expects and that story — putting action into a context of history and heart — dissipates resistance;*
- *that successfully defining the right-size task leads to successfully taking on the next-sized task;*
- *that tending the story is almost as important as doing the work, because the story shared inspires others to action;*
- *that story preserves the information and knowledge they gained;*
- *that activism in one area of their lives builds their sense of empowerment in all areas of their lives: they are more assertive citizens, and so are their families and their wider circle of friends, for they inspire each other into activism by giving each other hope.*

When the women attended a city council meeting to let their commissioners know they were adopting the creek, a local reporter picked up the story. At first, they resisted the idea of becoming a media event. "We're not doing this to get attention for ourselves, we just want to see what can be done about this one little stretch of water." After some thought, however, they decided it was important that the story get told so that others would decide to do something in their own backyards.

Stories start movements: Adopt a Highway is a story-to-action; Mothers Against Drunk Drivers is a story-to-action; foster grandparenting and school volunteer programs are stories-to-action. Storycatching is a movement. The list is beyond counting. Well, actually Paul Hawken tried to count it. At the Bioneers conference in October 2003, Hawken showed a video that listed the websites of nonprofit, community-based, nongovernmental organizations worldwide that are working to restore the planet and foster human community. The video is a visual of the earth in space, some soft music, and a scroll of organizational names and websites. If played in its entirety, the list would go on for three days. There are that many people in the network of restoration; there are that many stories.

Storycatching as an Act of Refuge

So if we believe that "life seeks order in a disorderly way," then all the upheaval and messiness that surround us become a sign of productive busyness. And if we can keep calm while "life uses processes we find hard to tolerate and hard to believe in — mess upon mess until something workable emerges," then we can let go of despair. Despair interprets messiness as chaos, as the loss of an order-seeking universe. Despair is a little box, way too small for the mind of *Homo sapiens*. Despair sucks the stories right out of our hearts. Despair discourages us just at those moments when we most need our courage and need to have enough heart energy in reserve that we can encourage each other. I say, enough of despair. Despair does not help.

No one has a right to sit down and feel hopeless. There's too much work to do.

— Dorothy Day

What we need is hope. Hope is the story that keeps us going. Hope says the world is still beginning, life is young and still getting organized. Hope says come on in, there's something only you can do, a story only you can share. Hope defines this time in history as a great turning; a time when human beings are taking our place as the earthly ones capable of wisdom and good judgment. Hope blows evidence of this capacity back into our hearts, and fills us with stories that inspire action.

The very least you can do in your life is to figure out what you hope for. And the most you can do is to live inside that hope.

— Barbara Kingsolver

There is a Ray Bradbury fable about a time when people are full of dread for the state of the world and what the future might bring. And one day in the midst of this dread, a young scientist comes into the city and stops in the center of town. When people gather around, he tells them the contraption he's hauling is a time machine. If they like, he will travel on their behalf into the future and see what has happened. Though fearful and ambivalent, the people tell him to go ahead. He jumps in his machine and it shakes and rattles and disappears.... After a while, the scientist reappears, steps out of the machine, and people assemble to receive the bad news. But the scientist looks happy. "Great news!" he tells them. "In the future there is peace and justice, there is enough food and water for all, people live in cooperation and walk gently on the earth." The people are stunned; this is not what they had expected. But something begins to stir in them — a sense of participation, a desire to do something to help this happen. They set off to create the future that has been promised them.

Years pass, and while life is not perfect, the world is indeed in better shape. So one day a young Storycatcher comes to visit the old, old scientist, who is sitting by the time machine now rusting in his garden. "Tell me about your journey," she asks.

The old man smiles, "My dear, I didn't go anywhere," he admits. "I just gave the people hope."

Hope is action; hope is doing something; hope is the story of a million creative, heartfelt responses in which we discover that choice is always present and human beings are always choosing. One of the great background delights of working on this book has been the hopeful stories that have come to my eyes and ears. The renewed life we long for is already residing in the hearts and minds of people all over the world; it's just waiting for us to believe in our capacity to live it.

Yet hope is tricky; like joy, it must include and befriend ambiguity. To live in denial, to proceed with false cheerfulness, avoiding the seriousness of our situation, will quickly dash any hope built on such a flimsy foundation.

As I travel around speaking with and listening to the Tribe of the Ambiguous, a story-based role is becoming clear: Storycatchers can serve not only as carriers of hopeful and thought-provoking tales, but also as receivers of confused and heartrending accounts of personal awakening. The movement aspect of storycatching is about creating interpersonal space in which we can hold story with each other. Like the circle of listening that frames chapter 2, we need to practice being in the now; we need a readiness to notice, to volunteer to listen and respond to each other while we speak our way into holding the complexity of the world.

Storycatching is at its root an act of refuge, a place to turn, an offering that we will be listened to while we hold our hearts like a talking piece in our hands; and then, we pay it forward — we become the listening ear for the next person, and the next. In this way, the skills of eliciting story, and skills of receiving story, grow among us. Story makes community: communities make story.

Get ready, I say. For the rest of our lives we, and others around us, are going to be falling out of our momentary resting places of security and surety, and every time that happens we need to help each other move from disorientation into story. We need to remind each other that this is what it feels like to enter the Spiral of Experience again and again, to be confronted with life events that have a sense of initiation.

GET READY. I was traveling out of SeaTac airport and the flight was delayed. Passengers were crowded into the waiting area and television screens were babbling the news over our heads. I found myself a seat with another row of chairs facing me. There was a retired couple to my left, a couple of businessmen on my right, and across from us another woman my age and a younger woman with a baby.

Though I was trying to read, there was too much distraction. I became aware that the news was bad, that some high-up government official was leaning casually against a lectern chatting about the right of the United States to use nuclear force if and when it deemed it necessary. He looked so at ease in this conversation, as though he was talking about something totally innocuous. I glanced down and there was the young mother, her baby held tightly to her breast and big tears rolling down her cheeks. She looked into my eyes and said, "I had this baby because I didn't think we were there anymore."

What will happen when the storytellers emerge?... They will sing our epic of being, and stirring up from our roots will be a vast awe, an enduring gratitude, the astonishment of communion experiences, and the realization of the cosmic adventure.

— Brian Swimme

The businessman got off his cell phone. "Don't worry," he said, "it's just rhetoric, posturing. The game is to convince the other guy you are capable of doing what you say... and then not blink and make him back down."

"Brinksmanship," said the retired man. "I spent my life playing it, went into the army to finish off Korea... stayed there thirty years and then worked security at U.S. embassies...." His wife smiles wanly.

"Wow," I say, "you must have a lot of stories. Tell us about a moment when things looked really bad but turned out well... tell us about a time when somebody made a good decision under pressure...."

The question calls the story, and this little group of strangers holds the space. The men talk... and other woman talks, the wife listens, and then the young mother asks me, "Do you think my baby will have a long life?"

"I don't know," I tell her, "but he's having a wonderful life right now, sheltered in your fierceness and love.... Let me tell you a little story: I was sixteen years old when the Cuban Missile Crisis happened, and it was a dark and stormy night..."

Get ready. Little moments and big moments are coming when we can offer and receive story that helps us hold each other steady in the untidiness of the world. So this is where I want to leave us: building the Storycatchers network, looking out for each other as we make our journeys home. We, the people, who know and practice and celebrate and preserve the power of story. We, the Storycatchers, who will never let the power of humanity's voice be silenced.

Story Time

Sunset is lingering in the western sky, clouds orange and lavender, and a line of mountains set like a wolf's jawbone along the horizon. I am walking on the beach with my beloved. Around this thumb of water called Puget Sound, where nearly five million people live within some kind of hailing distance, we are alone. We are silent, then exclaiming, then singing, our hearts so filled with beauty we feel inadequate to express it all. The whole world is playing out this ritual of day's end and we two humans are here to enjoy it. We call our wonderment into words because it deepens our joy to know we are accompanying each other in awe. Oh look, and look here, and look there.

Of course, we are not really alone on the beach. Our corgis are snuffling along the tide lines, birds are bobbing on the hued water, fish are swimming, crabs crawling, the teeming cities of tide-pool life are active just under the surface, aggregate anemones wiggle their tentacles in submerged privacy. Pebbles roll down the sheer cliff walls, a leaf drifts, sand shifts. Life is all around us. But only we, the human beings, look at it all. Only we get teary-eyed with wonder, reach for each other's hands, say Oh my God, say thank you. Only we appreciate it, try to make a story that conveys how it feels to stand awash in color, only we will write it down in a journal and three years later find this page and say, "Oh listen to this, Honey, remember that afternoon?" And we will remember.

Most of us feel this way thousands of times in our lives. Outdoors, indoors, blasted open by beauty, by love, by kindness, by acts of goodness and courage that we see occurring all around us. Enthralled with the world, we make story out of experience for the sheer joy of it, and because story is our job. Our niche in the great order of things is to appreciate, to notice, to call attention to beauty, attention to need, attention to something we can do. Without us — not the two of us, but the billions of us — there would be no one here to engage the story of it all.

How we lead our days is how we lead our lives.
— Annie Dillard

The sunset was doing its sky painting ten thousand years ago and ten million years ago, and it will be doing it ten thousand years from now and ten million years from now. No one will be reading this book. No one will be finding my journals or yours. No one will know the stories we seed so diligently into our lives and lineage. We will be long gone. And the earth will decide whether or not a creature that can imagine and appreciate and pray and conceptualize is worth all the rest of what we do. And yet, I believe our stopping on the beach in the glory of this moment changes the story — now and forever.

That's the point of this whole book: for us to notice how the story we make of the moment becomes the life we lead. I carry this sunset and this shared moment within me. It seeds the rest of my life, gives me a place of rest to return to in my mind. Someday I may be old, may be half-blind, may be far from here in a room where the window looks out on a brick wall, and my mind will paint the bricks orange and lavender, and I will rub my achy fingers together, remembering the feel of another's hand in mine.

I pick up a piece of beach glass and put it in my pocket to carry the now into the future. I will always remember the moment when I added this little green chip to my collection, I think; but I won't. This moment, this particular memory, will get buried and lost in a treasure trove of moments, and yet, remembered or not, it gives me strength to do the far more difficult things and to hold the far more difficult stories.

Satiated in this calm, we climb the stairs up the cliff to the little neighborhood of homes where we live. The colors fade.

Enough of this story: this story is enough.

What is the treasured moment you carry in your pocket right now?

Tell me that story.

Let's pause there.

Becoming a Storycatcher

Story is a search for community that allows us to share, build, and learn from each other. Intentional storycatching is a movement in the making, ensuring survival of the stories through oral and written traditions. Recognizing story as an act of citizenship, we know that the world can change on a word. Story can save us. We choose whether we want to live in hopefulness or despair. Storycatchers choose hopefulness, knowing that story has the power to change our lives.

Tell Me This Story...

These story beginnings can be used in writing or conversation to enhance storycatching in your life.

- What letter to the future and cache of common objects would you leave for others to find? Where will you place it?
- How else might you help story survive?
- How will you bring the world into your journal? Into your storytelling? What narrative do you want to preserve?
- What is right in front of you that would be the right-size activism to undertake? Organize this action and find the people to help you: tell your story.
- What practices of grief are you willing to explore? To help others explore? To make a ritual for acknowledgment so that it clears the heart for hope and beauty?
- What if you make a notebook of hope — collages, stories, photos — perhaps working with children to help them see all the good that is happening in the world?

- How many times a day, in how many creative ways can you express gratitude for your life and for life itself?
- Keep a little notebook by your bed and write down one blessing a day, one gift you have received. Tell that story.

Acknowledgments

In the ever-widening spiral that is story, there are people along the way who have been immeasurable help in bringing this book to the page. I want to thank first the people whose stories enliven these chapters, starting with my parents and family. My mother, Connie, is a champion for the work of my life; I honor her understanding of culture and family that has shaped me since childhood and her courageous sociability that is a light to many friends. My father, Leo, is a true sociologist, a student of the interconnectedness of social mechanisms, who from the time I was very young treated me as a thoughtful person and engaged my mind in questioning dialogue. My brother, Carl, is a man whose life speaks his story and I am grateful for his willingness to share his reflections on Viet Nam in chapter 5. His wife, Colleen, a dear sister of choice, stepped forward and shaped the Storycatcher questions found at the end of each chapter, researched hundreds of quotes to enhance the margins and serves as a primary reader, supporter, and help in bringing this work from book to movement. I thank my sister, Becky, for her loving perspective on the family stories shared here, and though our younger brother, Ric, doesn't have lines to speak in this book, I give thanks for his arrival when I was ten, and for all the wit and wisdom he has inserted into the family line. The solidarity and individuality of "the four of us" is a huge blessing in my life journey. Being brothered and sistered by these wonderfully diverse individuals has shaped my hopes for our generation and the generation we have parented.

I was delighted with how global the book became in the last months of writing. I loved being up before dawn with a tape recorder and a cup of tea talking with Marianne Knuth many time zones away having her afternoon tea in Africa. I thank her for letting me frame her life through the lens of chapter 6. Kit Wilson did the inner work of transforming her family story so that we could have a model for healing lineage in chapter 7 — go finish those memoirs, my friend! I am grateful for Toke Møller's sojourn through my house on his way across continents at just the moment I needed his global visions about organizations for chapter 8. I honor the spirited ministry of Episcopal priests The Reverend Donald Schell and The Reverend Richard Fabian, whose theology and practice gave me hope for religion when seeking a voice for chapter 9.

There are several other people who provided background material or support that I want to mention. I am grateful for the friendship of Margaret Wheatley, who introduced me to Marianne and Toke and opened my mind to living systems theory through her tutelage and writing. I thank Mary K. Sandford, professor of anthropology at the University of North Carolina, Greensboro, for helping me become an amateur anthropologist and providing a research frame for the material in chapter 3. Thank you to Tami Simon and Sounds True for recording *Lifelines*, my philosophy of writing and life story. That oral articulation laid out tracks for me to follow in this writing, like the basic beat under a complex piece of music. Thanks to cousin Bill Humphreys for family stories, to Walt Blackford for his genius at networking and relevant Internet forwards, and a bow to all the synchronicity that surrounds a project like this and the "chance remarks" that guided me on.

At home there are people who make writing possible by the ways they hold the rest of life in place. First of all, my love and gratitude to Ann Linnea for being my partner, inspiration, sister-writer, reader, and listener to draft after draft, a trusted wielder of the red pen, celebrant of wild words, and the one who calls me into the fullness of my capacities over and over again. Ann, and our office manager, Debbie Dix, carried on the business of PeerSpirit, Inc., providing me time to write. Debbie's ability to respond graciously to never-ending details and to interface with the Tribe of the Ambiguous by email and phone is an essential support we count upon daily. Thank you also to our fourth member of PeerSpirit, Margaret Rode, website wonder woman and storyteller at www.websitesforgood.com. Thank you to Cynthia Trenshaw, writer and neighbor extraordinaire, who has a knack for offering to cook supper on just the right days and who serves as a friendly outrigger to our busyness. Thank you to the APC and all my friends who waited out the year of writing with me and nurtured me in many ways, from prayers to patience. Thanks to the faithful little dogs, Glory and Gwen, who sat under my desk and took up all my foot room and then made sure we walked the beach.

As this book goes to press, the working association with New World Library enters the next phase. Great thanks to Jason Gardner, who is really an editor, a man who loves and supports his projects and his authors; to Munro Magruder, who is an equal champion in the marketing department; and to Kim Corbin, who does the work of delivering this book in sound bites and making sure *Storycatcher* gets its toe in the media door. These and other folks I am still coming to know are a great team.

And finally, a deep bow of respect and honor to the hundreds and hundreds of people who have sat with me in circles of story-making and who, with trembling courage, have offered their stories through voice and page to a ring of waiting faces. We are changing the world one story at a time. Blessings.

Notes

These notations are separated by chapter and begin with some of the background books and references that contributed to my overall thought process and writing, followed by specific citations of text and their sources. Please think of these notes as part of our ongoing conversation about story and visit www.storycatcher.net to read continuing updates and to contribute your own discoveries. I have resisted putting many websites in this list, as they are fairly changeable and search-engine technology is an evolving marvel for finding what we seek.

Chapter One. Following the Beeline

Dorothy Allison, *Two or Three Things I Know for Sure* (New York: Dutton, 1995).
Maya Angelou, *I Know Why the Caged Bird Sings* (New York: Bantam Books, 1997).
Donald H. Baldwin, *The Montana Baldwins: Saga of a Century* (private printing, 1986).
———, *"PA" Andrew W. Baldwin: His Life and Family* (private printing, 1996).
Yvonne Dewar, *The Hansons of Six Mile Grove* (private printing, 1988).
Marianne Hart Baldwin, *My Autobiography* (private printing, 1946).

11 *. . . among the Tzutujil Indians. . .* Martin Prechtel, *Secrets of the Talking Jaguar* (New York: Tarcher/Putnam, 1999).

11 . . . *In 1904, ten local Native girls* . . . Resourced from Linda Peavy and Ursula Smith, "World Champions: The 1904 Girls Basketball Team from Fort Shaw Indian Boarding School" (*Montana: The Magazine of Western History*, Winter 2001) and www.indiancountrynews.com, May 2004, article on cross-cultural dedication ceremony.

16 . . . *I have read the story of a tribe in southern Africa* . . . Extensive scholarly research was conducted concerning the customs and society of the Babemba people who were living in what was then called Rhodesia, during the colonial period of the first half of the twentieth century. This particular story was circulated on the Internet and incorporated into a number of articles and essays — everything from parenting guidelines to responses to the September 11, 2001, terrorist attacks. This version is now quoted in Jack Kornfield, *The Art of Forgiveness: Loving Kindness and Peace* (New York: Bantam, 2002).

17 . . . *Martin Buber, a great archivist* . . . Quoted from William J. Bausch, *Storytelling: Imagination and Faith* (Mystic, CT: Twenty-Third Publications, 1984), 54.

Chapter Two. The Ear in the Heart

Robert Atkinson, *The Gift of Stories: Practical and Spiritual Applications of Autobiography, Life Stories, and Personal Mythmaking* (Westport, CT: Bergin & Garvey, 1995).

Christina Baldwin, *Life's Companion: Journal Writing as a Spiritual Quest* (New York: Bantam, 1990).

———, *One to One: Self-Understanding through Journal Writing* (New York: M. Evans & Company, 1977; revised edition, 1991).

———, *Calling the Circle: The First and Future Culture* (New York: Bantam, Doubleday, Dell, 1995).

Laura Simms, *A Gift of Dreams: A Storytelling Kit* (audiocassette; Boulder, CO: Sounds True, 2001).

Marion Wright Edelman, *The Measure of Our Success: A Letter to My Children and Yours* (Boston: Beacon Press, 1992).

32 . . . *Under the guidance of* . . . Eliot Wigginton, ed., *The Foxfire Book* (New York: Anchor Press, 1972) and *Foxfire 2–12* (New York: Anchor Press, 1972–2004).

32 Wigginton, *Moments: The Foxfire Experience* (Washington D.C.: IDEAS, 1975).

35 . . . *People have always had the impulse* . . . Some of the material comes

from my own books on journal writing cited above, particularly the preface to the revised edition of *One to One.*

35 . . . *the first use of this . . . tool* . . . Riane Eisler, *The Chalice and the Blade* (San Francisco: HarperSanFrancisco, 1984), 71.

36 . . . BCE . . . Throughout this book I have used the culturally neutral terms BCE (before common era) instead of BC (before Christ); and CE (common era) instead of AD (anno Domini).

36 Leonard Shlain, *The Alphabet Versus the Goddess: The Conflict between Word and Image* (New York: Viking Press, 1998).

36 . . . *refugee cultures as the Hmong* . . . Anne Fadiman, *Spirit Catches You and You Fall Down* (New York: Farrar, Straus & Giroux, 1997). This book provides an understanding of the cultural demands placed upon people moving from isolated tribal life to modernity.

36 . . . *the story in English is not the story* . . . There is a horrendous history of genocide, eradication of culture, language, and story referenced in this sentence. While this chapter does not digress into this history, I hope the reader will. Indigenous people and their traditions are essential placeholders of legacy and wisdom. Dominant culture has destroyed these people at the gravest human cost and detriment to the world. Several recommendations include: Betty and Ian Ballantine, eds., *The Native Americans: An Illustrated History* (Atlanta: Turner Publishing, 1993); Annette James, *The State of Native America: Genocide, Colonization, and Resistance* (Boston: South End Press, 1992); Malidoma Patrice Somé, *Of Water and the Spirit: Ritual, Magic, and Initiation in the Life of an African Shaman* (New York: Tarcher/Putnam, 1994).

37 . . . *clerics and clergy learned to read* . . . It is interesting to contrast the illiteracy of early European Christian culture with the literacy of contemporaneous Jewish culture. The Jews were the first people to design a puberty rite of passage that admitted boys to manhood through the act of reading. Performed at one's thirteenth birthday, reading the Torah (the Law) before the community in the celebration of Bar Mitzvah signals the entry into Jewish adulthood and responsibility. In both cultures, literacy for women would take a few more centuries.

40 James Pennebaker, *Opening Up: The Healing Power of Expressing Emotions* (New York: Guilford Press, 1990).

41 Thomas Mallon, *A Book of One's Own: People and Their Diaries* (New York: Ticknor & Fields, 1984).

42 Deena Metzger, *Writing for Your Life: A Guide and Companion to the Inner Worlds* (San Francisco: HarperSanFrancisco, 1992), 254–55.

43 ... *The art of storycatching*... Some of the material presented here comes from my book *Calling the Circle: The First and Future Culture* and other writings on council and group process to be found at www.peerspirit.com.

Chapter Three. Tending Our Fire

Barry Holstun Lopez, *Crow and Weasel* (San Francisco: North Point Press, 1990).

Robert Jurmain, Lynn Kilgore, Wenda Trevathan, *Introduction to Physical Anthropology: Tenth Edition* (Belmont, CA: Thomson Wadsworth, 2005), "Chapter Eight, Primate Models for Human Evolution."

51 ... *ramble this ancient valley*... See Kilmartin House Museum website, www.kilmartin.org.

Iain Zaczek, *Sacred Celtic Places* (London: Collins & Brown, 2002).

53 ... *utilization of complex tools*... All definitions quoted or implied in this text are from the *Random House Dictionary of the English Language*, Second Edition, Unabridged (New York: Random House, 1987).

55 ... *Lest we get too enamored*... Stephen Pinker, *The Language Instinct: How the Mind Creates Language* (New York: William Morrow & Company, 1994), 18–19.

56 ... *behave intelligently*... Ibid., 19.

57 ... *for forty thousand years*... Ibid., 25.

57 ... *complex trains of reasoning*... Ibid., 26.

58 ... *all biologically modern humans*... Ibid., 353.

61 ... *to seek new lives in a new land*... The examples of lineage in this chapter come from my own bloodlines. I humbly acknowledge that throughout history, and still today, many people have lived through entirely involuntary relocations in their ancestral lines, and in their own lives.

66 Margaret Lynn Brown, *The Wild East: A Biography of the Great Smoky Mountains* (Gainesville, FL: University of Florida Press, 2000), 158–59.

67 ... *she had never been in an automobile*... Ibid., 161.

Chapter Four. It Was a Dark and Stormy Night

Anne Frank, *The Diary of a Young Girl* (New York: Doubleday, 1952).

Robert F. Kennedy, *Thirteen Days: A Memoir of the Cuban Missile Crisis* (New York: W. W. Norton, 1969).

Margaret Mead, *Culture and Commitment: A Study of the Generation Gap* (New York: Doubleday, 1970), quoted from *The New Beacon Book of Quotations by Women*, Rosalie Maggio, ed. (Boston: Beacon Press, 1996).

74 Sigmund Neumann, "The Conflict of Generations in Contemporary Europe," 1939.

81 ... *The illusion of powerlessness....* Paul Rogat Loeb, *The Soul of a Citizen: Living with Conviction in a Cynical Time* (New York: St. Martin's Press, 1999), 26.

82 ... *the problem that has no name...* Betty Friedan, *The Feminine Mystique* (New York: Dell, 1963).

84 ... *The politicians used to ask us...* Carrie Chapman Catt, founder of the League of Women Voters, 1919, speeches collected on LWV website.

88 ... *a gloomy and hopeful book...* Jane Jacobs, *Dark Age Ahead* (New York: Random House, 2004), 5.

89 ... *from forgetting what they had lost...* Ibid., 172–73.

90 ... *I am so honored to be alive...* quoted by Lynne Twist in "Waging Peace: A Story about Robert Muller," westbynorthwest.org Online Magazine, March 14, 2003.

Chapter Five. Riding Experience to Wisdom

Christina Baldwin, *Lifelines: How Personal Writing Can Save Your Life* (audio learning course; Boulder, CO: Sounds True, 2004).

95 Spelling notation: the name of the country Viet Nam is spelled as two words by the Vietnamese and as one word in standard American usage. I have chosen to honor the right of its citizens to determine how that country name is spelled even when translated into a different alphabet.

97 Annie Gottlieb, *Do You Believe in Magic? The Second Coming of the Sixties Generation* (New York: Times Books, 1987), 48.

Joseph M. Marshall III, *The Lakota Way: Stories and Lessons for Living* (New York: Penguin Compass, 2001).

98 A PDF version of the Spiral of Experience is available on my website, www.storycatcher.net.

104 ... *I'm just sitting here listening to the war...* The comments in parentheses made throughout this letter are direct radio transmissions Carl Baldwin inserted as they occurred in real time.

106 Rebecca Solnit, *Hope in the Dark: Untold Histories, Wild Possibilities* (New York: Nation Books, 2004), 29.

Chapter Six. A Story to Stand On

The quotes from Marianne Knuth are taken from telephone interviews and personal conversation. For information on Kufunda Village, see www.kufunda.org.

Louise DeSalvo, *Writing as a Way of Healing: How Telling Our Stories Transforms Our Lives* (Boston: Beacon Press, 1999).

Susan Wittig Albert, *Writing from Life: A Journey of Self-Discovery for Women* (New York: Tarcher/Putnam, 1996).

121 Annie Dillard, quoted in William Zinsser, *Inventing the Truth: The Art and Craft of Memoir* (Boston: Houghton Mifflin, 1987), 56.

130 ...*perepeteia*... Jerome Bruner, *Making Stories: Law, Literature, and Life* (New York: Farrar Strauss & Giroux, 2002), 16–17.

131 AIESEC is the largest student organization in the world with over 50,000 members, active on over 800 university campuses in 89 countries at the time of this writing. For more information see www.aiesec.org.

Chapter Seven. Writing and Talking in the Seven Generations

The quotes from Kit Wilson are taken from telephone interviews and personal conversation.

Angeles Arrien, *The Fourfold Way: Walking the Paths of the Warrior, Teacher, Healer, and Visionary* (San Francisco: HarperSanFrancisco, 1993).

———, *The Second Half of Life: Opening the Eight Gates of Wisdom* (Boulder, CO: Sounds True, 2005).

Allen Berger, "From Despair to Personal Integrity: The Therapeutic Value of the 12 Steps of Alcoholics Anonymous" (self-published booklet; Dr. Allen Berger, 2780 Skypark Dr. #205, Torrance, CA 90505).

Christina Grof, *The Thirst for Wholeness: Attachment, Addiction, and the Spiritual Path* (New York: HarperCollins, 1993).

Robert A. Johnson, *Owning Your Own Shadow: Understanding the Dark Side of the Psyche* (New York: HarperCollins, 1991).

Sharon Medhi, *The Great Silent Grandmother Gathering: A Story for Anyone Who Thinks She Can't Save the World* (New York: Viking, 2005).

Paula Underwood, *The Walking People: A Native American Oral History* (San Anselmo, CA: A Tribe of Two Press, Institute of Noetic Sciences, 1993).

143 ... *What is not integrated repeats itself*... Arrien's books are mentioned above; this quote is from my personal lecture notes, May 2003. See also www.angelesarrien.com.

153 ... *Forgiveness is simply returning*... Colin Berg, "The Art of Return," *Parabola Magazine*, Volume XII, Number 3, August 1987, p. 67.

160 Stuart Brand, *The Clock of the Long Now* (New York: Basic Books, 1999).
160 Barry K. Baines, *Ethical Wills: Putting Your Values on Paper* (New York: Perseus Publishing, 2001). See also www.ethicalwills.com for guidelines regarding this form of writing.

Chapter Eight. We Are the Ones

The quotes from Toke Paludan Møller are taken from telephone and personal conversations.

Tom Atlee with Rosa Zubizarreta, *The Tao of Democracy: Using Co-Intelligence to Create a World That Works for All* (Cranston, RI: The Writers' Collective, 2003).

Juanita Brown and David Issacs, *The World Café: Shaping Our Future through Conversations That Matter* (San Francisco: Barrett-Koehler, 2005).

Stephen Denning, *The Leader's Guide to Storytelling: Mastering the Art and Discipline of Business Narrative* (San Francisco: Jossey-Bass, 2005).

Parker J. Palmer, *Let your Life Speak: Listening for the Voice of Vocation* (San Francisco: Jossey-Bass, 2000).

Linda Stout, *Bridging the Class Divide and Other Lessons for Grassroots Organizing* (Boston: Beacon Press, 1996).

Margaret J. Wheatley, *Finding Our Way: Leadership for an Uncertain Time* (San Francisco: Berrett-Koehler, 2005).

167 Michael S. Malone, "Great Garages," *Forbes*, October 19, 2000, quoted from Forbes.com.
169 David Packard, *The HP Way: How Bill Hewlett and I Built Our Company* (New York: HarperBusiness, 1995), 79–80.
182 Herminia Ibarra and Kent Lineback, "What's Your Story?" *Harvard Business Review*, January 2005.
183 Jean-François Rischard, *High Noon: 20 Global Problems, 20 Years to Solve Them* (New York: Basic Books, 2002). The quote in the text is a paraphrase by Toke, referencing Rischard's speech and structure for developing a "networked global governance" for dealing with the level of crisis we find ourselves in.
185 See also www.artofhosting.org.

Chapter Nine. The Possible God

The quotes from Donald Schell and Rick Fabian are taken from telephone interviews and their video *Dancing with God*. See also www.saintgregorys.org.

Karen Armstrong, *The Battle for God* (New York: Ballantine Books, 2000).
Christina Baldwin, *The Seven Whispers: A Spiritual Practice for Times Like These* (Novato, CA: New World Library, 2002).
Joseph Campbell, *Thou Art That: Transforming Religious Metaphor* (Novato, CA: New World Library, 2001).
Tikva Frymer-Kensky, *In the Wake of the Goddesses: Women, Culture, and the Biblical Transformation of Pagan Myth* (New York: The Free Press, 1992).
Wayne Teasdale, *The Mystic Heart: Discovering a Universal Spirituality in the World's Religions* (Novato, CA: New World Library, 1999).

197 The quote and information regarding the Arawak people comes from Howard Zinn, *A People's History of the United States* (New York: The New Press, 2003).

203 George Lakoff, *Don't Think of an Elephant! Know Your Values and Frame the Debate* (White River Junction, VT: Chelsea Green Publishing, 2004), 102–3.

207 William J. Bausch, *Storytelling: Imagination and Faith* (Mystic, CT: Twenty-Third Publications, 1984), 94–95. This book is a wealth of story and structure for what Bausch calls "narrative theology."

211 Philip Gulley and James Mulholland, *If Grace Is True: Why God Will Save Every Person* (San Francisco: HarperSanFrancisco, 2003), 162–63.

212 Ibid., 186–88.

Chapter Ten. Storycatcher

John Graham, *Stick Your Neck Out: A Street Smart Guide to Creating Change in Your Community and Beyond* (San Francisco: Barrett-Koehler, 2005).
Marvin Thomas, *Personal Village: How to Have People in Your Life by Choice, Not Chance* (Seattle, WA: Milestone Books, 2004).
Margaret J. Wheatley, *Turning to One Another: Simple Conversations to Restore Hope to the Future* (San Francisco: Berrett-Koehler, 2002).

223 Margaret J. Wheatley and Myron Kellner-Rogers, *A Simpler Way* (San Francisco: Berrett-Koehler, 1996), 17.

225 Frances Moore Lappé and Anna Lappé, *Hope's Edge: The Next Diet for a Small Planet* (New York: Tarcher/Putnam, 2002), 18–19.

About the Author

Christina Baldwin's lifework addresses the deep need in modern culture to reestablish authentic and heartfelt dialogues. After graduating from Macalester College with an honors degree in English and Columbia Pacific University with a master's degree in educational psychology, she began her public career in the field of journal writing. Her classic books *One to One: Self-Understanding through Journal Writing* and *Life's Companion: Journal Writing as a Spiritual Quest* have helped tens of thousands of people articulate the dialogue they are having with themselves.

Her long study of personal growth and group dynamics led to her groundbreaking book *Calling the Circle: The First and Future Culture*. Her original contribution, PeerSpirit methodology, is based on ancient ways of council that help people have significant conversations with each other. Her book *The Seven Whispers: A Spiritual Practice for Times Like These*, invited people into a dialogue with soul. And now, in *Storycatcher*, she turns to the theme that weaves through all her work and writing: her utter belief in the power of story to renew how we are in the world on an individual to collective level.

Baldwin lives on an island near Seattle, Washington, where she and author/naturalist Ann Linnea, cofounded PeerSpirit, Inc., an educational company dedicated to building communities of reflection, adventure, and purpose. She is a frequent teacher and speaker throughout the U.S. and Canada and Europe. Please check the websites below for current calendar and teaching information.

www.storycatcher.net • www.peerspirit.com

Be Part of the Storycatchers Network
www.storycatcher.net

Did you know that a national story project was initiated in 2003 to help people record each other's stories? StoryBooths were set up in public places — like Grand Central Station in New York City — and in 2005 a StoryCorps caravan of mobile story booths began touring the country.

Did you know that many state historical societies and university library collections house personal diaries and journals as part of their archives?

Did you know about The Legacy Project, a national volunteer effort to preserve the letters and emails of active duty soldiers so that their stories are honored?

Do you know where to find the oral histories of former slaves recorded in 1936 to 1938?

Do you want to know how to preserve the stories in your family — how to transfer old journal entries off a five-inch floppy disk?

Have you heard about Conversation Cafés? Let's Talk America? Bookcrossing? These are all movements to help people engage and interact through story.

Do you want to share a storycatching resource you know about with others?

Go to **www.storycatcher.net** for the latest information about the network of Storycatchers who are speaking stories, writing stories, and propelling stories into the world to facilitate change. This website contains information about Christina Baldwin and her events and appearances, but it focuses on you — what you know, what you need, how to weave story into the fabric of your life. Reading and study guides are available to help you get started beginning conversations among your friends, family, or community. We welcome suggestions for the website. We seek to share resources and links in the midst of a grand story-gathering movement.

NEW WORLD LIBRARY is committed to preserving ancient forests and natural resources. We printed this title on New Leaf Eco Book 100 Natural Antique recycled paper, which is made of 100 percent postconsumer waste and processed chlorine free.

Using this paper instead of virgin fiber for the first printing of this book saved:

- 102 trees (40 feet in height and 6 to 8 inches in diameter)
- 43,329 gallons of water
- 17,425 kilowatt hours of electricity
- 9,384 pounds of air pollution
- 4,777 pounds of solid waste

We are a member of the Green Press Initiative — a nonprofit program supporting publishers in using fiber that is not sourced from ancient or endangered forests. For more information, visit www.greenpressinitiative.org.

NEW WORLD LIBRARY is dedicated to publishing books and other media that inspire and challenge us to improve the quality of our lives and the world.

We are a socially and environmentally aware company, and we make every attempt to embody the ideals presented in our publications. We recognize that we have an ethical responsibility to our customers, our employees, and our planet.

We serve our customers by creating the finest publications possible on personal growth, creativity, spirituality, wellness, and other areas of emerging importance. We serve our employees with generous benefits, significant profit sharing, and constant encouragement to pursue our most expansive dreams. As members of the Green Press Initiative, we print an increasing number of books with soy-based ink on 100 percent postconsumer waste recycled paper. We also power our offices with solar energy and contribute to nonprofit organizations working to make the world a better place for us all.

Our books are available in bookstores everywhere.
For a complete catalog, contact:

New World Library
14 Pamaron Way
Novato, CA 94949

Phone: 415-884-2100 or 800-972-6657
Catalog requests: Ext. 50
Orders: Ext. 52
Fax: 415-884-2199

Email: escort@newworldlibrary.com
www.newworldlibrary.com